The Transition to a Market Economy

The Transition to a Market Economy

Transformation and Reform in the Baltic States

Edited by

Tarmo Haavisto

Department of Economics, Lund University, Sweden

Edward Elgar

Cheltenham, UK • Brookfield, US

Published by
Edward Elgar Publishing Limited
8 Lansdown Place
Cheltenham
Glos GL50 2HU
UK

Edward Elgar Publishing Company
Old Post Road
Brookfield
Vermont 05036
US

A catalogue record for this book
is available from the British Library

Library of Congress Cataloguing in Publication Data
The transition to a market economy : transformation and reform in the
    Baltic states / edited by Tarmo Haavisto.
        Includes bibliographical references
        1. Baltic States—Economic conditions—Congresses. 2. Baltic
    States—Economic policy—Congresses. 3. Post-communism—Baltic
    States—Congresses.   I. Haavisto, Tarmo
    HC243.T73   1997   96–23174
    338.947'4—dc20   CIP

ISBN 1 85898 393 2

Printed and bound in Great Britain by
Biddles Limited, Guildford and King's Lynn

Contents

List of Tables and Figures   vi
List of Contributors   viii

1. Introduction   1
    Tarmo Haavisto
2. A Comparative Analysis of the Economic Transition in the
    Baltic Countries – Barriers, Strategies, Perspectives   17
    Niels Mygind
3. Introducing New Currencies in the Baltic Countries   66
    Seija Lainela and Pekka Sutela
4. Public Sector Development: Difficulties and Restrictions   96
    Hans Aage
5. The Future Trade Opportunities of the Baltic Republics   119
    Tor Wergeland
6. State-Owned Enterprises after Socialism: Why and How to
    Privatize Them Rapidly   150
    Pavel Pelikan
7. Investment Incentives in the Formerly Planned Economies   182
    Gunnar Eliasson
8. Structural Adjustment, Efficiency and Economic Growth   211
    Thorvaldur Gylfason
9. The Role of Institutions in the Transition to a Market Economy   222
    Michael D. Intriligator
10. Introducing New Currencies in the Baltic Countries:
    A Comment   241
    T.M. Rybczynski
11. Eastern Europe in Transition   249
    Oldrich Kyn
    Index   275

Tables and Figures

TABLES

Table 2.1:	Background conditions – before 1989	20
Table 2.2:	Trends in political development	26
Table 2.3:	Overview over stabilization and liberalization	36
Table 2.4:	Overview over privatization, 1989–1994	50
Table 2.5:	The development in production - J-curve	56
Table 2.6:	Economic results in the three Baltic countries	58
Table 4.1:	The composition of tax revenue in various countries (per cent of GDP)	97
Table 4.2:	Estonia 1991–1994: composition of government revenue and expenditure	105
Table 4.3:	Latvia 1991–1994: composition of government revenue and expenditure	106
Table 4.4:	Lithuania 1991–1994: composition of government revenue and expenditure	107
Table 5.1:	General statistics for the Baltic republics	127
Table 5.2:	Composition of trade in world prices, 1989 (million roubles)	128
Table 5.3:	Estimated potential trade levels for the Baltic republics	130
Table 5.4:	Human capital and labour force	134
Table 5.5:	International comparison of agricultural production	135
Table 5.6:	The industrial structure of the Baltic republics	137
Table 5.7:	Revealed advantages in Baltic exports	139
Table 5.8:	Integration with the former Soviet Union markets	141
Table 5.9:	The energy intensity of selected nations	142
Table 5.10:	Energy balances up to 2010	143
Table 7.1:	Institutions supporting property rights	184
Table 7.2:	The four mechanisms of economic growth	186
Table 7.3:	The risk hierarchy	190
Table 7.4:	Performance rates of the Swedish and East European firm	208
Table 8.1:	Static output gain as a function of the initial distortion and the ultimate share of industry in output	217
Table 8.2:	Economic growth as a function of the saving rate and the efficiency of capital	219
Table 11.1:	Marking to market	268
Table 11.2:	Index of real GDP	269

FIGURES

Figure 3.1: Foreign reserves 78

Figure 3.2: Monthly inflation rates in the Baltic countries 80

Figure 3.3: Exchange value of the US dollar in the Baltic countries
(domestic currency / US$) 87

Figure 5.1: 'The Diamond' with external influences 122

Figure 5.2: Changes in market shares 132

Figure 7.1: The links between property rights, investment incentives
and economic growth 185

Figure 7.2: Labour productivity distributions in small Swedish
manufacturing firms and subcontractors, 1989 204

Figure 7.3: Rates of return over the interest rate in 1989 in small
Swedish manufacturing firms and subcontractors 205

Figure 8.1: Output gain from agricultural trade liberalization 213

Figure 8.2: The path of output following structural adjustment 218

Contributors

Hans Aage, Roskilde University, Denmark

Gunnar Eliasson, The Royal Insitute of Technology, Sweden

Thorvaldur Gylfason, University of Iceland, Iceland

Tarmo Haavisto, Lund University, Sweden

Michael D. Intriligator, University of California, Los Angeles, USA

Oldrich Kyn, University of Boston, USA

Seija Lainela, Bank of Finland, Finland

Niels Mygind, Copenhagen Business School, Denmark

Pavel Pelikan, The Industrial Institute for Economic and Social Research, Sweden

Tadeus M. Rybczynski, City University, London, UK

Pekka Sutela, Bank of Finland, Finland

Tor Wergeland, Norwegian School of Economics and Business Administration, Norway

1. Introduction

Tarmo Haavisto

In 1992, the Nordic Economic Research Council initiated a research and development programme for the Baltic countries. This programme has resulted in a number of research reports which are now ready for publication as a special volume. In Riga on 4–5 November 1993 and in Bergen on 1–2 September 1994, the Nordic Economic Research Council arranged two scientific seminars. All the research reports in this volume contributed to those seminars.

The economic and political transformation of the former planned economies in the Baltic countries is unique in the sense that there are no identical cases in history. However, there are no historical events which are unique in the sense that they would have nothing in common with our earlier experience or that the analytical framework which is based on this experience would be completely irrelevant. We can always recognize certain regularities and phases of development, which are well known from previous empirical studies or have been discussed in the existing theoretical literature. This common knowledge can be used to analyse the new problems that present themselves, to make recommendations regarding what should be done and may also be used in relation to forecasts of expected developments in the future.

The aim of this book is to recognize such regularities and to use them to discuss the dynamics of the economics of transition in the Baltic countries, where the transition process has proceeded faster than in the other republics of the former Soviet Union. Their geographic position, inter-war independence and cultural traditions as well as separate languages have all contributed to the relatively rapid transition of the Baltic countries compared to countries like Russia, Ukraine, Belarus, or several other parts of the former communist empire. The trade between the countries around the Baltic Sea has always been lively with the exception of the post-World War II period until the collapse of the Soviet Union. The nations around the Baltic Sea have a long common history; Estonia has long historical ties to Finland, Sweden and Germany, and both Lithuania and Latvia have old political and economic relations with Germany, Denmark and Sweden. The common history and common traditions serve as a very useful platform when the Baltic countries are seeking ways to integrate their economies as part of the global framework of market economies. This background means that the Baltic countries have certain advantages compared to many other countries in transition and that the process of rapid transformation of economies seems more feasible in the Baltic case.

The economic transformation of the Baltic planned economies started in 1988. However, the process in Estonia, Lithuania and Latvia has not been identical, although there have been certain common characteristics of their subsequent development. In all three countries, the process started as a political liberalization movement, but the importance of economic issues has increased as political reform has continued. In each of the Baltic countries, the aim of the economic reform has been integration of the domestic economies with Western market economies. This means that the Baltic countries have also to adopt a similar institutional framework to that in operation in those market economies. In the Baltic case, in contrast to certain countries in their neighbourhood, this does not necessarily mean that there is a conflict between public opinion and those institutional requirements common to all countries that participate in global world markets. In the Baltic case, in fact, the opposite might be true. Because of the close links between political democracy and economic liberalism, economic reform and economic integration with international markets is one way of enforcing political reform.

Rapid integration of domestic markets into the global framework can be seen as an effective way of putting pressure on the domestic authorities to start the reformation of the institutional framework within the country. Especially in those cases where public opinion mistrusts both the intentions of the authorities and their capacity to reform the institutional system, economic reform towards a market economy might be considered as a necessary condition to accomplish this part of the political reform. At the same time, domestic firms (as well as the domestic bureaucracy) are forced into a rapid adoption of the technology, legacy and behavioural rules of the market economies.

In this book, we will both describe the process of transformation as it has been observed in the Baltic context and analyse certain common features of the dynamics of the economic transition. We start with three descriptive chapters. The first, by Niels Mygind, is a survey of recent developments in the Baltic societies. This chapter covers both the political and economical aspects of reform in these countries. Chapter 3 is by Seija Lainela and Pekka Sutela, who discuss the currency reform in the three Baltic countries as a part of the emerging financial markets. The focus of this chapter is on explanations of the rapid and successful implementation of the new currency systems in all three countries. Chapter 4 is by Hans Aage and describes the development of the public sector during the early years of transition. The fiscal transition in the Baltic countries has been another success story. Implementation of the new instruments of fiscal policy has proceeded rapidly and the process must be considered as rather trouble-free, at least compared to the massive failure in most developing countries during the 1970s and 1980s. Of course, it is easy to imagine that there is a close interrelationship between the simultaneous favourable reform of both the monetary and fiscal systems.

Mygind provides us with a brief history of the transition in the Baltic countries. This survey of Baltic experience is completed by an explicit analysis of the barriers to transition. It is easy to agree with Mygind that development in the Baltic countries must have been a disappointment to those people who were expecting a big jump towards a Western standard of living as the first and immediate consequence of the introduction of market economies. This has of course not been the case. Mygind makes an attempt to explain this development by studying the barriers to transition and his article presents a classification of the various barriers that stand in the way of an emerging market economy. The classification system used by Mygind is based on the basic functions of the economy. The first has to do with the institutional system, which had to be changed when the former planned economies were transformed to a market economy. In Mygind's framework the SLP approach (stabilization, liberalization and privatization) is also included as a part of the institutional system. The second element is the production structure of the economy in a broad sense. The massive Soviet-type industrial production is replaced by a new type of production structure based on small enterprises. It does not only imply a scaling down of the existing production units, but involves important claims on changes in human capital, transformation of the production structure from industrial production to service and trade sector, and so on. The third element is the social system and concerns the distributions of power, income and wealth. In the Baltic countries, this issue involves both the redistribution of power after the communist and Russian nomenclature within the titular population, and the problem with the large Russian minority which emigrated to the Baltic countries during the Soviet period, especially to Latvia and Estonia. The next element is the value system, and has to do with cultural tradition in the Baltic countries. These countries can be regarded as border countries between the East and West in Europe. The Eastern influence has been predominant since World War II and the influence of the russification programme and the command economy for almost half of this century does not vanish in a flash. The Eastern influence is, of course, also related to the geographic situation of the Baltic countries and affects the Baltic countries' relationships with their neighbours, called 'the surrounding world' by Mygind. This is the final part of his classification system. The Baltic countries were an integrated part of the Comecon system and their main trading partners are countries which are now in transition. However, in many of those countries the progress of the transition process has been considerably slower and the problems substantially bigger. As the Baltic countries are small economies and dependent on their foreign trade, the success of the transition process in the Baltic is dependent on the future development of transition in those neighbouring countries or on the emancipation of the ties between the Baltic countries and those 'transitional late-comers'. The latter means in turn, that the Baltic countries are under pressure to extend foreign trade with Western Europe in order to sustain the speed of the transition of their economies.

An alternative to Mygind's approach is to study the barriers to transition in terms of their durability. In such a system, the barriers are classified according to two criteria: the first, relates to the different 'time-patterns' shown by the barriers and the second concerns the nature of the barriers. There are types of barriers which tend to vanish more or less automatically as the process of transition progresses. Some of them may vanish quite rapidly and without active intervention, thus constituting only temporary obstacles to the reformation. Other barriers are more long-lasting and do not disappear without intervention. The first type of obstacle I would like to call frictional elements of transition or 'weak type of barriers'. They are eliminated as time goes by and their main influence might be that they disappoint those people who had expected a rapid transformation. As noted by Mygind, we should not underrate the importance of such disappointment, since it may threaten the entire reform programme. However, one should note that in this case, the threat to the reform comes from the disappointment caused by non-realistic expectations, rather than by the reform programme per se. Thus, the solution to this problem is more likely to be a pedagogical one. The second type of obstacle, that which requires active intervention in order to remove it, must be the most problematic and gives rise to the 'strong type of barriers'. The 'strong type of barriers' are barriers which the authorities must take charge of, while in the case of the 'weak type of barriers' we cannot be sure whether an intervention is useful at all. A typical 'strong type of barrier' contains those parts of institutional reform that are concerned with legislation or institutions that lower the political risks. An example of a 'weak barrier' would be those changes in market behaviour that follow the first phase of institutional reform. Such changes in behaviour must necessarily be an evolutionary process where mistakes are successively corrected by the market mechanism.

The role of fiscal policy in the transition countries is twofold. Fiscal policy should provide a social network for those individuals who are suffering from the hardships linked to the progress of structural change. The other main target must be to support the macroeconomic stabilization process. During the period of socialist rule, fiscal policy, in the sense that it was defined in the command economy, was functioning rather well and many activities were carried out by firms. Since independence, the design of fiscal policy has been determined largely by macroeconomic considerations. However, macroeconomic stability is also required to improve the fiscal stance in the long run. A more ambitious fiscal policy requires the sustainable growth of the tax base or higher taxation of the existing base. These requirements cannot be replaced by deficit financing. Therefore, it seems reasonable to consider the budget balance as a macroeconomic item, and the improved general welfare as a question of economic growth. In the long run, economic growth is required to increase the tax base and welfare policy is primarily a question of social transfers where a certain amount of this tax base is redistributed as a result of the political process to correct, but not to replace, the market mechanism. It is better to adjust government expenditure to the tax base and to the current budget restriction, than to believe that the tax base will adjust to social needs. However, in many countries in the initial state of transition the rapid erosion of the tax base together with the coincident increase in the needs of government social policy has resulted in fiscal crisis.

The distinguishing feature of the Baltic countries is that they have avoided such a fiscal crisis. As is described by Hans Aage, a dramatic decline has occurred in the profits of state-owned enterprises, which constitute the traditional tax base, at the same time as the needs of different kinds of social services have increased dramatically. Large budget deficits would seem unavoidable, since it is difficult to replace the revenue losses from the state-owned companies by other taxes in an economy that lacks an adequate accounting system. Moreover, political pressure and instability could result in large increases in government expenditure.

However, all the Baltic countries have succeeded in balancing government revenues and expenditures. This austere budget discipline implies that the real value of government activities has been in decline. As a share of GDP, revenue has declined in all Baltic countries, most substantially in Lithuania. As official real GDP has also been declining more than actual GDP, government revenues have thereby declined by approximately 50-75 per cent in real terms.

To restore the budget balance, the immediate consequence of the reduced revenues has been a sharp decrease in the level of expenditures. Although a substantial proportion of this reduction could be achived by abolishing all kinds of subsidies, the reduction in public expenditure has also produced hardship for the population: increased inequality and poverty, reduced health care and social security for old people, and even cuts in spending on education and infrastructure.

However, the hardships affecting the population should not lead to the conclusion that the government should abandon the budget restriction. Sound fiscal policy is needed for stability and growth. Government expenditures should not be expanded before the tax base expands again. It is only after the tax base has increased that the country will be able to choose an appropriate level of taxation that fulfils those ambitions it has regarding general welfare. The role of fiscal policy is not to redistribute resources which do not yet exist. The current hardship is a result of the necessary restructuring of the economy and the associated decline in production. There is no guarantee that fiscal policy can conjure up the missing production.

The hardship that those countries are currently experiencing is a severe problem. However, it is a temporary problem. When the economy starts to grow, it will be time to use fiscal policy to increase equality, eliminate poverty, improve unemployment benefits or do whatever else the Baltic people feel is desirable.

Besides those social needs caused by the economic recession, Hans Aage notices one other threat to budget discipline. In a sense, this second type of threat is a more serious problem from the dynamic perspective. As Aage observes, certain types of subsidies have been demanded by producers. If the government accepts the claims to reintroduce those subsidies, it will not be a temporary problem. In contrast to the discussion above, there is no mechanism that would lead automatically to lower subsidies in the future. On the contrary, such subsidies imply that the process of reconstruction is delayed. One important lesson from the post World War II period is that as firms get used to the subsidies, production becomes inefficient and politics will take over the most important function of the markets: the allocation of resources.

It is obvious that not so much could be done today by means of fiscal policy to improve general welfare in those countries. During the period of transition both fiscal and monetary policies must be aimed at supporting the macroeconomic goals of domestic price stability and stability of the foreign value of domestic currency.

We can see three main factors underlying the currency reform in the Baltic. The first factor might be labelled the sovereignty factor, the second one might be called the symbolic factor, while the third factor, a very practical factor, could be labelled the 'Russian disease'. This was related to the chronic state of monetary affairs in the Soviet Union, and to the attempts to prevent the spread of this disease by extermination of the disease carrier, the rouble.

We will start with the first factor. The new independent nations wanted to have the opportunity to design and control their own economic policy, both monetary and fiscal. These countries wanted to make their own fortune. A necessary condition for independent economic policy is that the country must have its own currency. The second factor was that a country's own currency, its own notes and coins, is regarded as an important national symbol by the newly independent nations. Hence, a country's own currency is not just a means of payment, but also an important part of the construction of a national identity. Both these reasons help to explain why the time schedule for the introduction was so tight. The collapse of the former Soviet Union was seen as a historical chance to free these countries from the Soviet system. All possible means should be used to emphasize this independence. In such a situation, economic reasoning need not necessarily have the highest priority. The first and most important task is to reach national independence and currency reform is seen as a vital part of this process.

However, in the Baltic states, as in the entire rouble zone, there were very good economic reasons for the rapid introduction of separate currencies, or at least for rapid severance from the Russian rouble. The economic reason was, of course, the very bad shape of the monetary system in Russia, the so-called 'Russian disease'[1]. The rouble was a disease carrier and could not serve as a currency unit in a stable monetary system. The stability of the monetary system in turn was an essential part of the successful transformation from planned to market economy.

One could argue that, although the monetary authorities in the Baltic countries needed some more time to learn the rules of the game, the risk that they would do worse than their Russian colleagues was limited. The subsequent course of events tells us that the monetary authorities in the Baltic states not only beat their Russian colleagues in their ability to implement monetary reform, but did very well even by international standards. It is not an exaggeration to say that monetary reform in the Baltic countries has been a success story. Although all the Baltic countries have been successful with regard to the transformation of the monetary system, they have not all followed the same route.

As pointed out by Lainela and Sutela (Chapter 3), the IMF warned about too rapid an introduction of the new currencies, because the successful introduction of currencies was dependent on fulfilment of certain preconditions. On the other hand, one could easily argue that the rouble zone

---

[1] The 'Russian disease' or the bad shape of monetary conditions has a very long history. Even during the classical gold standard, prior to World War I, the Russian rouble suffered chronic and severe problems in its aim to participate in the gold system.

was not an optimal currency area. Differences in the resource endowments, institutions and targets of the economic policies in the different republics of the former Soviet Union favoured a currency reform directed towards new national currencies. However, the attitude of the IMF reflected a high degree of caution, and the Fund pointed out that the completion of price liberalization and a balanced budget were preconditions which should be fulfilled before the new currencies could be introduced. In Estonia, as the first Baltic country, the new currency was introduced in spite of this restrictive attitude and without substantial support by the Fund. On the other hand, one should note that the IMF and the monetary authorities in the Baltic countries were to some extent addressing different issues. According to Lainela and Sutela, the IMF had a fullfledged central bank in mind, while the Estonian authorities planned for the implementation of a very simple version of a currency system, a currency board. Subsequent developments in the Baltic countries have shown that the strategy followed by the monetary authorities has been very successful. One is tempted to draw certain conclusions from the development of the monetary system for other sectors of the economy.

If the parallels from the monetary sector hold with regard to the other sectors, it seems that the lack of a complete institutional framework is not a sufficiently strong argument to delay the introduction of measures that would reform the system in the direction of a market economy. The currency reform supports this strategy by starting with a rapid reformation based on a simple institutional framework. This approach generates an evolutionary process of developing institutions, markets and instruments. To start by building up a complete institutional framework might be at least as risky as the alternative of a simple institutional framework. In the latter case, the risk is that the incomplete institutional framework does not work very well and this might cause problems for any further transformation. This disadvantage must be set against the advantage that the process is put in force rapidly. It takes a long time to build up the complete institutional framework of market economy, which would lead to substantial delays for the reform process. The problem gets even worse, when the delay results in the retention of old political and economic structure during this period of 'build-up' of market institutions.

As pointed out by Pelikan (Chapter 6), the capitalist system needs its capitalists, and a process which prevents the new political and economic structure from developing poses a threat to the transformation process. The old establishment is threatened by the movement towards a market economy and will therefore use every excuse to put obstacles in the way of the new structures.

If we return to monetary reform, there are two key words: simplicity and dynamics. Although the monetary arrangements implemented in those countries are simple to manage, they serve as a basis for emerging structures in the market economy. This simplicity is a guarantee that the authorities can manage the system while at the same time it becomes easier for the public to penetrate the system and thus implement the rules of the game regarding credibility and continuity.

However, the monetary system in the Baltic countries is fragile. A system with fixed exchange rates and free capital movements is very sensitive to large capital flows and external shocks. Consequently, the time that monetary authorities have at their disposal is limited and the process towards a fully-fledged central bank must proceed rapidly to allow a financial sector with a well-functioning market structure to emerge. Although, the currency reform so far has been a success, the reform has just began. The monetary system in force today can hardly be regarded as a sustainable system from the macroeconomic point of view. Nor can it be regarded as an optimal allocation system from the financial viewpoint.

The separation of the currency system was a very critical issue, since the foreign trade of all three Baltic countries was dominated by trade with the rouble-zone countries. Although this separation of the currencies from the rouble-zone could be harmful to the important trade with the rouble countries, it was also very important for the reallocation of the foreign trade from the former Soviet Union to the Western market economies. There were good reasons to believe that the reformation of the old system could continue faster in the Baltic countries than in the other parts of the communist empire after the collapse. This was of course one reason for dissociating the Baltic countries from the trade system between the other republics of the former Soviet Union. The other reason has to do with the dynamics of the reformation. As in the case of the currency reform, the exposure of the economy to initial shock can be seen as a part of an evolutionary process. By cutting down foreign trade with their former trading partners, firms were obliged to seek new partners in the West and in those former planned economies which had come further in their liberalization process. In the chapter by Tor Wergeland, the potential new trade areas are investigated. Wergeland studies future export possibilities for the Baltic countries and attempts to identify production areas where these countries could develop an international competitive advantage. This discussion makes use of both traditional and modern trade theory in discussing the future trade pattern for the Baltic countries. An empirical study is carried out by applying the gravity model to international trade. The aim of this study is to predict potential flows of foreign trade in future.

It is obvious, that the development of a new foreign trade pattern for the Baltic countries is of crucial importance for the future of the transformation process. To such small open economies, foreign trade offers large advantages for resource allocation and efficiency in the use of those resources. It is also of great importance that the restructuring of domestic production is carried out with regard to the integration of the Baltic countries into the global framework of international trade. It means that the domestic production structure is built up by using the comparative advantages, factorial endowments and other advantages that the Baltic countries have when participating in international trade. However, in the transition process, we must also consider one important dynamic aspect when discussing the opening of the former planned economies to international trade. Trade based on comparative advantages and free trade agreements with Western Europe and the Central European former planned economies, will be an important source of learning for the entrepreneurs of the new Baltic enterprises, as well as for the architects of the new institutional framework for the emerging Baltic market economies. Models such as the one used by Wergeland can never give us the exact answers regarding the products and countries which form the most important trade areas. It is not that easy to pick winners. However, those models serve as important instruments for an investigation of potential trade patterns, promising products and countries that are of special interest for Baltic trade. By looking at the empirical data, some idea of a feasible volume of foreign trade may be forthcoming. The approach is a very simple one, but it can provide some useful information about the future trade pattern.

The next three chapters deal with certain theoretical aspects of the economics of transition. The privatization and liberalization approach is the core of the reconstruction of the forthcoming production structure of the former command economy. The immediate effect of this process is a rapid decline in production volume. The old and inefficient production units are closed down and it takes time before new units are sufficiently established to match the production volume of the old units. This temporary decline in total production is not an excuse to avoid this process. The process is a necessary part of the transition and the restructuring of production cannot be carried out without the breakdown of the old production machinery. Moreover, the decline in production and the subsequent increase in unemployment and the scarcity of many basic goods, is not a reason for the authorities to intervene and to risk the stabilization part of the transformation. On this topic, we have first two papers that deal mainly with the microeconomics of the transition reconstruction issue: the papers by Pelikan and Eliasson. A third paper by Gylfason deals with economic growth and the initial fall in production. The paper written by Gunnar Eliasson focuses on the investment growth problem in the former planned economies. In particular, the institutions that define the investment climate of the economy are analysed; the incentive issue, property rights and risks are treated in a theoretical manner as well as illustrated by practical examples from the Baltic countries. In his chapter, Pavel Pelikan takes us to the very heart of the privatization issue; why the firms should be privatized and why it matters who owns them. Pelikan claims that the question of who are the proper owners of the firms during the transition is a very central part of the transition process and that the outcome of the process depends on whether the capitalists of the privatized firms are fully qualified in their role in the new, capitalistic system.

The first question to be answered is the time-sequencing of privatization. Should the privatization precede or follow restructuring? Pelikan argues that the privatization should precede restructuring. His arguments are based on the concept of economic competence and the apparent scarcity of this resource during the initial stage of restructuring. Pelikan notes that the role of the capitalist in the capitalistic system is often a neglected issue. The capitalistic system needs its capitalists and the economic competence of those capitalists is a very substantial part of the capitalistic market economy and its progress. If we agree that the capitalists and their competence, that is the role of the owners of the enterprises, is of major importance, the next question becomes how to put those forces to work. If private ownership is regarded as a requirement for successful restructuring, two conclusions follow. The management of the new capitalistic enterprises is a very special issue and very different from the management of the socialistic productions units in the command economy. There is no guarantee that the old managers of those socialistic production units are the right people to manage the new enterprises. The only way to check that and to find the right managers is to put the capitalist system into operation. This means that privatization must be implemented as fast as possible. There is no way of building a capitalist system without capitalists and it is highly undesirable for these emerging market economies to start with some kind of 'third' or 'mixed' way policies if the target is to establish a capitalist system. They should use this opportunity to start from scratch and build up an institutional structure that is in accordance with the target. The development of a capitalist market economy is an evolutionary process requiring both principals and agents and no one should underestimate the role of the economic competence of the owners and managers of the new enterprises in this evolutionary process.

The lack of financial markets is of course a considerable problem for rapid privatization and highlights the problem of the privatization method: how to transfer the control of the firms from government agency to the new owners in order to put the restructuring process to work. The post-socialist economies suffer from both a lack of capital markets and an extremely short supply of capital resources. Under those circumstances, Pelikan recommends an extraordinary method: privatization by freely distributed investment vouchers on the grounds that this is the most effective method to start an efficient allocation of economic competence.

Vouchers are just a technical solution to the initial problem of how to privatize the firms. However, they cannot be considered as a solution to the problem of the restructuring of production. Privatization by vouchers is the first step towards the introduction of market forces on the supply side of the economy. The second step is to put those market forces to work in terms of efficient resource allocation. This efficient use of market forces places demands on the design of the institutional framework. The most important institution supporting the investment incentives is the institution of property rights. Western market economies rely on credible institutions to protect private ownership; the owners' rights to manage their property, to access the profits and to trade in the property rights. If those requirements are not fulfilled, the investors face large risks. As a result, high expected returns are requested, leading to a scarcity of risk capital and low investments. The specific risk in the Baltic examined by Eliasson is that of political risk. Together with business risk and macroeconomic risk, it affects investment activity through the incentives to invest in those countries.

The next question is how to establish an institutional framework to attract both the domestic and foreign investment funds needed to permanently improve the supply of risk capital. The lessons learnt from earlier experience in the underdeveloped countries is that the solution is not primarily to supply more money, but to improve investment incentives. Eliasson provides an analysis of the necessary institutions required to improve the incentives for investment. It is again shown that fairly simple measures may do a great deal of the job and very limited legal codes are sufficient to cover the critical market functions.

The institutions that define the investment climate include legal codes, conventions and ethical norms. Since it seems impossible to design an optimal institutional framework that would 'facilitate the realization of all desired improvements', we need the opposite strategy; 'law should be formulated explicitly to prevent restrictions and hindrances to improvement'[2]. An appropriate way to support the investments is to design an institutional framework, which does not prevent investors from realizing their investment plans, rather than a framework that actively intervenes in the market in order to improve investments. The politicians, when designing the institutional framework, must be more aware of the risks of their interventions in terms of increased uncertainty and political risk that threaten investment incentives than the potential of the active measures in terms of increased investments.

---

[2]   Eliasson (in this volume p. 185).

The problem faced by the Baltic countries today is not how to design a complex of explicit codes to force the investors to supply those funds necessary for economic progress but how to make themselves legally and institutionally attractive both to domestic and foreign investors. The problems here are of course huge. Most of the institutions are lacking by definition; it is these institutions that are the real difference between market economy and command economy. The legal traditions are also quite different. The transition process means that those countries leave the socialist legal tradition where everything not listed in law was, in general, forbidden to a system where everything not explicitly forbidden is permitted. The Western legal codes can be considered as a guarantee system which provides your minimum safety, your rights. In many of the former planned economies, investments are limited both by the lack of those codes that define the rights of the investor, property rights, but also by the uncertainty of the design of the future legal system. In other words, there is a political risk. These factors combined with the macroeconomic risks that the investors face in the Baltic countries lead to the high level of discounting rates which puts an effective drag on investments in those countries.

Even the construction of the basic institutions to improve the incentives of foreign investors will take time, and so will delay the economic growth process. Thus, the governments of the Western countries must be involved, not by supplying money to the Baltic companies but by carrying part of the political risk involved in the direct investments made by Western companies in the Baltic countries.

Eliasson makes three recommendations. A set of enabling laws, a minimum set of codes to start the market economy, should be introduced until the more complete institutional framework is established. The aim of the enabling laws is to eliminate the growth drag from the old legislation and to provide a flexible and simple framework that will guide the investments to a sustainable growth path. Second, a temporary insurance arrangement is required to cover the political risks faced by the foreign investors. Opportunistic political behaviour gives rise to the political risk. This risk is linked to the fact that the old socialist legal system has not been completely abolished, and there is uncertainty about the legal usage today and about the design of the future system. Eliasson suggests that Western governments are needed to provide an insurance system that lowers the political risk premium of foreign investors and, thereby, lower the return requirements to the level of ordinary business risk. There is a risk that this kind of insurance system will delay the development of the institutional system. This leads to the third recommendation made by Eliasson. The design of the insurance system and the Western aid must include this problem as well as the problem of moral hazard. There are many ways to carry out the risk insurance and the

European Bank of Reconstruction and Development could have an active part in those arrangements.

The chapters reviewed so far have discussed the different aspects of the transition process. In the papers based on the empirical evidence from the Baltic countries, one can discern some scepticism about the rapid structural reform, while the theoretical arguments provided both by Pelikan and Eliasson support rapid reform and also offer solutions to the practical problems. However, structural reform is linked to heavy losses in production. Not only many productions units, but even whole sectors might turn out to be insolvent. This rapid decline in current production must imply welfare losses, which must then be weighed against the future gains of better resource allocation as a result of the implementation of the market economy. This topic is examined by Thorvaldur Gylfason.

Thorvaldur Gylfason shows how macroeconomic efficiency and economic growth are influenced by the liberalization of prices and trade. This liberalization affects both the price level, which has been suppressed, and relative prices, which have been administratively determined. Initially, aggregate supply contracts as a result of declining output and employment in the sectors with lower relative prices. The total output loss may even have involved spillover effects to the other sectors of economy. The new profit opportunities are, however, exploited by innovative entrepreneurs and the contraction is reversed. The point considered by Gylfason is whether the cure is worse than the disease. Is it possible to determine whether the losses which are temporary but occur currently outweigh the higher levels of output and productivity, which are permanent but will occur in the future. The analysis is based on a neoclassical general-equilibrium type of framework that emphasizes the structural adjustment and increased economic efficiency to promote economic growth. The economic distortion eliminated in this chapter is the price distortion which is removed by the liberalization of prices and trade. In this framework the focus is on the supply side and on the long-term effects of the price and trade liberalization.

Initially, output contracts and unemployment and bankruptcies increase. However, the relative price changes and new profit opportunities attract innovative entrepreneurs, so productivity rises, which in turn leads to a permanent gain in output, while the initial loss is only temporary. Thus, the paper suggests that the likely result of price and trade liberalization is not only a higher output level, but also a higher rate of long-term economic growth.

The conclusion of the paper by Gylfason is not that the rapid transition of the formerly planned economies is a guarantee to increased general welfare in the long run. This result depends on whether the restructuring of the economies leads to increased efficiency as a result of superior resource allocation and improved exploitation of the factors of production. Gylfason tells us that if productivity is increased then the initial fall in production need not be a problem. By plausible values on the discounting factors, he demonstrates that setting given increased productivity, the loss in terms of an initial, temporary drop is outweighed by the long-run effects in terms of increased productivity. Whether the transition really leads to increased productivity is not the point of his article. The arguments for increased productivity are provided by Pelikan and Eliasson as discussed above.

Chapters 9, 10 and 11 can be considered as reflections on the paper discussed above. All three authors participated the seminar in Bergen. The first of these three chapters is written by Michael D. Intriligator of UCLA, who comes with a critical view on the Big Bang approach to the transformation process. He discusses alternative paths for the former planned economies. Chapter 10 is by Tadeus Rybczynski of City University, London, who examines the emerging financial markets as a part of the transformation process in the Baltic countries. And finally, we have the chapter by Oldrich Kyn, of the University of Boston, dealing with the role of the SLP approach (stabilization, liberalization, privatization) in the successful transition to the market economy.

The point of departure is of course the role of the missing institutions. It seems that there is some confusion about what is meant by institutions. In some circumstances 'institutions' is used in the sense of actors in markets as with 'financial institutions' meaning banks, insurance companies, mortgage lenders and so on, while in some other circumstances, 'institutions' refers to institutions in the sense used here by Pelikan and Eliasson: the fundamentals of the market economy, such as property rights. There is of course a linkage between the fundamentals of the markets and the actors in the market: the fundamentals define the actors. However, it is clear that we should try to avoid confusion when discussing this issue. Intriligator points out that the lack of institutions, in the sense of certain market actors, is a reason to hasten slowly when introducing the market economy. Indeed, he goes so far as to recommend some type of 'third way approach' to avoid a collapse of the economy. Intriligator argues that there is a risk that the pace of destruction of the established structure of the former planned economies may be fast, while it may be a long time until the new market actors emerge. As a result, the economy will tend to slide into a chaotic state. Furthermore, it seems that authors like Intriligator believe that certain functions of the planned economy are vital and should be adopted in the new structure taking form in those countries. Thus, Michael Intriligator concludes that the Big Bang approach should be replaced by a third way approach.

This conclusion is in sharp contrast to the conclusions of several other chapters in this volume. A common conclusion reached in several papers is that only a simple framework is required to carry out the most basic functions of the market economy. Once those basic functions are implemented, the dynamics of the market economy are going to work in the same manner as they do in the Western market economies. The paper by Oldrich Kyn argues strongly for this latter view. We have both theoretical and empirical arguments to make us believe that the market economy and the Western type of democracy are the main reasons for the huge gap between the standard of living in the Soviet successor states and the market economies in the West.

Thus, the conclusions made by Kyn support a rapid implementation of the institutions of the market economies. The third way approach implies that certain functions of an economic system that never worked remain in force. A part of socialism is maintained in those countries to ease the hardships related to the restructuring of the economy. The problem here is obvious. The medicine recommended to alleviate the symptoms is in fact a part of the disease! It is easy to agree with Michael Intriligator that the lack of institutions is a huge problem in the process of transformation from socialism to capitalism, but as pointed out by Pelikan, Eliasson and Kyn, the maintenance of the old institutions of socialism is a greater threat to the successful transformation of those economies than are those temporary hardships arising from the transformation process.

Not only the needs of structural reform at the micro level support the desirability of rapid reformation of the economy. There are also macroeconomic reasons to force the reform. As Tadeus Rybczynski points out in his comment on Lainela and Sutela, the Baltic states have, for the moment, succeeded in their aim to stabilize both the domestic price level and the exchange rate by a combination of responsible fiscal policy and the adaption of pegged, undervalued exchange rates. However, he also reminds us that 'the time purchased is not unlimited and must be used for creating arrangements conducive to stable and non-inflationary growth'. This conclusion holds both at the micro and macro level.

2.   A Comparative Analysis of the Economic Transition in the Baltic Countries – Barriers, Strategies, Perspectives

Niels Mygind

2.1   INTRODUCTION

The political revolution in the Baltic states came as a surprise for most people. In a very few years these countries went from being parts of the Soviet Union to independent states. They went from a political system monopolized by the Communist Party to democracy. They went from being part of a centralized command economy to independent economies undergoing rapid transition to a market economy. The speed of the political change has been a surprise and even the problems of the economic transition have surprised many people. Although the economic transition has been both fairly rapid and quite radical, some people in the euphoria of freedom had expected that their country would take a jump into the Western market economy and the Western standard of living. These expectations have not been fulfilled. The economic transition has met serious barriers. In the first years of transition, production and the living standards of most people have been falling. It will take years to make a transition to a dynamic market economy that can catch up with what has been lost in the first years of transition, never mind what has been lost in the 50 years of Soviet rule.

What are the main barriers for the economic transition? What are the strategies followed in the three Baltic countries? What are the perspectives for the development of these countries? These are the main questions to be answered in this overview of the economic transition in the Baltic countries.

2.2   BACKGROUND CONDITIONS

In my book *Societies in Transition*, Mygind (1994), I have developed a model to analyse the dynamic process of transition and the interrelationship between different elements of society. I will shortly present some of the elements of my analysis as a framework for this article.

The *institutional system* is the set of formal rules governing the political processes and the coordination of the economy. On the political level this includes a new democratic constitution with rules for the distribution of political power between president, parliament, central and local governments and the rules for election to these bodies. On the economic level the transition from plan to market includes *liberalization*, that is: decentralization of decision, information and motivation to independent market units. This includes liberalization of prices, international trade, banking and so on, and it includes the legislative framework for the operation of private enterprises. Parallel to liberalization it will be necessary to achieve *stabilization* to secure macroeconomic conditions without inflationary pressure. Finally it is necessary to change the incentive structure in the state-owned enterprises. This includes *privatization*, which has turned out to be the most difficult task in the transition of former command economies.

The institutional system was integrated into the Soviet command economy. Most economic activities were governed from the centre in Moscow. Hence, the basic economic institutional conditions were quite similar for the whole Soviet Union. However, the Baltic countries, and especially Estonia, were during the period of perestroika used as a place to experiment with new forms of enterprises and elements of market economy. The Baltic countries, and especially Estonia, had the highest density of new cooperatives – small semi-private firms – and the highest numbers for 'individual employment' and joint-ventures (Aage, 1991a). These were the first steps towards a market economy. In the period of democratization, Gorbachev's 'demokratisatsia', there was a shift in power from the Soviet of the whole Union to the Soviets in the Republics. Especially after the semi-democratic elections in 1990, this was one of the main factors in the development towards independence for the Baltic countries.

The *production system* is the resources of society – nature, physical means of production and human knowledge. It is also the structure and the results of production. The production system in the three Baltic countries is heavily influenced by 50 years under Soviet rule. That means an underdeveloped service and trade sector, and an industry based mainly on very large firms built to supply the whole Soviet Union with specialized goods. Compared to the other republics in the Union, the Baltic countries, especially Estonia, have greater emphasis on light industry (Hanson, 1990). Both Estonia and Latvia were industrialized before the Soviet occupation. Tallinn and, more especially, Riga were already important trade centres at the beginning of the century. Lithuania, on the contrary, had a large agricultural population after

World War II and the industry here was mainly built up under Soviet rule. The land and climate in the Baltic countries provide good conditions for agriculture and forestry. Productivity was up to 50 per cent higher than in the rest of USSR (Hanson, 1990), and the countries were net exporters of goods from these sectors. They possess rich raw materials. An exception is Estonia's oil shale that has been the base for the production of electricity. Energy from oil shale represented about half of Estonia's energy consumption. However, the extraction and production process has left large areas with serious environmental problems. The Baltic states had a production per capita 10–20 per cent above the average for the whole Soviet Union. Output per capita in the USSR is very difficult to compare with the level in Western industrialized countries. Estimates for the 1980s lie between 10 and 50 per cent of the USA level (Aage, 1991a). Dellenbrant (1992) finds that Estonia and Finland in 1940 had about the same level of GDP, but in 1990 Estonian GDP was only around 40 per cent of Finland's. In the 1930s Estonia and Latvia enjoyed the same level of GDP while Lithuania was less developed. Therefore, economic development especially in Estonia and Latvia has been delayed because of the Soviet occupation. All the countries have a structure of production which needs substantial restructuring to fit a market economy.

The *social system* comprises the different social groups and their interaction with each other. This system includes the distribution of power, income and wealth. The social system in the Baltic countries was characterized by both the dominance of the communist nomenclatura and the dominance of Russians. In the period just before the Soviet occupation many people emigrated to the West. During the Soviet period, many Baltic people were deported to Siberia and there was massive immigration, principally of Russians, but also Ukrainians, Belorussians and so on. Immigrants from the rest of the Soviet Union got jobs in new large-scale industrial enterprises built to fit into the overall Soviet command network. In Lithuania there was still enough surplus labour from agriculture to supply labour to the new industries and hence there was only limited immigration from the rest of USSR. In Estonia and Latvia the Russian immigrants mostly settled in the new suburbs surrounding the big cities. They constituted about half of the industrial labour force and, particularly in Latvia, they also held some of the highest positions in the management of the enterprises. In Estonia the titular nationality had only 43 per cent of industrial employment, in Latvia they had only 38 per cent and in Lithuania 71 per cent. In Latvia other nationalities also had a strong position in sectors such as transport and construction, and even in administration titular Latvians comprised only 56 per cent of employment. In agriculture the titular populations dominated in all three countries.

The Transition to a Market Economy

Table 2.1: Background conditions – before 1989

	Estonia	Latvia	Lithuania
Production System			
population (mill.)[1]	1.57	2.67	3.72
land area (1000 km^2)[1]	45.1	64.6	65.2
NMP/cap USSR= 100 (1988)	117	119	110
energy production raw materials	electricity (oil shale) 50% of energy consumption	fully dependent on imports	50% of electricity from nuclear power station
industrialization	early	early	Soviet industrialization
employment (1990)[1]	796 000	1 409 000	1 853 000
industry	33%	28%	30%
agriculture	13%	18%	18%
Institutional System			
historical, foreign dominance During perestroika centres for experiments	especially Estonia many new cooperatives and individual employment		Strong state in medieval times
Social System[2]			
ethnic change during Soviet occupation	emigration to the West and deportations of Estonians, immigration of Russians to new industries	emigration to the West and deportations of Latvians, immigration of Russians to new industries	emigration of Lithuanians, but no large immigration of Russians – labour from agriculture to new industries
titular nationality / total (%)			
1939	92	77	76
1945	94	83	80
1989	61	52	79
in industry	43	38	71
state farms	84	69	84

transport	67	38	47
construction	81	46	61
administration	72	56	78
Value System			
language	Finnish/Ugrarian	Baltic	Baltic
religion	Protestant	Protestant	Catholic
foreign influence	mainly German	mainly German	mainly Polish/traditional
attitude to non-state sector: 1989, USSR 15% positive[3]	30% positive	22% positive	15% positive
Surrounding world[4]			
USSR trade % of NMP 1988	25% (X) , 29% (M)	24% (X), 27% (M)	24% (X), 27% (M)
trade deficit with USSR	748 mill. Rb, 18% NMP	695 mill. Rb, 10% NMP	1530 mill. Rb, 17% NMP
in world-market-prices	1 300 mill. Rb	1 300 mill. Rb	3 700 mill. Rb

Sources: 1) EIU country profile 1992/3, 2) Hanson (1990), 3) Aage (1991b) 4) Aage (1991a).

The *value system* is the basic culture of society. The values, norms and preferences of the inhabitants and the informal coordination of society. The value system is closely connected to the social system, since the social groups are heavily influenced by the ethnic divisions. For centuries, the special cultures of the three Baltic nationalities have survived foreign occupation. They were independent between the two world wars, but after 1945 the Soviet occupation challenged the Baltic cultures. The russification process did not happen only in the form of the massive inflow of Russian immigrants. Russian was in practice the official language and the main language in the educational system.

Although the long history of foreign occupation is quite similar for these countries, it is a mistake to understand them as one culture. There are important differences of language and religion: the Estonian language is quite similar to the Finnish language. Estonians are mainly protestant. Although Latvians and Lithuanians have a specific Baltic language, the two languages are sufficiently different to prevent direct communication. Latvians are mainly protestant, while Lithuanians are mainly catholic. This difference is associated with Lithuania's historic ties to Poland. Estonia and Latvia were more influenced by Germany (Andersen, 1992). This also partly explains the early industrialization the two most Northern countries.

Nearly half a century of a command economy creates special habits that must be changed in a market economy. This is borne out by, for example: hoarding of goods, different forms of corruption, focus on the quantity of production without paying attention to costs and quality, ignoring the demand side. Some of these habits change quite rapidly when the institutional system changes. For instance, when prices increase to the market level and the queues disappear, people stop hoarding. However, certain habits are probably more deeply rooted in cultural values. In the whole USSR, the percentage of respondents who had a 'positive attitude' towards cooperative and individual activity was 15 per cent in 1990. In the three Baltic Republics it was 30 per cent in Estonia, 22 per cent in Latvia and 15 per cent in Lithuania, (Aage, 1991b). These differences may reflect the fact that the Estonians had had more experience with market-oriented firms. They may also reflect the prevalence to a higher degree of individual values in Estonia as opposed to the more collective and egalitarian values held in Lithuania at the same level as in the rest of the Soviet Union.

The higher degree of market-oriented values in Estonia can also be connected to influences from *the surrounding world*. The close linguistic relationship with Finland gave Estonians the opportunity to follow Finnish television and radio. Many Estonians lived in exile in Sweden, Finland and North America. This was also to a certain extent the case with Latvians and Lithuanians but the language barrier meant that the influence of Western-style living was smaller in these countries. This has especially been the case in Lithuania with the most traditional agro-oriented culture. The economic ties between the Baltic countries and the West were quite small, and from a political and military point of view they were completely dominated by the centre in Moscow until the democratization period under Gorbachev.

2.3 MAIN POLITICAL DEVELOPMENTS UNDERLYING THE ECONOMIC TRANSITION

The rise of the independence movements in the three countries was closely related to Gorbachev's policy of 'glasnost' – openness – giving the opposition the possibility of expressing their protests against the ruling system. The first organized protests were concentrated around relatively less politically sensitive subjects such as environmental protection and, in Lithuania, conditions for the Catholic Church. In Estonia protests were held in 1987 against a planned phosphorite mine and similar demonstrations also took place in the other Baltic countries at that time. During 1987–8 the protests against the system changed directly to the question of autonomy for the Baltic states. A number of groups protested against the Molotov–Ribbentrop Pact and in 1988 Popular Fronts for independence were founded in all three countries (*Baltic Review* 1993:1).

The majority sections of the Communist Parties in all three countries changed their policy to support more independence. Developments were more radical in Lithuania where the local Communist Party in 1989 declared itself independent from the Soviet Communist Party. The strength of the Popular Fronts and the change in the local Communist Parties resulted in a change of policy by the Baltic Supreme Soviets: at the end of 1988 the titular languages were declared the official languages in all three countries. They started to use their traditional flags, and there was in 1988–9 a 'war of legislation' with Moscow about which legislation had supremacy – the republican or the all Soviet. In November 1989 the USSR Supreme Soviet adopted a decision on economic self-management in Estonia, Latvia and Lithuania.

The independence movement had broad popular support. In August 1989 two million people formed a 600 km human chain stretching from Tallinn to Vilnius. In February 1990 there were elections to the self-declared 'Congress of Estonia'. Only citizens of the prewar Republic and their descendants had voting rights. Later in the spring the first free elections for over 50 years took place in all three republics. The Popular Fronts and pro-independence groups won a majority in the three soviets. Shortly after the election, declarations of independence were adopted. Lithuania made the most radical declaration and this was answered by Moscow with the imposition of an economic blockade. In Russia, the beginning of the dissolution of the Union strengthened conservative forces, and the tensions between Moscow and the Baltic republics increased during the rest of 1990 culminating in January 1991 when Soviet troops seized the Radio and Television Centre killing 13 civilians. In the spring, an overwhelming majority voted for independence in referendums held in Estonia and Lithuania. It is worth noting that in Estonia around 50 per cent of the non-Estonian speaking people voted for independence (Andersen, 1992).

After the failed coup, the Baltic countries were recognized as independent states not only by Western countries, but also by the other states of the former Soviet Union. When the chains to the USSR were removed, differences emerged in the economic and political development of the three countries. I wish first to concentrate on the formation of political parties and the creation of political institutions.

After the election in 1990, the new Savisaar government in Estonia was dominated by experts working for Estonian independence. Many leading officials had a past in the Communist Party. They were working for a gradual but comprehensive economic transition, and they followed a fairly moderate line in confrontations with the Russians. Although the economic reforms in the areas of price liberalization and partial indexation of wages meant hardship for the population, the government was not met by resistance from the public or the parliament in 1990 and 1991. It was quite clear that the government, up to independence in 1991, had limited room for their decisions. In many respects the Estonian economy had developed quite well compared to the situation in other Soviet republics. The price reforms had meant high inflation but also more goods in the shops and improvements in the terms of trade with Russia.

However, the Baltic economies underwent a severe shock when Russia liberalized prices in January 1992, setting the prices of exported raw materials at the world market levels. The result was hyper-inflation during the first months of 1992, and a sharp reduction in the supply of energy and other essential raw materials. Many firms had to stop or drastically cut production, and in most houses and official buildings, the temperature was much lower than normal. Savisaar had to resign and a new government led by Vähi was appointed.

The new government continued the economic policy pursued by the former government, culminating with the introduction of the kroon in June 1992. However, the new government followed a more nationalistic line in the question of the Russian-speaking part of the population. In February 1992, the 1938 citizenship law was reinstated. Citizenship was given to citizens from before 1940 and their descendants. Later immigrants were required to have lived for two years in Estonia after 30 March 1990 – the day of the declaration of independence. They had to be able to speak Estonian to a certain standard. This meant that the large Russian minority had no voting rights at the referendum in June 1992, when the new constitution was approved, and no voting rights at the parliamentary election in September 1992. At this election, the national question still had a high priority. The nationalist parties won a victory, and a centre-right government was formed. The heir of the Communist Party failed to get into parliament. The economic strategy of the new government was neo-liberal, leaving very little scope for the role of the state. The programme of economic austerity was continued. Production fell further and the government quickly lost support among the population. In December 1992 a new Russian movement was organized. A referendum held in the summer of 1993 in the Narva district which has a large Russian majority, was organized to obtain more autonomy for the district. The 'aliens law' passed by parliament in June was also a step that escalated the national conflict. There were protests from countries both East and West, and President Meri refused to sign the first draft of the law. However, after some adjustments which gave the Russian-speaking population the right to stay in Estonia, it was passed (Andersen, 1994). The law considered the Russian-speaking minority to be foreigners, and gave them limited rights. Thus the national question continued to dominate the political scene giving the government scope in the economic policy.

Political developments in Latvia have many parallels with developments in Estonia. However, the Latvians have met more obstacles: Latvia and especially Riga was the stronghold of the Soviet troops, the Russians had a stronger position at the management level of the industrial enterprises (EIU, 1993:2), and Latvia did not have such close links to the West as did Estonia in relation to Finland. In 1992–3 there was a serious dispute with Russia about the ownership of the oil pipeline from Russia to the Latvian port of Ventspils. The conflict about Russian troops in Latvia was not solved until April 1994, when it was agreed that Russian soldiers should withdraw by the end of August except for a small group of soldiers at the Skrunda early-warning radar station. Russia was allowed to keep this base for four years.

After the election in 1990, a government was formed based on a majority from the Popular Front. In the following years the government had increasing difficulty in getting a majority behind its policy, because the Popular Front was split into different wings arguing about how to solve the problems of citizenship and economic policy.

The political conflicts made the policy for economic transition unclear. This was especially the case with privatization policy. The 'large privatization' did not really start, and the 'small privatization' was quite disorganized with the main decisions decentralized to local municipalities. Only privatization of agriculture proceeded fairly quickly. Part of the explanation for the latter is due to the minority question. Agriculture was dominated by Latvians. The Russian-speaking group were unable to obtain property through this privatization. In industry special concessions to employees and managers transferred a major share of ownership to the Russians. The political solution was to introduce a voucher system favouring Latvian citizens from before 1940. But the process was delayed and in the period before the election in 1993 the conflicts within the parliament intensified and some ministers resigned because they wished to show their disapproval of the unpopular prime minister, Godmanis. In this way the political deadlock intensified before the election in June 1993.

As in Estonia, the first election after independence was a victory for the nationalist centre-right. The government gave a high priority to closer integration with the West and rapid privatization. The national question continued to have a high priority on the political agenda. The debate on citizenship continued for months after the election. In July 1994, a new law

Table 2.2: Trends in political development

	Estonia	Latvia	Lithuania
I Fight for independence			
National Popular Fronts		Oct. 1988 Popular Front	Sajudis
Communist parties		split, strong pro-Russian party	strong independent line
1990 republic elections, independence referendum	pro-nationalists 77% pro-Russian 23%	pro-nationalists 65% pro-Russian 30%	pro-nationalists incl. CP 95%, pro-Russian 5%
Economic policy: from experiments to preparation for 'mixed economy'	IME programme: mixed economy with 'people's enterprises'		most radical declaration of independence => confrontation with Moscow
II After independence before elections			
national forces split, more complex choices on citizenship, constitution, economic policy => new conflicts, unclear interests, volatility IMF pressure => agreements autumn 1992	using part of old constitution, no citizenship or voting rights for Russians, liberal economic poli-cy, privatization slow, pressure for cutting ties with Russia => June 1992 intro-duction of kroon, shift in trade 1991–92	using part of old constitution, no citizenship or voting rights for Russians, privatization only fast in agriculture (no Russians), government – parliament in a deadlock on citizenship and economic policy disputes with Russia	introduction of citizenship law includes minorities, constitutional question splits, good relations with Russia, in spite of hardline policy, high egalitarian values => voucher privatization, but weak stabilization, IMF-pressure => stronger stabilization in autumn 1992

III After elections	Estonia	Latvia	Lithuania
more homogeneous and well defined interests	election, September 1992 new constitution approved, centre-right government	election, June 1993 centre-right government programme: continued reform, pragmatic nationalism,	Oct./Nov. 1992, presidential election, February 1993, centre-left government, continuation of
Russian troops out:	programme: ultraliberal, focus on	controlled	market-oriented policy with some
Aug. 1993 in Lithuania	the West, hardline nationalism, summer	privatization, May	moderation on
Aug. 1994 in Estonia and Latvia	1993, aliens' law Russian protests, Oct. 1993, local election failure for gov. parties, Sept. 1994, prime minister steps down after scandal	1994, local election nationalists win, July 1994, government crisis, Sept. 1994, centre-left gov.	stabilization, continued IMF pressure, Aug. 1994, opposition calls for referendum on privatization, but not enough votes

without strict quotas was passed[1]. This law gave residents born in Latvia the opportunity to apply for citizenship. During the summer, the government could not agree about tariffs to protect agricultural production. The crisis resulted in a new centre-left government.

In Lithuania the citizenship question was not so important because the titular population had a comfortable majority and the national question had a relatively limited role in the political debate. Instead the political discussion was concentrated on the question of the role of the president in relation to parliament. The result was a relatively strong president as in the French system[2].

At the same time, the Democratic Labour Party with roots in the former Communist Party was quite popular, contrary to the case in the other Baltic countries. There are several explanations for this popularity: the Lithuanian communists had followed a fairly nationalistic line in opposition to Moscow as early as 1989. Hence, the party and its leader, Brazauskas, were not identified with Soviet suppression as was the case in Estonia and Latvia. The

---

[1] In the spring of 1994 a proposal was passed which would have set very restrictive quotas. However, the international community protested and the Latvian president vetoed the law.

[2] The popular front, Sajudis, had a strong position in parliament in August 1991. The leader, Landsbergis had been the symbol of the confrontation with the Soviet system. But because of the depressed economy his popularity fell markedly during 1992. There were conflict, inside Sajudis on economic policy, and no clear strategy was followed. During 1991 and 1992 Sajudis was split into many parties.

period of Soviet rule was not considered to be an economic disaster to the same extent as in the other more developed Baltic countries. There was no threat from a large Russian minority with close links to the Communist Party. The early market reforms in Lithuania were a failure especially in the countryside. Therefore, the Labour Party had a surprising victory at the election in October/November 1992, obtaining an absolute majority in the Lithuanian parliament. At the presidential election, Brazauskas won 60 per cent of the votes. It was particularly in the countryside and among the non-titular Lithuanians that the Labour Party won its support. In this way, the flexible introduction of citizenship to all residents of Lithuania also contributed to the victory of the former communists.

As early as 1991 Lithuania started a rapid privatization programme based on a voucher system. On the one hand, this system showed a commitment to turn away from state ownership, while, on the other hand, it favoured a more equal distribution of wealth. Such a policy was possible because the question of citizenship was solved at an early stage. Stabilization policy was fairly weak in 1991 and 1992. This can partly be explained by the chaotic leadership of the ruling coalition and partly by the fact that there was no nationalistic shield over the economic policy. The people hit by the tough incomes policy represented a large part of the electorate. In Estonia and Latvia, a substantial proportion of the workers belonged to the minority without voting rights. The lower priority assigned to nationalism might also be one of the explanations behind the relatively slow introduction and stabilization of an independent Lithuanian currency. However, pressure from the IMF in particular resulted in a tougher stabilization policy from the autumn of 1992, and this policy was continued by the new government.

2.4 STABILIZATION AND LIBERALIZATION

The fight for independence was closely connected with the objective of transforming the command economy. The Baltic republics wanted to manage their economies themselves. The idea of decentralization led to the idea of a market-oriented economy.

These ideas were first developed in a comprehensive way in the Estonian 'IME' plan.[3] It was an outline for an independent Estonian economy with its own currency, central bank and a mixed ownership structure consisting of public firms, private joint stock companies and private employee-owned firms. During 1989 some of the 'plans' in the programme were given

[3]   The programme was put forward by the Estonian Planning Committee in May 1989. Translated into English the letters stand for: Economic Self-Management of Estonia. The Estonian word 'ime' means miracle.

legislative approval, including a law about leasing in agriculture and a law on joint stock enterprises (Hanson, 1990), and one of the leading authors of the programme was appointed the first chairman of the new Bank of Estonia.

In implementing Gorbachev's Perestroika, Estonia was also in the front line. By the end of the 1980s the Baltic countries had the highest proportion of employment in private firms in the form of 'cooperatives' and 'individual enterprises', and Estonia topped the list ahead of Latvia and Lithuania (Hanson, 1990). When there was a reaction in Soviet legislation against cooperatives in 1988, these legal changes were not approved in Estonia. In 1990, Estonia was well ahead in terms of Western investment. It had nearly as many joint ventures as the much larger Russia (World Bank, 1992).

Estonia did not have an independent stabilization policy before 1991, because up until this year the state budgets and monetary instruments were governed from the centre in Moscow. From January 1991, Estonia had its own state budget and a new tax system was implemented.[4] The fiscal policy was strict and the state budget had a surplus of 6 per cent in 1991 (World Bank, 1993a). This surplus was a result of both a disciplined economic policy and high revenues from profit taxes owing to the favourable terms of trade in 1991. In 1992, profits were squeezed by increasing input prices and a further fall in demand. Hence, the revenues from profit and incomes taxes fell, and the state budget deteriorated.

Monetary policy had only limited scope when Estonia was still in the rouble zone. As early as 1990, the Bank of Estonia had some freedom of action. In December 1990 the use of hard currency for commercial transactions was legalized. During 1991 the interest rate was gradually increased to match inflation. Before that time, the real interest rate had been strongly negative. In June 1992 Estonia introduced its own currency, the kroon. Following the 'currency board' principle, the quantity of kroons was strictly tied to Estonian reserves of hard currency and gold. The board principle has been followed strictly. It has been possible to keep a stable exchange rate of 8 kroons to one deutschmark. On the other hand the currency board put its limits on the money supply and credit policy. There was no room to expand the amount of money to stimulate investment. The

[4] The subsidy system was transformed from product subsidies to personal subsidies. A social security system was introduced taxing wage outlays at 33 per cent; company taxes and a 10 per cent value added tax were introduced. From January 1994 the tax system was simplified and included less redistribution since the progressive tax system which varied from 16 to 33% was replaced by a flat rate of 26% for all incomes (EIU, 1994:1). This was an example of the right-wing policy followed in this period which also included very low minimum wages, pensions and other social benefits. For more details see Aage, this volume.

central bank could not control credits, it could not make open market operations and it could not finance the budget deficit. The interest rate was set in the market outside the control of the central bank (Bennetts 1993, Lainela and Sutela, 1993). The kroon was made internally convertible, but there were still strong restrictions on capital movements. In 1993 it was made legal for enterprises to hold foreign currency accounts. Nearly all of the new kroons were exchanged with roubles at the exchange rate of ten roubles for one kroon. This meant a devaluation of around 10 per cent (Kukk, 1993). At that time the rouble was already strongly undervalued, measured in terms of purchasing parity. Hence, the kroon was also undervalued from the outset. This is another explanation why it has been possible to maintain a stable exchange rate since June 1992, although the price level in Estonia more than doubled in the following half year.

Wage policy has been strict in Estonia. Most wages followed movements in the minimum wage, which was fixed by the state. Wages have been regulated on several occasions, but insufficiently to adjust for inflation. The real wage was cut by 40 per cent in 1991 (World Bank, 1993a). As pointed out by Lipton and Sachs (1990), this does not mean a 40 per cent cut in living standards. Part of the real wage had no buying power because of the monetary overhang. Excessively high wages caused a lot of wasted time standing in queues. After the liberalization of prices, cuts in real wages, and the elimination of the overhang, there were goods in the shops and no queues at the beginning of 1992.

Prices increased by 2–300 per cent in 1990 as subsidies on food were reduced (Kukk, 1993).[5] In 1991 further liberalization took place for a broad range of goods. In 1991 inflation generally was more than 200 per cent. The biggest inflationary push came in the first months of 1992 following the liberalization of prices in Russia. The prices of raw materials imported from Russia were adjusted towards the level on the world market.[6] Following the hyperinflation of 88 per cent in January and 74 per cent in February (Kukk, 1993), inflation fell, rose slightly in the months following the devaluation and introduction of the kroon, but after September 1992, fell to single figures. By April 1993, the rate of inflation was down to 2.3 per cent. For 1993 as a whole, inflation was 90 per cent, although the trend was downwards. At the beginning of 1994 there was increased inflationary pressure because of rising prices of energy, rent and public transport. At the same time, the high foreign capital inflow following the introduction of the

---

[5] At that time the Estonian shops had more goods than the Russian shops, and the price increases were also a shelter against the Russians hoarding goods in Estonia.

[6] Estonia was still heavily dependent on raw materials from Russia both for direct supply of energy to households and for inputs to industry.

currency board resulted in an increase in the supply of kroons. Consequently, the estimates for inflation in 1994 had to be adjusted upwards. However, almost all prices had by then been adjusted to the market level and further inflationary pushes may be limited in the future.

The fall in inflation shows the success of stabilization policy. However, the cost has been a credit squeeze for Estonian industry combined with sharply falling demand on the domestic market. The disintegration of the former Soviet Union, and the transition to world market prices have led to a disruption of former trade links and serious problems on the supply and demand side for industry.

The growth of the banking sector has played an important role in economic development in Estonia. The first commercial bank, Tartu Commercial Bank, owned by other firms and individuals was established in 1988. By mid-1991 there were 12 commercial banks in Estonia. In 1992 the number had grown to 43. Many of these banks were in a difficult financial situation. Because of the decline in industry a large share of their assets consisted of 'bad loans' that would never be repaid, and many banks were in insolvency. During 1992, the Bank of Estonia gradually strengthened reserve requirements and in November three of the large banks were placed under official control. The bank crisis resulted in mergers and bankruptcies. The number of banks in the spring of 1993 fell to only 23. In the first half of 1994, the Central Bank intervened in relation to two large banks. This development shows the determination of the authorities to strengthen the conditions not only of the banking sector, but of all firms. They wanted a change from a regime of 'soft' to a regime of 'hard' budget constraints. If the banks themselves had a hard budget constraint they would pass this constraint to their debtor firms. In 1993 Estonia implemented a strict bankruptcy law which allowed creditors to start bankruptcy procedures. In the summer of 1994, 26 industrial enterprises had been declared bankrupt and it was estimated that a further 300 were undergoing bankruptcy procedures (World Bank, 1994).

The liberalization of foreign trade has been fairly rapid and comprehensive. In 1993 nearly all goods could be freely imported and exported. Licences were only required for the import and export of alcoholic beverages and tobacco and the export of metals. These goods were subject to tariffs. In December 1991, Estonia made a free trade agreement with EFTA on industrial goods and in May 1992 an agreement with the EC liberalizing trade for most industrial goods. In the summer of 1994, a free trade agreement was concluded with the EU for all the Baltic countries. In contrast to Latvia and Lithuania, Estonian free trade in industrial goods was able to start without an adjustment period because Estonia from the beginning had a very liberal trade regime. In relation to Sweden, Norway and Finland, there is almost completely free trade for all goods. The disintegration of the former Soviet Union and the opening up of trade with Western countries have resulted in a remarkable switch in foreign trade. In the 1980s Estonia's trade with Western countries was negligible. By 1992 Finland had became the most important trading partner followed by Russia and then Sweden and Germany. The kroon and the rapid liberalization process are the main factors behind this remarkable change. However, the switch to Western trading partners is also a strong objective of economic policy. This can be seen by exchange rate policy, by the fact that foreigners were allowed to buy Estonian land that was a part of a production unit in April 1993, and in the privatization policy that emphasized foreign investments. The internal trade between the Baltic countries has also developed, but from a low level. However, the neighbourhood status would suggest that there is still a long way to go in this respect. The development of a free trade zone between the three countries was speeded up after a summit in March 1994.

The balance of trade was negative in 1990. However, the rapid price liberalization improved the terms of trade with Russia for Estonian firms. After the liberalization of prices in Russia in January 1992 and the transition to world market prices, the terms of trade deteriorated for Estonia. This was partly neutralized by the switch to Western markets. For Estonian firms, the improvement of the terms of trade in 1991 compensated for the fall in sales volume. Therefore, profits did not drop before 1992 (World Bank, 1993a). The growth of foreign trade has been quite impressive. According to the Ministry of Economics, exports as a percentage of GDP increased from 32 per cent in 1991 to 67 per cent in 1993. However, it must here be noted that about one-third were re-exports, for example, of metals from Russia (Ministry of Economics, 1994). Continuing inflation and the fixed rate of kroon to deutschmark implied a declining competitiveness for Estonia. Hence, in spite of the restructuring of production, the net result in 1993 was negative for the trade balance (EBQR, 1993:4). The restructuring of industry and increasing productivity has not been fast enough to follow the real appreciation of the kroon. The trade balance continued to decline in 1994. However, the net result has been an inflow of capital, since foreign capital in the form of gifts, loans and direct investments has increased.

As in Estonia, Latvia achieved a high degree of fiscal autonomy from 1991.[7] The state budget in Latvia was in considerable surplus in 1991, although the situation changed dramatically in 1992 after the adverse movement in the terms of trade as a result of the increase in Russian prices

---

[7]   A new tax system was introduced, including tax on property, land and profits, 15–35 per cent progressive incomes tax, 38 per cent social security paid on payroll and a turnover tax, from January 1992 transformed to a VAT.

led to a decline in the tax base. After pressure from the IMF, the fiscal policy was strengthened. The stabilization programme for July 1992 to July 1993 included elimination of all subsidies on consumer goods, reduction of subsidies for agriculture, cuts in employment in the public sector and 15 per cent tariffs on imports (World Bank, 1993). After the election in 1993, it became clear that the budget deficit was increasing. Accordingly, VAT was increased from 6 per cent on food and 12 per cent on other goods to 18 per cent. The increase in food prices caused protests from the minority party in government, the Peasants' Union, and the increase in VAT on food was delayed until 1994 (EIU, 1993:4).

Like Estonia, Latvia only partly indexed state-controlled wages and transfer incomes. Hence, real incomes fell considerably in 1991 and 1992. Part of this fall was owing to the elimination of the monetary overhang. In industry, restrictions on wage payments were abolished in October 1991. This meant a sharp increase in wages but insufficient to catch up with consumer prices. In the second half of 1992, state regulation was more indirect through a tax-based incomes policy with very high tax rates on wage increases exceeding a certain level (Medvedevskih and Vojevoda, 1992). There have been no unions to protect workers against falling real wages. The old trade unions collapsed, the new Free Trade Unions Confederation of Latvia is fairly weak, and there is no central bargaining regulating wages and working conditions.

Because of the deadlock in Latvian politics, the stabilization policies of the government were not consistently implemented in Latvia. Hence, monetary policy has played a more important role. Since fiscal ties to the Soviet Union were broken, the Bank of Latvia has had a fairly autonomous position. Latvian roubles were introduced in May 1991 as a parallel currency to the Russian rouble.[8] In July, Latvian roubles (LVR) were declared sole legal tender in Latvia. At the same time LVR were made internally convertible and the exchange rate was also allowed to float against Russian roubles (Bleskina, 1993).

Because of the high inflation, LVR initially depreciated against hard currencies, but appreciated strongly against the Russian rouble. From the winter of 1992/3, LVR also appreciated against the DM and the US dollar – from 180 LVR per US dollar in October to 125 LVR in April. This is an indication both of the initial undervaluation of LVR and of the tough stabilization policy followed by the Bank of Latvia. The monetary policy was in line with the Estonian policy although without the ties of a currency board.

---

[8] The exchange rate was 1:1. The introduction was mainly explained by the lack of roubles to keep pace with increasing prices. The Latvians were dependent on the Russians because the roubles came from the Central Bank in Moscow.

This is the main explanation as to why inflation in Latvia fell to only 0.3 per cent in April 1993 (Shteinbuka, 1993).

The Latvian economic transition has similarities with developments in Estonia, although it has been slower and not so successful in switching towards Western markets.

In March 1993 LVR started to be phased out by 'Lats' at an exchange rate of 1 Lat = 200 LVR, and in July 1993, Lats were declared full legal tender so that all prices, accounts and so on were measured in Lats. LVR could still be used so there was no panic to get rid of LVR. In this respect, the introduction of Latvian currency has been more gradual than was the case in Estonia. In this way it has been easier to continue trade relations with former partners in Russia, Ukraine and so on (Bleskina, 1993). The appreciation of the Latvian currency continued and the value of Lats measured in dollars increased by 26 per cent in the second half of 1993. Latvia liberalized restrictions on convertability more rapidly than Estonia. As early as 1991, trade in foreign currency was free so that the most common shops in the centre of Riga were shops for currency exchange. Riga has developed into one of the main centers for currency trade including roubles in the whole of the former Soviet Union (Lainela and Sutela, 1993).

The price liberalization in Latvia was a little behind development in Estonia. It started in January 1993 when products were divided into three groups: one group with fixed prices based on costs and a profit margin, a second group subject to price ceilings set by government, and a third group with liberalized prices. Prices for goods and services increased by 218 per cent in the first half of 1991 (Shteinbuka, 1993). In December 1991, the liberalization of farm procurement and retail food prices was completed. In January 1992 prices on industrial goods were liberalized. For a period, there was some regulation of profit margins, because the monopolistic structure of production and important parts of the distribution system made monopoly pricing quite likely. The slow adjustment of prices to the steep fall in demand shows that this fear has not been without a basis in reality. There has been some attempt to implement a competition law, but at the same time the commercialization of enterprises giving the enterprises operational and financial autonomy has also given management new opportunities for monopolistic behaviour. The bankruptcy law has not yet been effectively implemented. There are many 'bad loans' in the banking system and at the same time inter-firm arrears have been increasing.

The growth of the financial sector in Latvia took off in 1992 and new banking legislation was implemented. The new commercial banks were at the outset fairly small and many of them were mainly servicing their owners, large state-owned enterprises. However, in spite of the economic depression in the rest of the economy, the banks developed rapidly and increased their reserves. In 1993, the capital of the commercial banks increased four fold. By the end of 1993, 61 commercial banks were registered (*Baltic Independent* 15 April 1994), although this number started to fall in 1994. In the first three months of 1994, three banks lost their licences and mergers will take place to fulfil the new reserve requirements consistent with EU rules to be fulfilled by 1998. In 1994 seven banks had more than the required 5 million ECU for reserves. The 13 largest banks had concentrated 89 per cent of the total assets in the banking sector (Arone, 1994).

Foreign trade has gradually been liberalized. At the beginning of 1992, all controls on imports were removed. All export quotas and licensing were abolished in June 1992 and replaced by a system of export taxes (IMF Survey, Nov. 1992). The programme 'Latvia 2000' envisages liberal trade except for agricultural products where tariffs and subsidies will be used to improve the incomes of farmers. The programme also includes plans for special free trade zones to attract foreign investments.

Production fell steeply: by 8 per cent of GDP in 1991 and 30 per cent of GDP in 1992. Industry in particular, and especially heavy energy-intensive industry, was hit by the deteriorating trade relations with the former Soviet Union and the steeply increasing energy prices in 1992. Trade with the former Soviet Union fell by more than 50 per cent in 1991, and this trend continued in 1992. In agriculture, production was hampered by reprivatiza-tion because of a lack of skills and equipment for the new small private farms, and the situation was worsened by a severe drought in 1992 (World Bank, 1993b).

Some of the trends in Estonia and Latvia can also be found in the economic development in Lithuania. This is especially because of the shared conditions in relation to the surrounding world. Price liberalization in Lithuania in 1991 and in Russia in 1992, and especially the increase in energy prices, produced the same terms of trade effects in Lithuania that have already been shown for Estonia and Latvia. The terms of trade with Russia improved in 1991 and worsened sharply in 1992. Steeply falling foreign trade with the former Soviet Union and falling production are part of a common picture. In Lithuania the conditions set by the IMF strengthened stabilization policy in the second half of 1992. The special feature of Lithuania was the relatively weak stabilization policy with delayed stabilization of wages and monetary policy compared to the other two Baltic states. Hyperinflation with double digit monthly inflation rates continued well into 1993.

Fiscal policy and the introduction of a new tax system is similar to the other Baltic republics. As a result of tough expenditure cuts the Lithuanian government achieved a budget surplus in 1992 (World Bank, 1993).

Table 2.3: Overview over stabilization and liberalization

STABILIZATION	Estonia	Latvia	Lithuania
fiscal policy	from 1991, tight budget policy, restricted by currency board	1990, transfers to Russia down, 1991, Latvian budget (balance), autumn 1992, tight policy	1991, surplus, 1992, both taxes and expenditures down, 1993, quite tight policy
tax system profit tax	Jan. 1991, new tax system graduated, 1994 26% flat progressive, 1994	Jan. 1991, new tax system graduated, lowest 25% for private	1991, new tax system, graduated, mostly 29% progressive, 1994
personal income tax	26% flat 1991	25% + 10% on high income	33% flat
social security VAT	33% on payroll 10%, June 1992 18%	38% on payroll 12%, 1994 18%.	31% on payroll 18% sales tax, 1994, 18% VAT
monetary policy	from 1991 increasing interest, in 1992 positive real interest, lack of credits for firms, Central Bank no interference owing to currency board	from 1992 tight money policy very high interest rates, 1993 Central Bank rates fall, but still high commercial rates, Treasury bills issue end 1993	1991–92, quite loose limited net domestic credits, monetization of Soviet credits, spring, 1993, tight policy, 1993/94, loosened winter
wage policy	min. wages fixed by state base for most SOE wages, tough incomes policy from 1991	partial indexation of wages => 91, fall in real wages, autumn 1992, tax-based wage policy	state min. wage benchmark, cuts in real wage delayed, autumn 1992, tough wage policy
exchange rate policy	kroon from June 1992 currency board, fixed 8 EEK = 1 DM then real terms appreciation	July 92, independent floating LVR, appreciation against rouble , appreciation against DEM, July 93, Lats, 1994 1 Lat = 1.25 SDR	May 1992, start issuing Talonas, Oct. 92, sole legal tender, June 93, Litas legal tender, April 94, currency board, 4 Lits = US $1
LIBERALIZATION			
legislation	Nov. 1989 enterprise law, June 1990, law on ownership, 1993, real estate law, Dec. 1993, new civil code, June 1993, competition law	Sept. 1990, entrepreneurial law, Aug. 1990, private ownership, Dec. 1990, enterprise law, Jan/Feb. 1991, company law, July 1992, part of civil code 1937	May 1990, enterprise law, July 1990, joint stock law, June 1992, accounting law, Oct. 1992, const. Property rights, July 1994, new joint stock law
budget constraint	Sept. 1992, bankruptcy law favourable to creditors, Nov. 92, 3 banks in	stop for state orders, budget support, administrative loans,	early 1992, SOE independence and financial autonomy,

	bankruptcy, 1993, 26 enterprises, 1994, 200–300 in proceedings	inter-firm arrears increasing, Jan. 1992, bankruptcy law no implementation	Sept. 1992, bankruptcy law strengthened, autumn 1993, implementation?
Price liberalization	spring 1990, start liberalization, 1991, further lib. Also wholesale, 1992, fuel, transport, rent not free 1994, liberalization completed	Jan. 91, start liberalization Dec. 91, free prices on food, Jan. 92, on industrial goods, 1992, public utilities, rent not free	Jan 1991, start liberalization, Oct. 1992, 15% controlled (energy, transport, tele.), 1994, stop for remaining subsidies
bank system	Jan. 1990, Central Bank, Jan. 1992, Gosbank out, Dec. 1988, first semi-private bank, 1992/93, strict control => commercial banks 43 => 20	Bank of Latvia, commercial functions to 93/4, Savings Bank has 95% of household savings, 1994, converted to Unibank,	Feb. 1990, Bank of Lithuania, Savings Bank, Agricultural B. Start of capital market with Investment Funds (vouchers), Sept. 1993, start stock exchange
foreign trade agreements with EFTA Dec 91 EU May 92, July 94	from 1992, liberal trade regime, July 1992, free trade with Norway, Sweden and Finland, Jan. 95, Free trade with EU	Jan. 1992, deregulation import, from licence to tax on export, Sept. 1993, 15–30% tariffs, adjustment period to free EU trade	1992, import quite liberal, July 1993, tariffs 10–30%, July 1994, higher tariffs on food
convertibility	internal convertibility with introduction of kroon, still restrictions on foreign capital account, loosened 1993	Nov. 1990, free currency trade LVR internally convertible, liberal regime for foreign exchange, Lats now fully convertible	October 1992, Talonas internally convertible
foreign investment	Sept. 1991, amended Dec. 1993, law on foreign investment, few restrictions, tax benefits	Nov. 1991, amended, March 1993, law on foreign investment, tax benefits	December 1990, legislation February and June 1992, further liberalization

However, it was difficult to implement a tough incomes policy in Lithuania. Unlike the other Baltic countries real wages were not cut in 1991. After IMF pressure, real wages were first cut in the second half of 1992. The target was a fall of around 30–35 per cent but, according to the World Bank (1993c), the fall was even steeper. This was bad timing for the government. The election was held at a time of sharply falling real wages and with inflation still out of control. The new government promised to stop inflation and to improve real wages. In the spring of 1993 wages were increased several times although not completely adjusted for the increase in prices. It was not because of a tough incomes policy that inflation was stabilized in the early summer of 1993, it was because of a change in monetary policy.

Lithuania stayed in the rouble zone a few months longer than the other Baltic countries. In May 1992 it introduced its parallel currency the 'Talonas'

– coupons to cover the deficit on Russian roubles. In October the Talonas were declared 'sole legal tender' with a floating exchange rate in relation to other currencies. In the first few months, the Talonas followed the depreciation of the Russian rouble. This can be explained by a relatively weak stabilization policy up to the end of 1992. Monetary policy was quite loose. Although net domestic credit growth had been limited, it was still possible for the enterprises to monetize non-convertible correspondent accounts with the former Soviet Union countries.

In this way the central bank gave cheap credits to firms without sufficient security. In the spring of 1993 a new chairman of the Bank of Lithuania, Visokavicius, was appointed, and the government was committed to stabilizing the currency prior to the introduction of the new Lithuanian currency the 'Litas'. By limiting credits to firms, increasing reserve requirements and taxing foreign currency incomes, the policy was successful in terms of stabilization.

Inflation was halved every month from 25 per cent in April 1993 to 3 per cent in July in spite of the gradual phasing-out of the last subsidies on bread and sugar (EIU, 1993:3). The Litas were introduced on 25 June and made sole legal tender. The austere monetary policy exerted strong pressure on industry because of limited loans and the subsequent appreciation of the Litas. State enterprises and other parts of the state bureaucracy reacted against the policy and Visokavicius was dismissed in the autumn of 1993 (EIU, 1993:4). This incident also shows that the central bank in Lithuania was subject to strong influence from parliament and government. From April 1994, Lithuania has imitated Estonia, by introducing a currency board linking the Litas to the dollar. It seems that this step was not necessary since at this point the Litas had fairly high credibility and was relatively stable. On the other hand it was a signal to the surrounding world of commitment to a tough stabilization policy.

Price liberalization started in February 1991, and by October 1992 only 15 per cent of prices were controlled. This included energy, telecommunications and public transport. In July 1993, 10–30 per cent tariffs on imports replaced the earlier licensing system. The commercialization of state-owned enterprises started early in 1992 by making the firms formally independent and giving them financial autonomy. In 1992, a bankruptcy law was introduced, a competition law was passed and a special Competition Council was established (World Bank, 1993c). Although the growth of the banking system was slightly slower compared to the other Baltic countries, this sector was the first one in Lithuania to use Western-type accounting systems and in 1994 the private commercial banks were able to provide most of the services known in the West. In September 1993, the first Baltic stock exchange opened in Vilnius. Because of the rapid privatization the turnover of shares and other securities was increasing but from a low level.

The overall picture of Lithuania is of a somewhat more hesitant stabilization and liberalization than was the case in Estonia and Lithuania. The politicians have been under greater pressure from the groups suffering from the initial stages of transition. Pressure from the IMF, a relatively balanced finance policy and a tough monetary policy resulted in a fairly effective stabilization.

2.5   PRIVATIZATION

The change of ownership from state ownership to decentralized private ownership is the most fundamental part of the transition. The main objective behind privatization is to move away from a system where the decision-takers received detailed commands and complex incentives from the higher levels in the bureaucracy to a system where the people taking decisions are economically responsible for the consequences. To make this responsibility system work there must be certain signals and pressures working on the market (see Mygind, 1994). The owners must be able to control the management of the firms directly in a closely held ownership structure or indirectly through a well-functioning capital market. The financial institutions perform an important indirect ownership role by ensuring that the firms meet their financial obligations. Competition in the markets for inputs and outputs of the firm is a necessary element. It takes time to build up these institutions and to develop a competitive structure. This is an important barrier to privatization.

There is no one dominant model of privatization for transitional economies. Different types of assets have been privatized in different ways, and different models have been used especially for the privatization of the large-scale enterprises dominating the production system of the command economies. 'Small' privatization covers small firms and removable assets like trucks and other machines that can be used in other product lines. These assets are relatively easy to value, and even with limited private savings it is possible for a large proportion of the population to finance a takeover. Therefore, it has been possible to implement small-scale privatization rapidly in most countries in transition, and the usual method has been sale by public auction. Privatization of large enterprises has been slow in most countries. This has especially been the case in countries where the model has been sale for cash. In these cases, as in Hungary and Estonia, lack of domestic capital meant that a large proportion of the privatized companies was taken over by foreign capital. The German experience makes a special case. East Germany was taken over by the West Germany. There was no uncertainty about legislation and institutions, and there was a massive transfer of capital from the West. Even under these conditions the net revenue of the privatization agency, Treuhandanstalt, was negative (Finanzbericht (1992), Treuhand-anstalt)!

In Czechoslovakia, Lithuania and Russia, the problem of lack of capital and the distributional problem were solved by introducing a 'voucher' system. For a symbolic amount, people received vouchers to be used as payment for assets. In this way the demand for the assets to be privatized increased, and a rapid privatization was attainable. In some countries, investment funds have been set up to administer the shares of the population. In countries such as Russia, Lithuania and Slovenia a concessionary element has also been used in relation to the employees of the firms. They have been given the opportunity of obtaining or buying a certain share of their firm at a preferential price (Frydman et al., 1993). Another method of privatization without selling for revenue is simply to give back the property to the former private owners. Such 'reprivatization' or 'restitution' is seldom straightforward because the assets have often been physically changed. Other conditions may also have changed, so it is difficult to define what to give back to the former owners or their descendants. Restitution has been used especially in relation to housing and agricultural land.

The national dimension is essential to any understanding of the large differences in the development of privatization in Lithuania compared to Latvia and Estonia. The difference lies in the fact that the Russian-speaking minority is much more important in the two countries to the north. The privatization policy has changed as relationships with the USSR and later Russia changed. In Estonia and Latvia privatization has been closely related to the fight for independence and an increase in the titular population's control of productive resources.

This relation seems to be most clear in the case of Estonia. In the period when Estonia was still dependent on Moscow's goodwill and on the whole population living in Estonia, the strategy for privatization was to transfer ownership from the USSR to Estonia. The workers were good allies in this process, and at the same time the claims for market economy were not so radical. Therefore, employee ownership in the form of 'people's enterprises' played an important role in the IME programme from 1989. The idea of people's enterprises 'was seen as an intermediary step between all-union and republican subordination, and was designed to make the desired transfer of control less threatening to Moscow and the current directors' (IMF Survey, 1991, p. 234). It was believed that most work collectives in the enterprises would oppose privatization. In 'people's enterprises' the work collective leased the enterprise. In this way the workers had an important role in the first privatizations. However, only seven enterprises became 'people's enterprises' but these were relatively large (Elenurm et al., 1993). The policy soon changed giving less influence to employees. In the General Principles of Privatization presented to the Supreme Soviet in October 1990 it became possible to sell up to 20 per cent of shares to the employees on preferential conditions (Terk, 1993), although privatization was to be mainly based on direct sale with voucher systems in a secondary role. In this way, the interests of the workers were phased down at a quite early stage when the independence movement started to gain some momentum. An exemption from this trend was the privatization of another seven large enterprises in 1991 on an experimental basis. In some of these enterprises, the employees secured a majority of the ownership, but the shares were often divided into non-voting shares for the majority of employees and voting shares for management. An explanation of the move away from employee ownership might be that most of the workers were not titular Estonians, and at the same time the workers' union was losing its legitimacy.

The legislation for 'small privatization' was passed in December 1990.[9] Firms with less than 500 000 Rb in book value could be privatized for cash. There were special pre-emptive rights for employees giving them the first option to buy. The law was amended in May 1992. The limit was increased to 600 000 Rb and the special rights of insiders were abandoned. There was, however, a fear among the dominant Estonian parties, that the direct sale of assets could attract large amounts of Russian roubles from all over the former Soviet Union. This is probably an important explanation as to why privatization was quite slow at this stage. In January 1992 only 208 units had been sold (Frydman et al., 1993).

In the summer of 1992, the climate towards the sale of enterprises for cash changed because of the successful introduction of the Estonian kroon. The government developed a new scheme for the sale of enterprises inspired by the method used by Treuhandanstalt in Germany, and the parliament passed

[9] As early as the winter of 1986–7, the economic experiments in Estonia opened up the establishment of independent enterprises with close relations to their state owned 'mother companies'. At the beginning of 1991 there were about 700 such small 'private' enterprises (Frydman et al., 1993). In this way a considerable asset stripping activity was made possible. During the winter of 1990–1, the government approved legislation concerning renting equipment and facilities of state-owned enterprises to cooperatives and private companies. According to Elenurm et al. (1993) this system was vulnerable to corruption. There were several cases, where top managers of SOEs set up private companies, which rented the assets of their 'mother companies' for a low fee. How widespread 'wild privatization' has been is difficult to estimate. A few cases have been discussed in the press or taken to court but this covers probably only a fraction of all cases.

resolutions supporting this scheme just before the election in September 1992. The kroon functioned as a shield against a massive inflow of roubles, and gave Estonian citizens a preferential position as bidders for the assets to be privatized. During the rest of 1992 and in 1993, small-scale privatization accelerated so that the finance minister in April 1993 noted that 50 per cent of small businesses had been privatized (EIU, 1993:2). During 1993, 243 small enterprises were sold for 120 million EEK (*Øst Nyt*, 7:94). At the end of 1994 nearly all of the more than 1 500 small enterprises had been privatized (*Baltic Independent,* 13 Jan. 1995).

In November 1992, 38 large and medium firms were announced for sale in Estonia and in leading international newspapers. The sale was organized by a new institution: the Estonian Privatization Enterprise (EPA),[10] which was supervised by experts from Treuhandanstalt. Of the 103 bids received 53 were from foreign investors (Terk, 1993). These bids were chosen not only on the criterion of the highest price, investment plans and job-guarantees were also given considerable attention.

The government continued the Treuhand strategy and the actual settlement of contracts also gained momentum at the end of 1993 and during 1994 bringing the total number of deals concluded up to 163 in September 1994. The total sales revenue was around 80 million US dollars and total guarantees were around 20 000 for jobs and 45 million US dollars for investment (*Baltic Independent*, 23 Sep. 1994). The speed of sales was impressive. However, the same cannot be said for selling prices and the guarantees. Most of the enterprises were sold without debt. Thus the net revenue for the Estonian Privatization Agency, was often negative (World Bank, 1994). This is similar to the results of Treuhandanstalt which ended up with a negative balance of 275 billion DM. Of the first tender, the enterprises sold as whole units had employment guarantees varying from 17–120 per cent with an average of 58 per cent of the employment at the time of announcement. Foreigners went into the deals on the same terms as domestic investors except that Estonians could buy by instalments. To open up further for foreign investment it was decided in April 1993 to allow foreigners to buy the land related to their production units. The Director of EPA estimated that 20 per cent of the privatized capital was sold to foreigners and, if the foreign capital behind some Estonian buyers was included, the percentage would increase to about 40 per cent,[11] (*Baltic Independent,* 29 April 1994).

---

[10] In June 1993 a new law strengthened the authority of the Privatization Enterprise from now on called Estonian Privatization Agency (EPA).

[11] The strategy shows the emphasis on core investors. This has a particular advantage in a situation without a developed capital market. However, the low sale prices and

In April 1993 a law was passed that entitled residents over the age of 18 to vouchers in proportion to the number of years they had worked in Estonia to be used towards the purchase of their apartments. The distribution of vouchers in relation to working years meant that immigrants received less than the typical titular Estonian. The vouchers were mainly intended to be used for privatizing housing, but in 1994 the idea of selling minority shareholdings of large enterprises for vouchers was supported. The first public share offering of an enterprise partly for vouchers took place in September 1994, and later in the autumn, minority shareholdings in the largest department store in Tallinn and the largest brewery in Estonia were offered for voucher sale.

Compensation vouchers from restitution could also be used like other vouchers to buy shares in enterprises, housing, shares in investment funds, bonds of the special Compensation Fund or bonds of the Pension Funds. The vouchers were freely tradeable and could be sold to Estonian citizens and permanent residents as well as legal entities registered in Estonia. The vouchers were mainly distributed in 1993 and 1994. However, the main tranche of the assets for purchase with these vouchers was not ready before late 1994 or 1995 or later (Purju, 1994). Thus, when trading increased in the autumn of 1994 the price was relatively low. Another reason was that many poor people sold their vouchers in the initial stage so depressing the price.

The nationalistic parties in parliament emphasized the restitution of property nationalized after the Soviet occupation. In June 1991, legislation on restitution was passed. The first priority was to return the assets to the former owners or their descendants. If this was not possible, they got special compensation vouchers. Since it often took a long time to resolve the questions about former ownership, some of these vouchers were paid after a considerable delay. This is one reason why it was also possible to buy bonds in the special Compensation Fund financed by some of the proceeds from privatization. The questions surrounding restitution were often very complicated. Many people claimed the same property. In January 1992, the deadline for claims, there were claims for twice the total area of Estonia and the claimed property had often been changed during the last 50 years. At the end of 1992 out of 200 000 claims only 1 000 had been settled. Such unsettled restitution claims were an important barrier to the privatization process.

Restitution was especially important in agriculture. Before World War II Estonia had 140 000 private farms (EIU, 1993:2). Because of the complete

the concentration of capital leads to very unequal distribution of wealth and the majority of the population might feel that they are being cheated in this process.

dominance of titular Estonians in this sector there was no national problem. Although privatization was faster here, the complications surrounding restitution played a major role. According to the Ministry of Economics (1994) instead of 360 collective farms there were in November 1993 4 313 private farms, 1 218 shareholding farms and 769 cooperative farms.[12] Only 1 700 farming properties had been returned to former owners, because of the problems of restitution. Figures from the Statistical Office show that the private share of agricultural production increased from 24 per cent in 1990 to 46 per cent in 1993.

Part of the pattern from Estonia is found in Latvia where the national question has also played a major role in privatization. Here, large privatization has been even more slow and hesitant but it was speeded up during 1994 and a higher priority given to vouchers. There are also important differences: privatization of agriculture has been quite fast and foreign investment plays a smaller role compared to Estonia.

More than half of the industrial workers in Latvia have Russian as their main language as is the case in Estonia. However, in contrast to Estonia, a significant number of the industrial managers and most of the new private capitalists are non-titular Latvians. According to Nørgaard (1992), between 75 per cent and 82 per cent of private capital belongs to non-titular Latvians and among the eight richest people, there are no titular Latvians. This could be an important factor behind the higher priority given to vouchers in Latvia. The voucher system is designed so that immigrants since 1945 receive a relatively small share.

Large privatization has been rather slow, and at the same time commercialization has given the managers of the enterprises substantial freedom of action. The managers can even buy and sell assets, and it can be assumed that 'asset stripping' has taken place on quite a large scale. This was especially possible under the former Soviet law on leasing (Frydman et al., 1993). The scope for action by managers has been extensive because the organization of privatization has been quite chaotic in Latvia. Much of the small-scale privatization has been decentralized to local municipalities, the responsibility for many of the large and medium firms has been placed in different often sectoral-oriented ministries. This gave the management of the enterprises in cooperation with their contacts in the bureaucracy ample opportunities to arrange deals, including privatizations, for their own benefit. Most of the large privatizations made according to the old legislation were of the type of leasing with the option to buy. When the 'cream was skimmed' they did not resist the centralization of the organization of privatization. This

---

[12] According to the National Land Board there were 10 153 private farms at the end of 1993, probably on another definition, and they covered 10 per cent of the land.

was decided by the new law of privatization of March 1994. The Latvian Privatization Agency became the new centralized authority for privatization.

Legislation of the small-scale privatization was passed in November 1991. It covered firms below a certain size defined by different measures – most important being that there were under ten employees – and the firms were sold for cash through auctions. This should have favoured the new private capitalists belonging to the group of non-titular Latvians. However, national Latvian interests were safeguarded by the fact that bidders had to have at least 16 years' residence in Latvia. Most of the privatization was organized by local municipalities. The small-scale privatization proceeded quite rapidly, so that 60 per cent of the firms were privatized in November 1992 (World Bank, 1993c) and 90 per cent were privatized in January 1993 (EIU, 2:93). The Latvian government indicated that 83 per cent out of 3 500 small enterprises had been privatized by August 1994; 882 enterprises had been sold and 2 011 were leased with an option to buy after five years. Many of the firms were sold or leased to the employees who up until an amendment of the law in February 1992 had the first right to buy (Vojevoda and Rumpis, 1993). The statistical office calculated that out of a total number of 902 firms privatized in August 1994 in trade, catering and services there were 125 employee-owned enterprises and most of them were established in the first years of transition.

The employees also received part ownership in some of the few large enterprises that were privatized in the period 1991–2 and a few firms were also partly privatized as joint ventures with foreign firms. The first privatizations by the newly created Department of State Property Conversion was followed by a public uproar over 'give-aways', and the Department was dissolved after only six months of operation in November 1991 (World Bank, July 1993). After this the large privatization came to a standstill. In August 1992, the government announced a programme for the privatization of 846 firms using different methods, but the procedure for the formulation and approval of privatization plans for each enterprise was very cumbersome. The process of decentralization to various ministries was very slow so that only 46 large state-owned enterprises had been privatized by January 1994 (Shteinbuka, 1994). However, the process was speeded up so that according to the Latvian Privatization Agency there were 256 large enterprises which had followed the old path to privatization in 1992–4. During 1994, 240 enterprises with 20 000 employees were transferred to be privatized under the custody of the Privatization Agency. At the agency's first international tender in November 1994 45 objects were offered. The first public offering partly by vouchers was implemented at the end of 1994.

In November 1992, a law on vouchers was passed. However, the distribution started as late as May 1993 and it did not really take off before the summer of 1994. This delay could be used by the above-mentioned alliance of managers and bureaucrats to 'skim the cream'. The people received one voucher for each year of living in Latvia after the war. Prewar citizens and their descendants got 15 vouchers on top of this while 5 vouchers were deducted from people who immigrated after the war. The deduction was payment for 'the use of Latvian infrastructure'. People connected to the Soviet Army or KGB did not get any vouchers. Because of this distribution 87 per cent of the vouchers went to Latvian citizens – people with voting rights at the June election (EIU, 1993:2). It is possible to sell the vouchers but there is a special tax of 2 per cent and a fee must be paid to the bank administering the special privatization account (*Baltic Independent,* 14 May,1993). Trading of vouchers started in August 1994. In the first months the market price was less than 10 per cent of the nominal value. With some similarity to Estonia, this reflects partly the lack of clarity about what the vouchers could be used for. Only very few investment funds had been formed; the legislation about voucher privatization of housing had not been passed in 1994; and there were also large uncertainties about the privatization of enterprises for vouchers. The strategy of the Privatization Agency was to try to find a core investor and sell around 50 per cent of the shares for vouchers. Another reason behind the low voucher price was the lack of information and the high need for means of consumption in the poorest part of the population. As in Estonia a concentration of wealth was rather strong in the initial months of the free trade of vouchers.

The legislation about foreign ownership of land has been quite restrictive giving foreigners only the possibility of leasing for 99 years. However, with this exception the legislation for foreign investments has been quite liberal and at the end of 1994 the legislation for foreign ownership of land was liberalized.

The commercial banks of Latvia are not completely private. About one-third of the capital of the ten largest banks was owned by state-owned enterprises in June 1994. Hence, they will not be privatized before their owners themselves are privatized. The banks often function as agents for their owners to organize the short-term finance of trade flows (World Bank, July 1993). Up to 1994, the Bank of Latvia covered the major part of commercial banking through special commercial branches. In December 1992 the commercial branches were transferred to the Bank Privatization Committee. In 1993 the privatization of these commercial branches were completed; 49 branches was privatized of which 22 were merged to form a new 'Unibank' (Arone, 1994).

Until now restitution has been most important in housing and agriculture. However, as was the case in Estonia, restitution claims have been a barrier to rapid privatization in nearly all fields.

Privatization of agriculture has been fairly rapid in Latvia. In this sector there have not been national problems, because nearly all the farm workers were titular Latvians. Privatization has been mainly based on restitution although there is also an element of employee ownership in the process. The process started in November 1990, with a land reform that outlined the rules for restitution of land. The deadline for claims was June 1991. There were around 300 000 claims for farms and small plots of land. In the same month, the collective farms and state farms were transformed into joint stock companies by a property reform. The shares were divided between the workers and former owners, and it was foreseen that many of the large units would be split up into smaller units. In the spring of 1992 about one-third of the land was restored, divided into 41 000 private farms with an average area of 15 hectares and 71 000 small plots with an average 4.5 hectares. At the end of the year the numbers were 50 000 and 100 000 respectively. When the farms were split up into small units, there were often problems owing to lack of skills, machinery and inputs. This explained part of the fall in agricultural production. In the large farms, too, uncertainty about possible division made it difficult to shape a rational plan of production (Abele, 1992).

The privatization process in Lithuania has been very different from developments in Estonia and Latvia. Privatization has been much faster and more comprehensive. In fact, privatization in Lithuania has been one of the most rapid in all the Eastern countries. Already by the end of 1992, 56 per cent of all assets had been privatized (EIU, 1993:1). Vouchers and employee ownership have played a more important role, and direct sales and foreign investment have had a smaller role. Considerations regarding the fair distribution of ownership have been stronger, and the policy has placed much more emphasis on the interests of the workers. The main explanation behind this development lies in the fact that non-titular Lithuanian groups have played a limited role. Almost the whole population was united in the fight for independence. Once this fight was won, the nationalist parties had a much weaker position than was the case in Estonia and Latvia. The focus was on economic problems and questions concerning distribution rather than the problem of a large Russian minority.

The cornerstone in the fast privatization in Lithuania has been the voucher scheme.[13] The Law on the Initial Privatization of State-owned Property

---

[13] The first privatizations were in the form of transfers of shares of leased enterprises to employees. The amount transferred was the sum of the leasing fees paid, plus delayed wage payments invested in production plus part of the social funds. Almost 60 enterprises were included in this programme. Another early transfer to employees was included in a law from December 1990. Enterprises with capital exceeding a certain amount could sell up to 10 per cent of their capital to

(LIPSP) was passed in February 1991 at a time when the result of the fight for independence was far from clear. The privatization plan was one of the elements in the fight for independence in Lithuania. The scheme signalled a determination in the struggle for economic self-management. It included the privatization of enterprises formerly owned and controlled by the central authorities in Moscow. The vouchers and the cash quotas, described below, were only given to residents. This formed an effective barrier against the flow of roubles from the rest of the (former) Soviet Union into the privatization process.

The voucher scheme was probably inspired by Czech discussions and their plan for a similar system. However, the Lithuanians were the first to implement the system. The vouchers were distributed in April 1991, the sale of enterprises started in September 1991 and investment funds were approved in December 1991 at the time when the Czech voucher system took off. The distribution of vouchers was dependent on the age of the citizens. People below the age of 18 years received 1 000 roubles, while the people of the age of 35 or higher received 5 000 roubles, and between these groups the amount was increased step by step from 1 000 to 5 000 roubles. The voucher rights and all the transactions were recorded in special accounts in the public Savings Bank. The nominal amount has been revalued on two occasions increasing the nominal value of the vouchers by eight times since their introduction to compensate for inflation and the revaluation of the assets to be privatized (KPMG, 1993).

The account system was made to control the limited transferability of vouchers; the vouchers could only be transferred to relatives. However, it subsequently became possible to use vouchers in exchange for outstanding loans for housing. A loophole was also made in relation to investment funds. These funds were established by private initiative in the autumn of 1991, and the law was amended in December 1991 to legalize their functions. People could invest their vouchers in the funds. In return they received shares in the funds. The funds invested the vouchers in different firms. Investment-fund shares could be sold for cash (World Bank, 1993c). In March 1994 about 33 per cent of the privatized capital was owned by investment funds (Visokaviciene, 1994). Since the shift of government, the investment funds have played a fairly passive role because certain temporary restrictions were imposed on them and new permanent legislation was delayed.

The vouchers could be used both in the auctions for small enterprises as well as in the share subscriptions for large enterprises, and in the

employees. Part of this could be paid by vouchers. 50–60 per cent of the state enterprises used this method in the initial stages of privatization up to July 1991, when another programme started (Frydman et al., 1993).

privatization of housing. The assets were sold for a combination of cash and vouchers. The cash quota connected to the vouchers set a limit on how much cash a person could use to bid for the assets to be privatized. By February 1994 about 30 per cent of the vouchers had still not been used and it was stipulated by law that vouchers not used for buying assets would be converted to state bonds at the end of the planned privatization period. However, such a solution would have been very expensive for the state budget. Instead it was decided to extend the deadline, prepare the remaining firms to be privatized, set an expiry date for the vouchers of July 1995 and terminate their value if they were not used for buying the remaining assets.

Small-scale privatization of enterprises with a book value below a certain amount was carried out by auction, where vouchers and cash quotas could be used. There were special conditions to secure the continuation of the current activity for at least three years, and layoffs of employees were restricted to a maximum of 30 per cent in the same period. By August 1992, 1 300 small enterprises had been privatized (World Bank, 1993c) and by October 1994 the number had increased to 2 498 (Ministry of Economics).

From the start, 10 per cent of the shares could be sold to the firms' employees at concessionary prices. This percentage was increased to 30 per cent in April 1992 and in February 1993 the new government further increased the percentage to 50 per cent of which 20 per cent were without voting rights. According to data from the Ministry of Economics, in the first period 461 large enterprises were privatized and only a few shares went to employees.

In the next period, from April 1992 to February 1993, 945 large enterprises were privatized of which about half had no employee shares and about one-third had 30 per cent or more employee shares. From February 1993 to November 1994, out of 950 large enterprises 79 per cent had 50 per cent or more employee ownership. These enterprises represented 67 per cent of the capital privatized in this period under the Labour government. According to the normal procedure for privatization the enterprise initially draws up a privatization plan that must be approved by the Central Privatization Commission often represented by Privatization Committees of regional governments. In most cases 89 per cent of the shares are for sale. The initial offer for the first round is based on the book value revalued by an inflation parameter. If the bids do not reach within 10 per cent of these price, the price is regulated up or down, and a new round of bids takes place. It has been most difficult to sell the large energy-intensive enterprises in heavy industry that have close relations to the former Soviet Union. There have been attempts to break them up into smaller units, and some of them have been put up for sale for foreign currency. In August 1992, a list of 114

Table 2.4: Overview over privatization, 1989–1994

	Estonia	Latvia	Lithuania
wild privatization	'experiments' from 87 SOE subsidiaries from ultimo 1989 joint stock	Institutional control unclear,commercialization gives high autonomy for managers to buy and sell assets	distribution high priority, high speed of privatization can give lack of control in implementation
reprivatization	Dec. 1990 law, pre-1940 property to citizens, by April 1992, 200 000 claims, Feb. 1994, 100 000 validated, compensation vouchers	deadline for claims agricultural land, June 1991, on firms, July 1992, for housing, Oct. 1994, compensation vouchers	only 'immovable' property, deadline for claims, Jan. 1992, no trade of land for 5 years
small privatization	Dec. 1990 law, amended, May 1992, book value< 600 000 Rb slow at start, Oct. 1991, only 95 (IMF), April 1993, 50% privatized, 1993, sold 243 125 mill. EEK, 1994, sold 1 000, nearly all privatized	Nov. 1991, legislation partly by local municipalities, below 10 employees, auction bidders >16 years residency trade, catering, service 83% privatized, Aug. 1994, mostly to the employees	vouchers and cash quotas can be used in auctions, conditions: employment cannot be reduced more than 30% and same activity 3 years, Aug. 1992, 1 300 sold, Aug. 1994, 2 425 sold (70%)
large privatization	1989 IME, people's enterprises, 1991, 7 SOE experiments, 1992, EPE Treuhand model, June 1993, law strengthens EPA, Nov.1992 – Nov. 1994, announced 375 SOEs, 110 000 employees, 1993, sold 54 for 340 mill. EEK guarantees: 9 000 jobs, 220 mill. EEK Investment, 1994, sold 109.1 bill. EEK guarantees: 24 000 jobs, 650 mill. EEK investment Public auction of minority shares for vouchers started autumn, 1994	Mar. 1991 Decree, 1991, 6 SOE sold to employees, standstill sale decentralized to ministries, Apr. 1993, 20 SOE sold/leased, Jan. 1994, 46 SOE sold/leased, 1994, about 180 SOE sold/leased, Mar. 1994, new law, centralization of authority at Latvian Privatization Agency, Nov. 1994, first int. tender, autumn 1994, sale for voucher/cash, Aug. 1994, start voucher market, one voucher/year in Latvia, + 15 if citizen, - 5 if not	Feb. 1991, LIPSP privatization law, voucher legislation, Sept. 1991, sales begin, sale of shares through vouchers and cash quotas, Dec. 1991, Investment Funds, the share employees can buy at preferential terms increased from 10% to 50% Jan. 93, Aug. 1992, 50% privatized, 114 SOE foreign cash sale, Aug. 1994, 71% of enterprises and 48% of capital privatized, 2 241 large SOEs sold voucher sale to July 1995

banks	most commercial banks started as privately owned	commercial banks mixed owners, 1993–4, Bank of Latvia's commercial branches privatized	1993/94, commercial branches of Central bank and Savings Bank privatized
land/property /housing	Apr. 1993 law, vouchers for each year worked in Estonia, payment per squaremeter, July 1994, 10 000 out of 460 000	restitution or main part to be sold for vouchers: ½ m² = 1 voucher, start Jan. 1995	restitution or sold for vouchers and cash, Dec 1992, 89% private, 1993, finished, 1994, large real estate market
agriculture	1991, law on land reform quite slow privatization mainly through restitution, 1993 only 10 000 private farms, June 1993, preferential rights to farmer coops for food industry	start in 1989, restitution, Nov. 1990, land reform, usufructus, June 1991, property reform collectives and state farms => joint stock companies, shares to employees and former owners, 1993, 2/3 land private, 57 500 mainly through restitution	1989, law on land rights, usufructus to 6 000 former owners, July 1991, land law, restitution compensation also possible, Sept. 1992, 500 000 applicants, ult. 1993, only 1/5 settled green vouchers to farmers
foreign investment	Sept. 1991, foreign investment law, April 1993, foreigners can buy land but not trade it, tax benefits	Nov. 1994, foreigners can own land with production facilities, tax benefits	only Lithuanians can own, foreigners 99 year leases, tax benefits
new firms	rapid development, lack of finance, 1993, 10 000 start-ups	not widespread in industry, but in trade, construction, services, most non-Latvian entrepreneurs	not widespread in industry, but in trade, construction, services

state-owned enterprises for unrestricted sale for foreign currency was published. By March 1994, only 38 of these enterprises had been sold. This type of privatization has been relatively slow and foreign sale can only be considered as a supplement in Lithuania.

The Ministry of Economics has estimated that there were 8 484 state enterprises with a total book value of 1 608 million Lits, of which 6 464 enterprises with a value of 1 069 million Lits were included in LIPSP. By October 1994, 74 per cent of the enterprises and 67 per cent of the book value included in LIPSP had been privatized.

Privatization of housing has also been very fast in Lithuania. The voucher system played an important role in this process. Already in December 1992,

89 per cent of the apartments were in private hands (EIU, 1993:1). About 43 per cent of the redeemed vouchers were used for apartments (KPMG, 1993). By December 1993, 94 per cent of the apartments planned for privatization had been privatized (Martinavicius, 1994). This rapid privatization has opened up a fast developing real-estate market in the cities.

Restitution was also an element in the privatization of housing, although it has been most important in agriculture. Privatization of agriculture has many similarities with the process in Latvia. In 1989, there were 835 collective farms and 275 state farms in Lithuania. The same year a new law on land rights transferred the usufruct rights to 6 000 small plots of land to the farmers. They were not allowed to trade the land. The new Land Law in July 1991 opened up agricultural land for full private ownership, and it gave priority to former owners or their descendants to take over the land. There was a maximum limit of 80 hectares, the new owner had to farm the land and could not sell it within five years. In March 1992, the restrictions on leasing of land were taken away. In some cases the former owners received compensation instead of physical assets. There were about half a million claims on land and other assets, and it took a long time to settle these claims.

According to Frydman et al. (1993) the reorganization of the farms began in November 1991 and by autumn 1992 it was almost complete. The collective workers received vouchers in relation to the number of years worked for the collective. In some cases the actual workers took over the collective or separate units, for example, large dairy barns. On the whole, the privatization of agriculture was quite chaotic. Many inefficient small-scale farms with unskilled people from the cities were established resulting in a fall in production. The uncertainty of the future for collective and state farms resulted in bad planning and falling production.

The transition of the legal structure and basic institutions proceeded slowly. This was related to the relatively slow and weak stabilization and liberalization policy. Therefore, the positive effects of privatization were initially quite limited. A direct relation between control and responsibility for the economic results – a change in ownership – is not enough to give a fundamental change of incentives. The managers of the enterprises must be monitored by the owners – the majority group of shareholders. Competitive pressure is also needed to give the right incentives. The chosen methods of privatization gave the employees of the firms a relatively big share of the ownership in Lithuania. It will be interesting to see whether this will make employee ownership only a temporary type of ownership, or whether employees' participation will be a permanent feature of the Lithuanian economy.

2.6   THE DEVELOPMENT IN PRODUCTION AND UNEMPLOYMENT

In all Eastern countries in transition, production has fallen sharply in the first years after the start of the transition. This has also been the case for the three Baltic countries. In 1990–92 GDP fell by nearly 40 per cent in all three countries. Part of this fall can be explained by the lack of registration of the new growing private activities and underreporting of the results in state-owned firms. The new private firms and some state-owned firms may have had an incentive to underreport to avoid taxes. For firms facing privatization the managers might have wanted to give a bad picture of the results, if they had an interest in a low price being set for the enterprise.

The time-profile shows the fall to be a little earlier in Estonia compared to Latvia and a little lower compared to Lithuania, but apart from this development has been paralleled by an accelerating fall up to 1992. *Table 2.5* shows on one side, the main factors behind the fall in production, and, on the other side, the possible factors that it is hoped will make production recover. Hence, the results would then form the characteristic J-curve – with production on the vertical axis and time on the horizontal axis. The specific relevance for each of the three Baltic countries is indicated by 'E', 'Lat' or 'Lit'.

The factors behind the fall can be divided into the demand side and the supply side: the main factor behind the fall in aggregate demand was the very tough stabilization policy, which was implemented in all three countries. Estonia was the first to tighten both fiscal and especially monetary policy with Latvia following shortly after. In Lithuania stabilization was somewhat delayed, but from the second half of 1992 and in 1993, an austere stabilization policy had a great impact on demand in Lithuania. Incomes policy can in this context be included on the demand side, because it had only been implemented for public sector wages and transfer incomes. However, this covers the main part of personal income in society, since the private sector was small at this initial stage. On the supply side incomes policy did not have much positive effect because of the monopolistic structure of production. Real incomes were cut considerably in all three countries, again with some delay in Lithuania.

The elimination of the monetary overhang induced a shift in demand behaviour. Consumers and enterprises no longer had an incentive to hoard. This meant that demand fell initially as people reduced their stockpiles instead of buying new goods. This adjustment of hoarding behaviour might have been delayed in the period with very high inflation, when people hoarded goods because they expected the high inflation to continue.[14] In Estonia and Latvia, the adjustment of inventories was probably most important in the second half of 1992 with the steep fall in inflation. In Lithuania this occurred about half a year later.

The general development in 1990–92 was a sharp fall in the demand from Russia and other republics in the former Soviet Union and also from other countries in Comecon. Most of the trading partners, especially in the former Soviet Union, simply could not pay for the goods. This resulted in increasing inter-firm arrears and a change to barter trade, but initially it resulted in a sharp fall in trade. All three Baltic countries were seriously hit by this development. As a result of the economic blockade in the spring of 1990, Lithuania experienced the first blow. The next blow of disintegration hit all three countries. The transition to trade in convertible currencies hit Estonia and Latvia in the summer of 1992, when their currencies were taken away from the rouble-zone, and both the Estonian kroon and the Latvian rouble started to appreciate strongly against the Russian rouble. Some of these tendencies could be seen in Lithuania, when the Talonas were made independent from the rouble. However, it was in the spring of 1993 that the Lithuanian currency first appreciated strongly in relation to the rouble. The industries for military production were hit hardest by the changes in trade. Other hard-hit sectors were the producers of railway carriages in Latvia and of electronic equipment in Lithuania.

External demand also includes trade with Western countries. However, there was no negative demand shock. On the contrary, the trade barriers were relaxed and the growth in Western trade was initially not restricted by demand, but by the supply side. On a longer perspective, the degree of liberalization of trade with the West and economic development in countries like Finland will have a major impact on the production in Estonia. As early as 1992 Norway, Sweden and Finland entered into free trade agreements with the three countries. In December 1991, EFTA made an agreement for a considerable liberalization of trade, and in May 1992 the EU reached an agreement liberalizing many industrial goods. In the summer of 1994, free trade agreements with the EU were concluded covering most goods except textiles and food products. This was implemented in January 1995 with a certain adjustment period for Latvia and Lithuania. Since Estonia already had a very liberal foreign trade regime, no adjustment period was needed there.

---

[14] A special situation occurred in the Baltic countries, because they started liberalization of prices before Russia. There was for a period extra demand from Russians, who faced empty shops in their own country. This was the case in 1991, when the Baltic countries had already taken important steps towards liberalization but still belonged to the rouble-zone.

Finland was already the main trading partner by 1992 indicating a dramatic shift in trade from the former Soviet Union.

Although the demand side caused a large decline in production, the supply side was at least as important. Even if aggregate demand had not changed, production would have fallen, and prices increased because the supply side could not respond to the change in the composition of demand, and to the change in the incentives of production after the commercialization of enterprises and the liberalization of prices. The enterprises had to buy their inputs and sell their outputs at market determined prices. They might not have had an incentive to maximize profits but they did have incentives to try to cover costs and maintain employment, since in many cases the management did not have the opportunity to cut employment. They could, however, employ the workforce part time with only part-time wages. There is, therefore, reason to believe that even without privatization, the incentives would have changed so that enterprises would have tried to maximize revenue and cover expenses. At the same time, the credit squeeze made it difficult for firms to cover their deficit by bank loans. They had to cut down production that could not be sold at prices covering costs. As pointed out by Hare and Hughes (1992), part of production did not even cover the costs of the inputs excluding labour inputs – value added was negative measured in world market prices. It was not production but destruction of valuable inputs to low-valued outputs. Much of this production, and production not covering wages, was cut in the initial stage of commercialization. Further cuts followed privatization and the implementation of a hard budget constraint requiring firms not only to cover costs for inputs of materials and labour but also to pay a return on capital.

The shift in demand and cost structure makes it very profitable to produce in certain fields of production. This will tend to give rise to bottlenecks for a limited period. In the initial stage, competition will be limited in such fields because of the monopolistic structure of production and limited foreign competition, as long as the currency is strongly undervalued. Therefore many firms can behave like monopolies with high prices and relatively low supply.

The sharp appreciation in real terms of the currencies in all three countries has gradually increased the competitive pressure from foreign firms. In Estonia this resulted in quite high deficits in foreign trade in the last months of 1993 and in 1994.

Table 2.5: The development in production - J-curve

DEMAND SIDE			
tough stabilization	E		more expansive economic policy
monetary policy	Lat		when inflation is under control
fiscal policy	later		
incomes policy	Lit		
downward adjustment of inventories			temporary
fall in external demand from former	E		recovery of Russian trade,
Soviet Union, collapse of payment	Lat		liberalization of trade with the
1991/2	Lit		West
Russian roubles undervalued		E	
SUPPLY SIDE			
restructuring production:			resources => new activities
commercialization	E		
=> adjustment	Lat		releasing credit squeeze and
quick to cut down	Lit		foreign capital =>
slow to start new production, lack of capital		E	increasing investment
privatization,	Lit		
hard budget => closures	E	all	new firms started up
lack of competition,	Lat		enterprises split up new, firms,
monopolies exploit			real appreciation of currency =>
bottlenecks,	(E)		intensified competition
no supply effect of	(Lit)		=> supply response
cuts in real wages,			
undervaluation of currency =>			
foreign competition low			
restructuring foreign trade			
fast break-down of tradelinks, slow		E	increasing trade =>
build-up of	Lat,	later	exploiting competitive
new trade links,	Lit	Lat	advantage especially in the West
terms of trade shock		Lit	
energy prices	E, Lat		
	Lit		

In all three countries, the restructuring of production has caused a decline in output combined with upward pressure on prices. However, it is very difficult to estimate the exact impact of restructuring, and the relative importance in each of the three countries. Commercialization has been implemented in all three, and part of the production that could not be sold has been cut down. The next step has been taken only in Estonia where fairly severe bankruptcy procedures have been implemented. In Lithuania privatization has been extended, but the other institutions necessary to develop full market incentives have not been developed at the same speed as privatization. However, the growth of financial institutions can help to monitor the managers of firms. In all three countries, there will still be strong pressure for the closure of unprofitable firms and a fall in production, when the hard budget constraint is fully implemented. The monopolistic structure has been especially emphasized in Latvia (see Nørgaard, 1994). However, since the production structure in all three countries was dominated by large monopolies operating in the whole of the USSR, monopoly behaviour is probably a big problem in all countries.

The main problem of restructuring is that it is much easier and quicker to close down than to build up new production. The question is, how successful the countries are in starting up new production in existing firms and establishing new firms, and how successful they are in splitting up the former monopolies. Estonia leads both in relation to the development of new firms and in attracting foreign capital. Another ground for optimism is the increase in imported capital goods in 1993 and 1994. An important barrier to investment is the strict monetary policy. Bank loans are nearly always short term and at very high interest rates (Sutela, 1994). This means that the enterprises have to finance their investment from internal accumulation or from capital injections from their new owners.

Disruption of the trade links with the former Soviet Union has, as already noted, meant a considerable fall in production in all three countries. The fall in trade accelerated in 1991 and peaked in 1992 with sharply increased import prices from the former Soviet Union. There was a severe energy price shock strongly affecting the supply side of the Baltic industries. Trade with Western partners fell in 1991 because of the unstable political situation, but since then Western trade has developed rapidly. Baltic imports of Western goods are restricted on the demand side by the lack of purchasing power and finance. This is not the case with Baltic exports to the West. At the prevailing low wages the Baltic countries are highly competitive, although exports are still at a rather low level. Estonia is in front principally because of the sharply increased trade with Finland. Latvia has also experienced an important shift of trading partners. According to the State Statistics Committee of Latvia,

Table 2.6: Economic results in the three Baltic countries

	Estonia					
	1989	1990	1991	1992	1993	1994
GDP growth %[1]	-1	-8	-11	-26	-8	5
unemployment average %[3]	0	0	0	1.1	2.5	2.0
inflation %[1]	6	23	211	1 076	90	47
average wage $ Dec.[3]			16	65	77	178
minimum wage $ Dec.[3]			4	23	22	38
real wage growth %[1]	4	1	-36	-45	5	11[5]
state budget surplus[1] % of GDP	2.8	2.9	4.6	0.5	-1.4	0
balance of trade[1]% of GDP		-2.5[2]	8.4[2]	-2.9	-7.4	-16[7]
current account[1]% of GDP				3.2[8]	1.5[8]	-7.0[8]
% of export to CIS[4]		94	82	34	30	30[5]
% imports from CIS[4]			72	40	22	20[5]
local currency/$ Dec.[3] June 1992=100				102	109	97
foreign investment mil. $[1]				58	122	294[7] 187[8]
private sector[5] % of employment					44[3]	55[1]

	Latvia					
	1989	1990	1991	1992	1993	1994
GDP growth %[1]	7	-3	-8	-34	-12	3
unemployment average %[3]	0	0	0	1.2	5.2	6.2
inflation %[1]	5	11	224	951	109	36
average wage $ Dec.[3]			12	52	118	188
minimum wage $ Dec.[3]			3	9	25	52
real wage growth %[1]	5[2]	5[2]	-16	-16	1	14[5]
state budget surplus[1] % of GDP	1	2	6.4	0	1	-2
balance of trade[1]% of GDP	-4.7[2]	-6.8[2]	2.7[2]	3.7[2]	2.5[5]	-7.4[5]
current account[1]% of GDP	-10[2]	-5.3[2]	5.5[2]	1.6	8.4	-3.1[7]
% of export to CIS[4]		95	97	45	47	43[5]
% imports from CIS[4]		75	87	38	39	30[5]
local currency/$ Dec.[3] June 1992=100				100	70	64
foreign investment mil. $[1]				43	60	220[7]
private sector[5] % of employment		8	12	31	47	53[1]

	Lithuania					
	1989	1990	1991	1992	1993	1994
GDP growth %[1]	2	-5	-13	-38	-16	2
unemployment average **%**[3]	0	0	0	0.7	1.3	2.4
inflation %[1]	2	8	225	1 021	390	70
average wage $ Dec.[3]			10	27	70	115
minimum wage $ Dec.[3]			3	5	13	16
real wage growth %[1]	8	7	-18	-33	-9[5]	14[5]
state budget surplus[1] **% of GDP**	-3.8	-3.7	4.9	0.7	-5.2	-4.9
balance of trade[1]**% of GDP**	-8.4	-8.8	9.1	3.4	-8.6	-1.6[7]
current account[1]**% of GDP**				3.4	-6.2	-8
% of export to CIS[4]		94	85	65[5]	57[5]	47[5]
% imports from CIS[4]		80	83	79[5]	67[5]	50[5]
local currency/$ Dec.[3] June 1992=100				200	223	229
foreign investment mil. $[1]				5	40	125[7]
private sector[5] **% of employment**	5	6	16	42	54	61[1]

Sources: 1) EBRD, 2) World Bank, 3) *The Baltic Independent*, 4) ECE, 5) National
           Statistics, 6) IMF, 7) EIU, 8) Bank of Estonia

MER (1993), the CIS's share of trade fell from 81 per cent in 1991 to 47
per cent in 1992. 'Other' countries, especially Western countries, increased
from 7 per cent to 46 per cent of trade in the same period. Lithuania is a little
slower in restructuring trade. Imports from the CIS have been quite stable at
around 80 per cent and for the first time in 1993–4 this percentage was
significantly reduced. For Estonia and Latvia this percentage was halved as
early as 1992 (EIU, 3:93). It can be expected that, as production is
restructured, exports to the West and a recovery of trade with the CIS and
Eastern Europe will make an important contribution to growth.

   In the initial stages of transition, employment has not followed the steep
fall in production. The enterprises have kept their workforces although they
have cut down production. However, the workers have often been sent home
for a time without pay and without being registered as unemployed. This has
been the case in all three countries. In Estonia the rules for unemployment
benefit are quite restrictive and the benefits rather low. Therefore, only
around one-fifth of those actively seeking jobs are registered and receive
unemployment benefits (Purju et al., 1994). In 1993 more unemployment

emerged, especially in Latvia (EIU, 1993:4), and in Lithuania official unemployment started to rise in September 1995 (*Baltic Independent*).

2.7   ECONOMIC AND POLITICAL PERSPECTIVES

For centuries developments in the Baltic countries have had many parallels with each other. Since their independence in 1991, there are, however, important differences in their path to and destination for a market-based economy. Estonia has chosen the most liberal model with a very limited role for the state, a low level of social benefits, emphasis on foreign capital, and very limited room for 'popular capitalism' or employee ownership in privatization. Lithuania is not so oriented towards the West and puts an emphasis on more widespread ownership by the population in general and by the employees of firms.

The main threats especially for Estonia and Latvia are associated with the conditions and possible integration of the Russian-speaking minorities. If the Russian question is handled with care, and if a nationalist government fails to appear in Russia, there is hope that the large Russian minority will be gradually and peacefully integrated into Estonian and Latvian society. The Russian withdrawal of the military in August 1994 might imply that the 'Russian question' will have a lower profile in the political debate. On the other hand a strengthening of the nationalistic right wing both in the Baltic countries and in Russia may cause tensions to increase. The conflict level will also depend on developments in production, because high unemployment may intensify social conflicts. Enterprises with many Russian workers in particular have to restructure production and cut employment. In this way the social conflicts of transition combined with the national question could make a dangerous cocktail which might result in political and economic instability and drawbacks for the transition process.

Drastic cuts in living standards for pensioners, the unemployed and workers in the troubled enterprises are important social problems in all three countries. Unions are weak and lack legitimacy and the workers are split, especially in Estonia and Latvia because of the national question. In Estonia, the neo-liberal policy has neglected the social problems. In spite of modifications in this policy in the autumn of 1994, the election in the spring of 1995 was expected to see a popular reaction. In Latvia, the government has given a higher priority to social problems and in Lithuania a turn to the left had already taken place in the elections at the end of 1992.

Stabilization policy is balancing on a knife edge, where on the one hand, too weak a policy might mean continued inflation, and on the other hand, too tough a stabilization policy can result in further social deprivation and in persistent unemployment and 'hysteresis'. High unemployment and low tax revenues from the increasing private sector might mean continued pressure on the state budget resulting in further cuts in social transfers and public employment in health, education and so on. There is a risk that all three countries will be caught in such a low growth trap. On the other hand, inflation has fallen in all three countries and will probably reach an acceptable level in 1995 or 1996. This may give room for an expansionary policy. A recent fall in interest rates might indicate a relaxation of the credit squeeze on investment. An investment and export upswing is probably on its way most strongly in Estonia but also in the other two countries.

All three countries seem to be determined in their transition to the market. Liberalization is nearly finished in most fields and privatization has taken a large step especially in Lithuania and recently also in Estonia. The upswing in foreign investment, especially in Estonia, is an indicator of the development of legislation and the necessary institutions. The other countries are following close behind. However, there is still some way to go in developing clear rules for investors and in developing a well-functioning financial system in all countries. Unclear rules about private property, contracts, taxation and especially weak public instruments to control adherence to the laws still provide ample opportunities for different forms of criminal networks. Criminality has increased very much in all three countries. Payment of protection 'tax' to different mafia gangs is widespread in all sectors. The threat is that such structures establish roots deep in the private sector and in the public sector. On the other hand, there is a hope that when privatization is finished and the agents have clear legal rules to follow there will be less room for the black economy. Estonia is in the forefront of developing a legal framework and tightening budget constraints on enterprises.

In the production system it seems that all three countries have reached the bottom of the J-curve. Investment and export-induced growth, restructuring of existing enterprises and the growth dynamics of the new private sector are probably most developed in Estonia but the other two countries are following close behind. Initially Estonia was in a better position with a higher output per capita and with higher potential for close cooperation with the West, especially with Finland. The increase in unemployment was delayed in relation to the steep fall in production. Officially the former first started to increase in Latvia in 1993, whereas in Lithuania this happened in the autumn of 1994, and in Estonia the official registration still shows very low unemployment. In reality unemployment is probably quite high and increasing in all three countries.

The main threat from the surrounding world is still a reaction in Russia resulting in a nationalistic policy where rebuilding of the old Soviet Empire is the main goal. In a situation where the Russian Federation itself is at risk of being split such a development is unlikely. However, the Russians still consider the Baltic countries to belong to their sphere of influence, and politicians in Russia often express concern about conditions for the Russian-speaking minorities in the Baltic countries. If the reforms come to a standstill in Russia, and if the Russian economy continues to be in a chaotic situation, this could have a strong negative impact on the Baltics. If, on the other hand, Russia develops a stable market economy, trade links with Russia and other CIS states could have a positive impact on the Baltic economies. Because it has better political relations with Russia, Lithuania has an advantage in this respect.

Estonia is ahead in switching its trade to the West. There is a risk that economic problems in the West could result in limited demand and some protectionist actions. However, the main trend is still for liberalization of trade. If the liberal trade regime is extended to cover the Baltic countries it will mean a good opportunity for these countries to start an export-induced growth. Western firms will find opportunities to invest in the Baltic countries and use the cheap, highly qualified Baltic labour force.

The interaction between the different systems can be summarized in a vicious and a beneficial circle: in the worst case escalating social conflicts, either because of national tensions or because of disappointed expectations, may result in political deadlock. The countries could end up in a low-growth trap because of the failure of stabilization and of restructuring enterprises. High unemployment could intensify social conflict and a big proportion of the population could be expelled from the active labour force. The destruction of physical capital might be followed by destruction of human capital. Halfway reforms and bad habits from the command economy might result in an economic system where corruption and non-economic 'mafia-methods' would be necessary elements of transactions. Political instability, development of authoritarian governments, tensions with other countries and protectionism might diminish the possibility of exploiting the advantage of foreign trade and increase the risk connected to foreign investment.

An important element in the positive circle is a compromise between different social groups creating a stable political climate. This widens the possibility of a balanced economic policy and the fulfilment of institutional restructuring. Clear and stable rules and creation of the necessary market institutions could create a good climate for investment, both domestic and foreign, and people might learn quickly to act under market conditions. The competitive advantage of low wages and good qualifications could be used to generate strong export-led growth made possible by open Western markets and renewed trade links with the CIS. Growth and mutual economic dependency might diminish the social and ethnic conflicts and stabilize the new democracies.

Neither the negative nor the positive circle is very likely to happen in any of the Baltic countries. The probable outcome lies somewhere between the two extremes. At the time of writing, in November 1994, development is closer to the positive circle. The different elements have different weights in the three countries. In Estonia and Latvia national conflict combined with high unemployment are the most serious risks. The social consequences of the neo-liberal policy in Estonia increases this risk. In Lithuania, on the other hand, the main problem might be too slow restructuring.

2.8   REFERENCES

Aage, H. (1991a), *The Baltic Republics*, NATO colloquium 1991, Brussels.

Aage, H. (1991b), Popular Attitudes and Perestroika, *Soviet Studies,* 1:91.

Abele, D. (1992), *Über gegenwärtige Lage in Landwirtschaft Lettlands*, Working Paper, Institute of Economics, Latvian Academy of Sciences.

Andersen, E.A. (1992a), *Estland, Letland og Litauen – en landebeskrivelse*, SNU.

Andersen, E.A. (1992b), De baltiske lande i verdensøkonomien: ressourcer, problemer og perspektiver, *Økonomi og Politik*, 3:92.

Andersen, E.A. (1994), *De baltiske land i 1993 – fremgang trods alt*, Øststatus 1993, Østeuropa-instituttet, Københavns Universitet.

Arone, I. (1994), *Brief Economic Survey of Latvia*, Working Paper, Deutsch Lettischer Bank, Riga.

Bennett, A.G.G. (1993), The Operation of the Estonian Currency Board, *IMF Staff Papers*, 40:2, 2.

Bleskina, T. (1993), Latvians Buying New Purses, *The Baltic Review*, 2:93.

Coopers & Lybrand (1993), *The Legal, Regulatory and Institutional Framework for Business and Investment in Albania, Bulgaria, the Czech and Slovak Republics, Estonia, Hungary, Latvia, Lithuania, Poland and Romania*, Report prepared for the Commission of the EC.

Dellenbrant, J.Å. (1992), Estonia's Economic Development 1940–90 in Comparison with Finland's, chapter 10 in Åslund (ed.), *Market Socialism or the Restoration of Capitalism*, Cambridge University Press.

EBRD (European Bank for Reconstruction and Development) (1994), *Transition Report*, October 1994, London.

EBQR (*Estonian Bank Quarterly Review*), Tallinn.

ECE (Economic Commission of Europe) (1993*), Economic Survey of Europe in 1992–1993*, UN, New York.

EIU (Economist Intelligence Unit) (Selected Years), *Country Reports*, London.

Elenurm, T. et al. (1993), *Employee-Owned Firms in the Transitional Economy – the Case of Estonia*, Working Paper, EMI, Tallinn.

Frydman, R. et. al. (1993), *The Privatization Process in Russia, Ukraine and the Baltic States*, Privatization Reports, Vol. II, Central European University Press, Budapest, London, New York.

Hanson, P. (1990), *The Baltic States,* The Economist Intelligence Unit – Briefing, London.

Hare, P.G. and Hughes, G. (1992), Industrial Policy and Restructuring in Eastern Europe, *Oxford Review of Economic Policy*, vol 8., 1:92.

IMF (1991), *IMF Survey*, vol. 20, no. 15, p. 234.

IMF (1992), Latvia is first Former Soviet State to Adopt a One-Year Stand-By Arrangement, *IMF Survey*, November.

IMF (1993a), *Latvia – Recent Economic Developments,* International Monetary Fund, 6 April.

IMF (1993b), *World Economic Outlook*, October.

KPMG (1993), *Lithuanian Domestic Privatization,* Peat Marwick, Policy Economics Group, PHARE.

Kukk, K. (1993), Out of Hyperinflation: The Estonian Experience, *The Baltic Review*, 2:93.

Lainela S. and P. Sutela (1993), Introducing New Currencies in the Baltic Countries, *Review of Economies in Transition*, vol. 8, Bank of Finland.

LDA (1994), *Business with Latvia*, April 1994, No. 2, Latvian Development Agency, Riga.

Lipton D. and J. Sachs (1990), Creating a Market Economy in Eastern Europe: The Case of Poland, *Brookings Papers on Economic Activity*, 1:90.

Martinavicius, J. (1994), *Privatization in Lithuania: Legislative and Political Environment and Results Achieved*, Working Paper, Vilnius University.

Medvedevskih, Z. and L. Vojevoda (1992), *Actual Problems of Latvian Industry*, Working Paper, Institute of Economics, Latvian Academy of Sciences.

MER (Ministry of Economic Reforms) (1993), *The Survey of Latvia's Economy in 1992 and Prognoses for 1993*, Riga.

Mygind, N. (1994), *Omvæltning i Øst* (translated as: Societies in Transition, Copenhagen Business School), Samfundslitteratur, Copenhagen.

Nørgaard O. (ed.) (1994), De baltiske lande efter uafhængigheden. Hvorfor så forskellige? (The Baltic countries after independence. Why so different?), *Politica*, Århus.

Nørgaard, O. and I. Ostrovska (1992), Kampen om kornet: bistandspolitik og nationalisme i Letland, *Vindue mod Øst*, no. 21.

Purju, A. (1994), *Privatization with Vouchers in Estonia*, Working Paper, March 1994, Stockholm Institute of East European Economies.

Rajasalu, T. (1994), *Estonian Economy: Summer 1994*, Report, no. 2, Institute of Economics, Estonian Academy of Sciences, Tallinn.

Rosati, D.K. (1992), The Politics of Economic Reform in Central and Eastern Europe, *CEPR Occasional Paper*, no. 6.

Shteinbuka, I. (1993), Latvia in Transition: First Challenges and First Results, *Review of Economies in Transition*, vol. 8, Bank of Finland.

Shteinbuka, I. (1994), *Privatization in Latvia*, Working Paper, Ministry of Finance, Riga.

Sutela, P. (1994), Production, Employment and Inflation in the Baltic Countries, *Communist Economies & Economic Transformation*, vol. 6, no. 2.

Terk, E. (1993), Privatization in Estonia: Will the Economic Approach Prevail?, *The Baltic Review*, 2:93.

The Baltic Independent (weekly paper), Tallinn.

Van Arkadie, B. and M. Karlsson (1991), *Economic Survey of the Baltic Republics*, Stockholm.

Visokaviciene, A. (1994), *Survey of the Current State of the Privatization Process in Lithuania*, Working Paper, Vilnius University.

Vojevoda L. and L. Rumpis (1993), *Small Privatization in Latvia*, Working Paper, Institute of Economics, Latvian Academy of Sciences.

World Bank (1992), *Foreign Direct Investment in the States of the Former USSR*, Washington DC.

World Bank (1993a), *Estonia: The Transition to a Market Economy*, A World Bank Country Study, The World Bank, Washington DC.

World Bank (1993b), *Latvia: The Transition to a Market Economy*, A World Bank Country Study, The World Bank, Washington DC.

World Bank (1993c), *Latvia – Informal Study of the Enterprise and Financial Sectors*, Mission report.

World Bank (1993d), *Lithuania: The Transition to a Market Economy*, A World Bank Country Study, The World Bank, Washington DC.

World Bank (1994), *Estonia – Finance and Enterprise Sector*, Mission Report Privatization.

3. Introducing New Currencies in the Baltic Countries

Seija Lainela and Pekka Sutela

3.1 ABSTRACT

This paper offers an overview of the currency reforms in the Baltic countries. After surveying the arguments for introducing national currencies, the differing solutions applied in the three countries are analysed. Estonia opted for a modified currency board, while Latvia has pursued policies that are institutionally liberal but stringent in terms of stabilization. Lithuania has followed Latvia in adopting a piecemeal reform strategy. The pros and cons of both approaches are discussed. Nevertheless, it is concluded that although escaping from the rouble zone has not only been possible but desirable, there is more than one way of achieving this goal.

3.2 BALTIC STATES INTRODUCE THEIR OWN CURRENCIES

New currencies were introduced in the Baltic states during the summer and autumn of 1992. Estonia was the first to introduce its own currency, the kroon. Latvia and Lithuania left the rouble zone a little later when they declared the parallel currencies that had been circulating alongside the Russian rouble to be the sole legal tender. These interim currencies were to be replaced with true national currencies, the lats in Latvia and the litas in Lithuania. The introduction of the lats was started in March 1993, and the litas followed during the summer of 1993. This was largely seen as a technical operation involving the exchange of banknotes – and changing price scales – without any fundamental change in the monetary system as this had already taken place when the Russian rouble was abandoned. As the Estonian experience shows, however, one should not underestimate the socio-psychological importance of finally having a 'real' national currency in circulation. Moreover, the new notes are much better protected against counterfeiting than those of the parallel currency had been.

The Baltic currencies, as the monetary authorities of these states would be the first to emphasize, are not entirely new in the sense that all three states had their own sovereign currencies between the world wars. In Estonia the currency was initially the markka and subsequently the kroon, in Latvia it was the lats and in Lithuania the litas.

There are several valid economic arguments for the introduction of national currencies in countries which were formerly part of the rouble zone (see, for instance, Fieleke, 1992, Hansson, 1993). 1) A national currency allows the pursuit of a more independent economic policy, while at the same time underlining the responsibility of national decision-makers for the development of their own economies. 2) There is no reason to think of the rouble zone as an optimal currency area. The resource endowments, probable exogenous shocks, institutions and policy goals of the former Soviet republics vary markedly. Having different currencies is therefore a more natural arrangement than the rouble zone ever was. 3) The rapid depreciation of the rouble has made it necessary for these countries to buffer themselves against the rouble crisis. 4) Particularly during the early months of 1992, the rouble zone suffered simultaneously from an excess supply of deposit roubles and a shortage of cash roubles. Supplementary currencies were duly introduced in several of the former Soviet republics for transactions purposes. There was a probability that regional or enterprise-based monies would have appeared in the Baltic countries without the introduction of sovereign currencies. That would have greatly complicated the conduct of economic policy. 5) The existence of a national currency also introduces the possibility of garnering government revenue in the form of seigniorage.

Apart from such economic considerations, Baltic currencies were also viewed from a wider perspective. A national currency has great importance as a symbol of national independence. The enthusiasm shown by the Baltic states for their own currencies is easy to understand and should also be respected from this point of view. Evidently, the endogenous population of countries like Estonia and Latvia, where stringent stabilization policies have proved very popular in the voting sense, has been willing to accept greater hardship in the name of defending the value of one's own currency than would ever have been possible under a different monetary arrangement. National sentiment, a seemingly irrelevant factor in economic policy making, may thus have had great importance in widening the sphere of the feasible in economic policies.[1]

Outside understanding of Baltic currency plans was rather less than complete in 1992. The International Monetary Fund (IMF) and the European

---

[1] Naturally, there is an interesting asymmetry. Those perhaps worst hit by stabilization do not always have the chance to vote in elections.

Community (EC) are understood to have urged the Baltic states to be cautious in introducing their own currencies. In the Baltic states this was widely, even if incorrectly, interpreted as opposition in principle to national currencies. Hansson and Sachs (1992) argue that the IMF 'tried at first to delay the introduction of Estonia's currency, arguing that the country was not yet ready'. Only after having seen that the Estonian authorities 'proceeded on their own', did the IMF provide them 'with some last-minute technical support'. They would seem to be well placed to make the comment, as Hansson was a member of the official three-member Estonian Currency Reform Committee at the time that the kroon was introduced.

However, the IMF has vehemently contested this interpretation (Odling-Smee, 1992). The Fund does not try to deny that – as evidenced by Hernández-Catá (1992) – the IMF originally took a highly cautious attitude towards the introduction of national currencies in the former Soviet Union. The Fund at that time argued that 'certain key elements would need to be in place to improve the chances for success, including, inter alia, completion of the price liberalization process and a balanced budget'. Not all such preconditions were present when the kroon was first introduced. The difference in the monetary reform schedules implied is partly explained by the fact that the Fund seems to have been thinking along the lines of establishing fully-fledged central banking, while Estonia basically chose to pursue the shorter and narrower road of a currency board. As such, the IMF naturally never questioned the sovereign right of Estonia to choose its path. The introduction of a national currency is a matter for sovereign decision-making in each independent country. What has changed since early 1992 is the emphasis given to national currencies as policy instruments. While the IMF recommended careful consideration to the Baltic countries in early 1992, the Fund was in early 1993 understood to be pushing such unwilling former Soviet republics as Belarus and Kazakhstan towards the introduction of national currencies as a condition for full-scale Fund support (see also Hernández-Catá, 1993). Indeed, if the technicality of having notes printed is satisfied, there is no economically acceptable reason for not introducing a national currency in any former rouble-zone country. The example of Ukraine perhaps shows that it is possible to manage the monetary system on one's own in an even worse manner than has been the case in the rouble zone, but that is not really a valid argument against national currencies. As pointed out above, the existence of a national currency not only creates new policy instruments, but also highlights the responsibility of domestic authorities. This is obviously a good thing in itself.

The Baltic states are only now in the process of developing institutions and instruments for the pursuit of monetary and foreign exchange policies.

This process will inevitably take a long time, as experience, know-how and other resources remain scarce.

The IMF also stressed the need to negotiate payment arrangements with the rouble-zone countries prior to the introduction of national currencies in order to prevent the dislocation of trade between these countries. In negotiations, Russia was cooperative in relation to the technical issues of exchanging kroons for roubles, but trade issues proper have been repeatedly bogged down by various economic and political conflicts of interest. All Baltic states have seen a collapse in their trade with the rouble-zone countries, especially Russia. However, trade had already started to decline before these countries left the rouble zone. Thus the Baltic states' own currencies were not a decisive factor in this regard, although they did give rise to some technical difficulties and payment delays. Russian monetary disorder has surely been a more serious trade obstacle.

Opinions differ in the Baltic states concerning the pace at which foreign trade could and should change from almost complete dependence on Russia to a more balanced geographical distribution. It is generally accepted, however, that there is a need to continue trading with Russia and other CIS states. Agreement has been reached on payment arrangements between these, although negotiations between the Baltic states and Russia were hampered by various political disputes and problems concerning, for example, the servicing of outstanding debt commitments. Much of the actual trade between the countries is conducted outside official channels, often using barter or mutually acknowledged convertible currencies. Consequently, not all of this trade is recorded in statistics.

It is widely held in the Baltic states that the decline in trade with Russia is mainly owing to the serious economic situation in Russia as well as to political measures taken by Russia that are regarded as being anti-Baltic. On the other hand, the outcome of the parliamentary elections in Lithuania in the autumn of 1992 demonstrated that, at least in that country, people felt that their own government could also do more to maintain and develop traditional trade relations.

Currency substitution, the parallel use of foreign currencies in domestic circulation (dollarization), can be interpreted in different ways. Under certain circumstances, it may be the only possible path to monetary stability. At the same time, it transfers seigniorage abroad and removes money supply from among the instruments of economic policy. Where possible, governments usually seek to avoid currency substitution. In this respect, the introduction of national currencies and the consolidation of their position have been most successful in Estonia, where the kroon has replaced practically all the roubles and convertible currencies in circulation. The Estonian kroon enjoys the confidence of the population, as is evident in the extensive exchange of cash convertible currencies for kroons and the increase in kroon deposits since the currency reform.

Convertible currencies can still be used in Latvia and, until August 1993, they could be used in Lithuania as well. In Latvia, for a lengthy period after the currency reform, a large share of transactions was made in convertible currencies. This presumably still remains the case. There have also been Russian roubles in circulation. The Latvian monetary authorities sometimes deny seeing this as a problem. In a Hayekian vein, they argue that there should be a choice of monies. Corresponding information is not available concerning Lithuania, but it seems probable that the position of the national currency has not been any stronger there.

The stability of the new currencies in the longer term is difficult to assess at this point. The Estonian kroon has from the beginning been pegged to the deutschmark and as a result of the general European currency turmoil it has strengthened along with it. The Latvian currency floated until early 1994, although the central bank was quite active in the markets, and the exchange rate against the dollar strengthened steadily. In Lithuania, the national currency floated until April 1994, when the Parliament decided to peg it to the dollar. Before that, the value of the national currency appreciated or remained stable after readjustments in monetary policy in the spring of 1993.

Against the background of Russia's monetary chaos, the introduction of the Baltic currencies stands out as a crowning achievement. In 1993, the annual rates of inflation in the Baltics varied between 35 per cent (Estonia and Latvia) and 190 per cent (Lithuania), which contrasted with the rate of inflation of 840 per cent in Russia. Even at worst, monetary reform could hardly have made the situation in the Baltic states any worse than it is in Russia. It became increasingly evident during the course of 1992 and 1993 that escaping from the rouble zone was the wise thing to do. The uphill struggle to stability and beyond to prosperity is, however, still in its early phase. The Baltic states clearly lack effective instruments for macroeconomic management and expertise in such areas as monetary and fiscal policies. This might still undermine the credibility of the new currencies. A separate, but potentially serious problem, is the rekindling of inflation since the autumn of 1993.

While stabilization policies will determine the worth of the new currencies in the short run, the ability of the Baltic economies to earn foreign exchange is of crucial importance for the stability of the new currencies in the longer term. Structural reforms in the economy and the reorganization of production are therefore important tasks. However, the countries' own resources will not be sufficient in themselves, and external financial support will remain necessary in the coming years.

It is sometimes assumed that the size of a country correlates positively with the possibilities of establishing the necessary credibility of new currencies (see Bofinger et al., 1993). The Baltic experience, especially when counterposed with Ukraine, does not support this assumption. It may actually be that small, compact countries with a high degree of homogeneity and commonly shared goals are in a better position in this respect than large countries with deep divisions. The relatively small exchange reserves needed may be easier to mobilize and some of the technicalities of transition are certainly much simpler in a small setting.

3.3 THE ESTONIAN KROON

3.3.1 Background

Discussion of a national currency started in Estonia in 1987 when a group of four high-ranking government officials and scholars published the so-called IME programme, aimed at securing Estonia's economic independence.[2] A national currency was part of this programme. The economic and political obstacles to the introduction of Estonia's own currency were, however, insurmountable as long as Estonia was part of the Soviet Union. In spite of this, preparations for the introduction of the kroon got under way in 1990 when the Estonian central bank, Eesti Pank (Bank of Estonia), commenced operations. When Estonia gained political independence in August 1991, the way was open for the introduction of the country's own currency.

As already mentioned above, the IMF closely followed the preparations being made for the Estonian currency reform during the spring of 1992. The IMF had earlier supported the idea that the rouble should be retained in the republics of the former Soviet Union but later in the spring relaxed its opinion and in the final stage assisted in the practical issues involved in the introduction of the kroon. The Russian government also changed its attitude towards the introduction of national currencies in the former republics in the course of the spring. Because of the uncontrolled monetary policies pursued in some of the republics, the Russian government now felt that a shrinking rouble zone was in Russia's interest. For this reason Estonia and Russia found it fairly easy to reach agreement on the technical issues related to the introduction of the kroon.

---

[2] For the political and economic background of Estonia and Latvia, see Misiunas and Taagepera (1983), Van Arkadie and Karlsson (1992). For early Estonian economic policies, see Hansson (1992a). An authorative account of the Estonian currency reform is provided by Kallas and Sörg (1993).

The introduction of the country's own currency has been strongly supported in Estonia for both economic and political reasons. It may not be too much of an exaggeration to conclude that almost magical efficiency-enhancing properties have been attached to sovereign currency among segments of the public at large. In the longer term, however, such expectations could turn out to be a problem if greater independence in economic policy fails to bring about the rapid increase in stability and the standard of living which the Estonians expect. Two years after the currency reform, however, Estonia is already seemingly firmly on the path of economic growth.

3.3.2   Estonia's New Currency System

In introducing the kroon, Estonia basically adopted the currency board system. A currency board is arguably the most simple, credible and pressure-resistant way to introduce a national currency in undeveloped monetary conditions. It is an arrangement whereby the introduction of the currency is the responsibility of a currency board, that is, an independent monetary authority that is either distinct from the central bank or at least separate from the central bank's other activities. The currency board undertakes to convert all the national currency offered to it at a fixed rate into the currency chosen as the reserve currency. The domestic currency in circulation is fully backed by foreign exchange and can only change according to changes in the foreign exchange reserves. Monetary policy is thereby not exercised, since the supply of money is endogenous to the market (see Osband and Villeneuva, 1992, and Walters, 1987).

The aim of the currency board system is to achieve currency convertibility and a fixed exchange rate and thereby help to stabilize the economy, bring about structural change and integrate the country into the world economy as quickly as possible. As the currency board is a technical arrangement which is not associated with any economic or political discretionary power it ensures adherence to the fixed exchange rate. Political pressures, to which a conventional central bank is exposed, cannot affect a currency board. Indeed, if they do, the arrangement collapses. For the same reason, inflationary financing through central bank lending to the government cannot take place either. The government can only run budget deficits if it is able to finance them in the money market. As a country like Estonia lacks well-developed markets where the government may raise deficit finance, a currency board and a balanced budget become natural companions.[3]

---

[3] But paradoxically, a currency board system might help to pave the way to the abandonment of balanced budgets by enhancing the credibility of the government

A currency board's strength and weakness thus lie in the fact that it completely ties the hands of the currency issuing authority. In so doing, it economizes on scarce policy resources and in a limited sense borrows the credibility of the reserve currency chosen. On the other hand, it subjects possible economic policies to stringent constraints.

The great advantage of the currency board system is that it is simple to operate and does not require experts in monetary policy. This is particularly important in former socialist countries, where the ways and means of the market economy are generally less than perfectly understood.

It is essential for the success of a currency board that it is credible, that is, that the market shows confidence in its ability and will to exchange currency at a fixed rate. The country issuing the reserve currency may choose to support the currency board country here, as may also international organizations and other countries. Foreign support may become crucial in countries with a low capacity to earn foreign exchange and large variations in its foreign exchange earnings. Without support, such fluctuations would be directly reflected in the domestic money supply, which might be impossible to accept for cyclical reasons.

The currency board model in a post-communist country is naturally also open to different kinds of criticisms. It may be judged as too harsh a solution for an economy in the process of adjustment because the only way to increase the supply of money is by attracting foreign exchange into the country, either through exports or capital investment. When inflationary financing is impossible and the exchange rate is not flexible, other factors – domestic interest rates, prices and wages – must adjust. Softening adjustment by inflation and money illusion is impossible as a policy line. This puts the functioning of the economy and the political acceptability of the currency board to a severe test. Perhaps not surprisingly, currency board solutions have proved to be unacceptable to large countries. There are also examples of failed currency boards. They are thus neither sufficient nor necessary for successful stabilization. Most stabilizations have been achieved without a currency board.

Currency board arrangements have been applied in various parts of the world, mainly in former British colonies where the mother country's currency has been the reserve currency. More than 70 such boards once operated. Among the best known examples of countries which still have a currency board of some kind are Hong Kong and Singapore. In both of these cases, however, the currency board has developed a long way towards being an ordinary central bank over the years (Fieleke, 1992, pp. 20–21). Argentina

thereby facilitating market-based deficit financing. In the Estonian case, this phase may already have been reached.

adopted the currency board principle in the spring of 1991 and it has succeeded in curbing its high inflation rate and bringing down interest rates.

Before the currency reform in Estonia, there were doubts about the applicability of the currency board model in Estonia as it lacks the foreign exchange earning capacity typical of the countries cited as examples. It was suspected that money supply would become a random process in an Estonian currency board. So far at least, such fears have proved to be unfounded.

In May 1992, the Estonian Parliament passed three laws: the currency law, the law on backing the Estonian kroon and the foreign exchange law (see Eesti Pank, 1992). These laws establish the principles of Estonia's currency system. As they make the running of the Estonian currency board the task of the central bank, which also retains the opportunity to pursue monetary policies, the Estonian case is best characterized as a hybrid form of currency board (Bennett, 1992).

This fact has given rise to peculiar discussions. On one hand such prominent supporters of the currency board principle as Hanke, Jonung and Schuler (1993) argue that the Estonian case should not be characterized as a currency board at all. On the other hand Fieleke (1992) points out that no 'pure' currency boards currently seem to exist. The purist argument therefore looks suspiciously like an attempt to make a principle immune to criticisms from the real world.

According to the above-mentioned Estonian laws, the kroon is fully backed by gold and foreign exchange. The Bank of Estonia can change the amount of notes and coin in circulation only to the extent that there are changes in the gold and foreign exchange reserves. The Bank of Estonia undertakes to convert all kroons offered into foreign currencies. In the early stages of the currency reform the central bank operated in only one currency, the deutschmark. This arrangement was applied because of its simplicity. After some time the central bank shifted to the normal practice whereby it operates in several convertible currencies.

The exchange rate of the kroon is fixed and the kroon is pegged to the deutschmark (1 DM = 8 EEK). The exchange rate is allowed to fluctuate within margins of 3 per cent. The Bank of Estonia quotes an official exchange rate for the kroon against the deutschmark and unofficial rates against other currencies.

Right after its introduction, the Estonian kroon was convertible within the country as regards current account operations, that is, the convertibility covered the current foreign exchange transactions of Estonian enterprises and individuals. According to the Bank of Estonia's instructions, the kroon was convertible into foreign currencies when the customer could present documentary evidence of a journey abroad or of an import transaction. In practice, however, these documents were not always requested. Foreign exchange earnings had to be surrendered within two months of their receipt. Enterprises engaged in foreign trade could, however, obtain the Bank of Estonia's permission to keep foreign exchange in foreign banks for a longer period.

During 1993 these restrictions were gradually lifted, and Estonia moved closer to total convertibility of its currency, also in relation to capital account transactions. In March 1994, the last restriction prohibiting private persons from opening foreign currency accounts in domestic banks was eliminated.

There are no restrictions on the transfer abroad of dividends or foreign capital invested in Estonia. The permission of the Bank of Estonia is required for raising foreign loans.

The core of Estonia's foreign exchange reserves consists of the gold reserves which the country had deposited in Western central banks before 1940. During 1992, Western countries have returned these reserves, totalling about 11.3 tonnes, to Estonia either in the form of gold or foreign exchange. The Bank of Estonia is required to publish information once a month on the gold and foreign exchange reserves and the amount of notes and coin in circulation. A decision has also been made in Estonia regarding the eventual use of the country's forest reserves to back the kroon, if necessary, but the practical implementation of this decision is likely to be difficult.

3.3.3 Implementation of the Currency Reform

Technically, Estonia's currency reform was a notable success. A reform whereby the entire amount of notes and coin in circulation is changed at one time requires very complex practical arrangements. In the practical exchange of one currency for another, a large number of volunteer workers assisted at conversion points in different parts of the country. The aim was to make sure that the rules and arrangements were as unambiguous as possible so as to minimize the scope for discretionary decisions and abuse. In a small country with an educated population, the authorities were able to implement the practical exchange in a speedy and orderly fashion.

In carrying out the currency reform there was the risk that large sums of roubles might flow into the country from Russia for the conversion. This danger was avoided by restricting the amount of cash that each inhabitant could exchange and by separately investigating all unusually large transfers made between bank accounts before the conversion. It may also be that in the end the possessors of large amounts of rouble notes decided not to place their trust in the new currency of a small nation.

The currency reform was carried out between 20 and 22 June 1992. The rouble ceased to be legal tender in Estonia with immediate effect on 20 June and the only legal tender since then has been the kroon. All persons residing in Estonia who had registered their names for the conversion were allowed to exchange 1 500 roubles at a rate of 1 kroon per 10 roubles in the period from 20 to 22 June. The amount was equivalent to about 12 dollars. Larger amounts of roubles could be converted into kroons at a rate of 1 kroon to 50 roubles in the period from 26 to 30 June. After this the roubles could no longer be converted into kroons. Apparently, the Tallinn authorities believed that Estonians would use any remaining surplus roubles for shopping in Russia. The central bank of Russia, however, forbade the import of roubles from Estonia to Russia after the currency reform. The non-implementability of such restrictions is not a major problem in the case of such a small state as Estonia. This fact helped to make the reaching of agreement between the Tallinn and Moscow authorities easier than in case of, for instance, Ukraine.

Bank deposits held by residents were also converted into kroons at the rate of 1:10. The only exception was deposits of more than 50 000 roubles made after the beginning of May. The conversion of such deposits was decided on a discretionary basis. Roubles held by enterprises were also converted into kroons at the rate of 1:10. As soon as the currency reform began, stores marked their prices in kroons and, for example, all hard currency stores started to sell their goods in kroons only.

Foreign currency accounts held by enterprises or individuals remained valid and foreign currencies in such accounts could be used until the end of 1992. The accounts were, however, closed as regards new foreign currency entries, which had to be converted into kroons. From the beginning of March 1993, Estonian firms were again allowed to open settlement accounts in foreign currencies in authorized Estonian banks. According to the Bank of Estonia, this measure was made possible by the strengthened position of the kroon.

Since the introduction of the kroon, the official exchange rate quoted by the Bank of Estonia has been one deutschemark to eight kroons. The exchange rate between the kroon and the deutschemark was set at the level of the so-called market rate of the rouble at the time of the currency reform. This meant that the kroon was undoubtedly undervalued. The rouble's market rate which was determined in interbank auctions was undervalued as a result of the scarcity of currencies offered and an abundance of roubles. The undervaluation of the kroon follows the example of many other currencies that were undergoing rapid economic liberalization. It should facilitate economic development by promoting exports and protecting home markets from import competition. On the other hand, it is one possible explanation for the continuation of Estonian inflation.

A crude way of assessing the feasibility of the current exchange rate over a longer period of time is to look at Estonian competitiveness in terms of wage levels. Currently average Estonian wages are approximately US$ 80–

90 per month. Taking the Polish level of some US$ 200 per month as the benchmark, Estonia could still at least double its cost level while maintaining the current exchange rate.

Altogether about 2.2 billion cash roubles were converted into kroons (Hansson, 1992b). The amount is of about the same magnitude as estimates of the amount of roubles in circulation in Estonia at that time, on which no accurate data were available. It would seem that only small amounts of roubles were converted into kroons during the second stage of the conversion at the more unfavourable rate.

The implementation of the currency reform required discussions with Russia beforehand on practical arrangements related to the issue of the kroon. The Bank of Estonia agreed to return the roubles collected during the conversion to the central bank of Russia without compensation. Because of problems connected with payment arrangements, this was never done. Owing to high Russian inflation, and particularly after the rouble note reform of August 1993, the whole issue became academic.

3.3.4   After the Reform

The currency reform can also be considered to have succeeded fairly well in achieving goals other than technical ones. This is indicated by the fact that the kroon immediately became the only currency in circulation. Since the currency reform, significant amounts of foreign exchange have flowed into the Bank of Estonia. During the first months after the currency reform, the foreign currency converted into kroons consisted mainly of cash held by residents and the magnitude of these sums came as a surprise to the authorities.

Later on, enterprises also started to repatriate their foreign exchange funds. In July, the Ministry of Economy estimated that Estonian companies held foreign exchange in foreign bank accounts to the equivalent of US$ 65 million (Baltic News Service, 24 July 1992). Other estimates put the sum as high as US$ 100 million. Currency was evidently transferred abroad at an accelerating pace prior to the currency reform because companies were uncertain as to how foreign currency holdings would be treated.

On 16 July 1992, the Bank of Estonia published its balance sheet for the first time. It showed foreign exchange reserves of US$ 98 million. By the end of 1993, the reserves had already increased to US$ 362 million. The kroon is actually overbacked relative to the currency board principle adopted. Developments in the Baltic states' foreign currency reserves are shown in *Figure 3.1*.

Criticism of Estonia's currency reform came mainly from economists and spokesmen for the business sector. The level at which the kroon's exchange rate was fixed aroused criticism. It was argued that the undervaluation of the kroon makes imports too expensive, with the result that a large part of production becomes unprofitable (Rajasalu, 1992). It should be noted, however, that this criticism has not been levelled at the choice of a currency board as such.

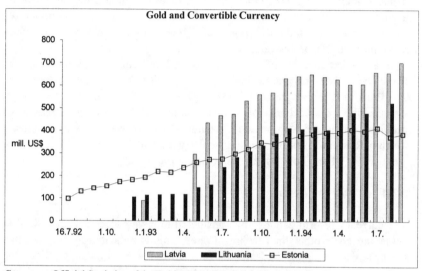

Sources: Official Statistics of the Baltic Countries, Baltic News Service

Figure 3.1: Foreign reserves

The criticisms of enterprises and banks refer to problems caused by the practical arrangements associated with the conversion and the new exchange rate system. Large companies engaged in trade with Russia are unhappy about the obligation to convert all of their roubles as this hampers their trade with Russia. Altogether, companies exchanged 700 million cash roubles into kroons in connection with the reform.

As regards commercial banks, problems were caused in the beginning by the central bank's practice of operating only in the deutschmark and not in other foreign currencies. Commercial banks had to convert other currencies deposited in accounts with them into deutschmarks before presenting them to the Bank of Estonia for conversion into kroons. The operation took time and weakened banks' liquidity as they nevertheless had to immediately pay the corresponding amounts in kroons to their customers (Otsason, 1992).

3.3.5 Impact of the Reform on the Foreign Trade Sector

As the rouble is not a convertible currency, the Bank of Estonia does not quote an exchange rate for it. According to the banking agreement between Estonia and Russia, payments between the two countries may be effected either in roubles, kroons or other currencies (*Estoniya*, 1992). The aim is to have payments related to trade with Russia handled by commercial banks. Accordingly, Estonian banks have been authorized to open correspondent accounts in Russian banks. There are three ways in which companies engaged in trade with Russia can spend the roubles they have earned: they can keep them in Estonian banks' correspondent accounts in Russia, exchange them for convertible currencies in the Russian currency auctions or find a buyer on Estonia's currency exchange. Even after the reform, there are still currency exchanges operating in Estonia where banks, acting on the instructions of companies, buy and sell kroons and convertible currencies, primarily against roubles.

Trade between Estonia and Russia has declined sharply over the past few years. Difficulties have been encountered in importing goods from Russia as well as in receiving payments for export deliveries. Hence the introduction of Estonia's own currency has not been crucial for trade with Russia, although the new payment arrangements have not apparently functioned especially smoothly. It is obvious that a substantial part of trade between Estonia and Russia that is excluded from official statistics is based either on barter or convertible currencies.

Payments with other CIS states are effected through correspondent accounts kept in the central banks and commercial banks. It is the intention of the Bank of Estonia that commercial banks gradually take over all these arrangements. In practice, trade is now partly conducted in cash convertible currencies as well. It has been agreed that payments between the Baltic states are made in convertible currencies.

3.3.6 Implications of the Reform for Other Sectors

In connection with the currency reform, the turnover tax in Estonia was raised from 8 per cent to 18 per cent, the corporate income tax was raised by 10 percentage points to 35 per cent and personal taxation was tightened. Wage rises were also restricted. These measures are part of the economic stabilization programme which the Estonian authorities drew up together with IMF experts. The stabilization programme is based on restrictive monetary policy and tight fiscal policy aimed at improving the budget balance.

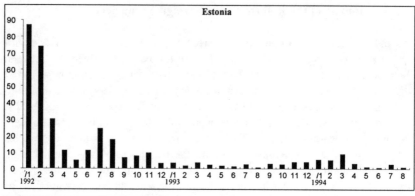

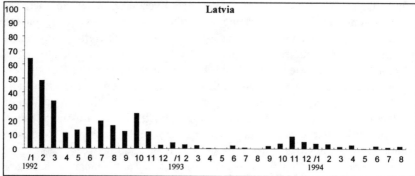

Source: Official Statistics of the Baltic Countries.

Figure 3.2: Monthly inflation rates in the Baltic countries

As a result of these measures, living costs rose by almost a quarter between June and July 1992. For the whole of 1992, the rate of inflation was 953 per cent. In 1993 the yearly inflation came down to 35 per cent, which is a remarkable achievement. However, it seems that Estonia has not been able to bring its inflation completely under control. During the first six months of 1994, consumer prices increased by 27 per cent. For monthly inflation rates see *Figure 3.2*.

There are several possible explanations why the currency board did not immediately bring about price stability. One contributing factor to the rapid rate of inflation after the currency reform has been the larger-than-expected inflow of currencies into the Bank of Estonia. This turned into a rapid increase in the amount of currency in circulation. These currencies came from both larger-than-expected original cash reserves and from exports, including the reportedly very profitable trading of metals and other commodities imported from Russia.[4] The share of exports in the economy has thus at least temporarily been larger than expected. Performance on the real side of the economy has, however, remained weak, and output fell continuously until at least early 1993. The rapid rate of inflation has reduced the substantial original undervaluation of the kroon, which had in its turn allowed the existence of inflation. Finally, one should note that Estonian price liberalization has proceeded step by step. This has also continued to feed inflation in spite of the balanced budget.

Commercial banks may set interest rates freely. Nominal interest rates on loans fell in 1993 together with the decline in the rate of inflation. At the end of the year, average loan rates were about 25 per cent (two Estonian banks, Hansapank and Hoiupank, *Estonian Economy*, 1994). Real interest rates continue to be negative. Bank-specific variations in interest rates are large. The Bank of Estonia does not quote any interest rate that might be taken as an official policy guideline.

The application of the currency board system in the Estonian conditions over the longer term will involve special problems. As already mentioned, the foreign currency reserves have grown faster than expected both because the size of domestic foreign currency cash funds was larger than expected and because export earnings had been boosted by receipts from trading. In theory it is possible that export earnings will continue to increase at a faster rate than domestic production in the future, in which case the currency board system could turn into a mechanism sustaining inflation.[5]

---

[4] The share of such re-exports reported to the authorities and of currency revenue repatriated remains a mystery.

[5] Naturally, the currency board principle only sets an upper limit on money supply, leaving it to the discretion of the monetary authority to decide which share of currency revenue should be 'activated' in money supply. As seen in *Figure 3.1*, the Bank of Estonia has not issued money up to the limit set by the currency

Perhaps partly in recognition of this danger, the central bank, which is responsible for the currency board's functions in Estonia, has also retained monetary instruments at its disposal. Most important of these involves commercial banks' reserve requirements at the central bank. In April 1993, the Bank of Estonia started to issue certificates of deposit, which it auctions regularly. However, their significance lies more in providing commercial banks with safe instruments to place their extra reserves in than in regulating the amount of money in circulation. Hence, these measures do not have any significant role as instruments of monetary policy. In principle, however, a potentially unstable combination of a currency board and a central bank pursuing monetary policy might be emerging. It is very probable that the currency board principle will be regarded as too strict in coming years, as the credibility of the kroon will no longer be a problem and politicians, not least for good economic reasons, increasingly come to learn to love budget deficits. The transition from the present arrangement to something much more like an ordinary central banking system is a question which will perhaps soon be occupying Estonian policy planners.

A more probable outcome than oversized export revenue will be the drying up of income from trading Russian commodities on international markets. In such a case, adherence to the currency board would lead to a contraction of money supply in an economy which has already undergone a statistical decline of some 50 per cent in production. This might be the time for the Tallinn authorities to gradually abandon the currency board, which at least some of them have always understood to be a temporary vehicle for creating credibility and borrowing time for the development of central banking instruments and policies proper.

The Banking Department of the Bank of Estonia has already intervened strongly in the banking system. Several banks, among them three of the largest, had to be liquidated or consolidated in the first round of a post-socialist banking crisis. These moratoria following insolvency translated into illiquidity were owing to general incompetence, unduly high inflationary expectations and the loss of currencies in the Moscow VEB debacle. It was not yet a case of a bank crisis induced primarily by bad loans. That is still waiting in the wings.

3.3.7   Estonia: Concluding Remarks

Hanke, Jonung and Schuler (1993) cite three criteria for a genuine currency

inflow. The accumulation of reserves – say for the case of a banking crisis – might, however, become politically difficult to sustain in some circumstances.

board. The monetary base must be fully backed by foreign reserves, the currency must be fully convertible and the exchange rate fixed. In their view the Estonian case fails on two counts. At the time that they wrote the article, kroon convertibility was not complete even for current-account transactions, and the kroon was not convertible for capital-account purchases by Estonians. Furthermore, the kroon exchange rate is not fixed but pegged; it can be changed.

There is no doubt that the Estonian case is not that of a pure currency board. But, as Fieleke (1992) argues, it seems impossible to find a pure currency board anywhere. Moreover, it seems that Hanke and others may exaggerate the ease with which the kroon exchange rate can be changed.[6] Finally, their case is weakened by their insistence that 'when the pegged exchange rate of the Estonian monetary system is altered, as we believe will occur in the near future, the currency board system should not be blamed, since Estonia does not have that'. As all good utopians know, the only way any system can remain beyond failure is to define it in such a way that it would never be subject to empirical judgment.

Nevertheless, as the above discussion ought to make clear, Hanke and others are very probably right in seeing current Estonian monetary arrangements – however one decides to define them – as being transient.

Fieleke (1992) tends to judge the adoption of a currency board by economies in transition as being in a sense superfluous. If the authorities can commit themselves to reform, why would they require so drastic a remedy? If they remain inclined to inflate, why would they agree to a currency board?

But surely, as we have already indicated, the alternatives are not that simple. First of all, the Baltic countries are clearly cases where the authorities have not reformed themselves. It is a question of genuinely new authorities, with possibly genuinely new frames of mind. Second, and more important, the most important lesson that may be drawn from the Estonian case seems to be that money is indeed not only money, but also a crucial national symbol. It is highly improbable that the Estonians would have accepted as stoically as they did the policies of balanced budget were it not for the sake of maintaining the value of the kroon. The currency board principle made 'The Only Stable Currency in the North of Europe' possible, and national pride helped to make drastic stabilization policies feasible.

---

[6]   '. . . the governor of the central bank has warned that he would have to devalue the kroon if the Estonian parliament approved a high minimum wage' (Hanke, Jonung and Schuler, 1993). He can do no such thing, because according to existing legislation, the Bank of Estonia is prohibited from devaluing the kroon.

3.4   THE LATVIAN ROUBLE AND THE LATS

3.4.1   Implementation of the Currency Reform

Latvia's intention of introducing its own currency was first made public in the first economic reform programme drawn up by the government in 1990. The Latvian currency reform is not as well known abroad as Estonia's. This might be because roubles were gradually replaced by the national currency in Latvia, and initially this took place through the introduction of an interim currency. In Latvia there was no single conversion operation that might have attracted a lot of publicity. In contrast to Estonia, the Latvians opted for a stepwise reform. The introduction of Latvia's true national currency, the lats (divided into 100 santimi), was only started in March 1993.

The issue of the interim currency, the Latvian rouble or 'rublis', was started in May 1992. Latvian roubles were introduced alongside roubles at the exchange rate of 1:1. The immediate reason for the introduction of Latvia's own currency was a severe shortage of rouble notes, a shortage which was felt throughout the entire rouble zone, especially in the early part of 1992.

From May 1992, wages were paid in Latvian roubles. The position of the Latvian rouble gradually strengthened during the summer. In July, retail stores started to give change in Latvian roubles only, and the Savings Bank of Latvia started to take deposits from individuals in Latvian roubles only. Russian roubles could still be withdrawn from savings accounts, however. The Bank of Latvia exchanged cash roubles for Latvian roubles until mid-July at a rate of 1:1.

As from 20 July, the Latvian rouble became the only legal tender in Latvia. Bank deposits of both enterprises and individuals were automatically converted into Latvian roubles at the rate of 1:1. At the same time the Russian rouble became a foreign currency and regulations regarding foreign currencies applied to it. The use of foreign currencies inside the country was not forbidden altogether although all prices had to be given in Latvian roubles and, because of their legal tender status, Latvian roubles had to be accepted for payment. Wages could still be paid in foreign currencies. According to the sparse information available, enterprises – particularly the all-Union ones formerly subordinated to Moscow – continued to use Russian roubles to a large extent in their payments. Accurate data on the scope of the use of Russian roubles and convertible currencies are not available, but the Riga authorities have cited figures claiming that at the end of 1992, half of all transactions – according to other information one-third – were still in convertible currencies and perhaps some 15 per cent in roubles.

Hard currency shops were obliged to start selling their goods in Latvian roubles as well. However, shops effectively circumvented this obligation by pricing their products so high in Latvian roubles that it paid customers to exchange their roubles for foreign currency in exchange offices and pay for their purchases in foreign currency. Exchange offices – Polish-style kontors – are plentiful and competitive. Central bank officials refer to the freedom of markets and claim ignorance of the volume of the Riga cash market. It is believed to be probably the largest in the former Soviet Union.

The practical implementation of the currency reform in Latvia was successful, although for reasons very different from those in Estonia. Latvia chose a very simple method of gradually replacing Russian roubles with the new currency. This method nevertheless entails certain dangers: with bad luck, Latvia could have been faced with a flood of roubles from Russia and other former Soviet republics. The value of the new currency would then have collapsed. Fortunately for Latvia, there was obviously little confidence in the new Latvian currency outside the country, and thus foreigners were not interested in acquiring Latvian roubles.

The Latvian rouble was always intended as an interim currency before the lats was introduced. According to the authorities, the lats would be issued as soon as inflation had been brought under control and the exchange rate stabilized. However in the autumn of 1992, the governor of the central bank asserted that this would possibly take place in the latter part of 1993 (as cited in *Estoniya*, 9 September 1992). Considering that the original plan was to introduce the lats in 1992, it is evident that, somewhat unexpectedly, the Latvian roubles temporarily lost their interim nature and became relatively permanent. This also created a serious technical problem as the Latvian rouble notes were easy to forge.

The announcement of the gradual introduction of the lats was made – after much speculation – in early March 1993. The official reason given was that as the economy had been stabilized, the time for the lats had come. Remembering what was said above about the socio-psychological importance of the kroon in Estonia, there is also some reason to wonder whether the June 1993 elections were not a contributing factor. Finally it seems clear that the flow of counterfeit Latvian rouble notes was much bigger than expected.

The rate of conversion of Latvian roubles into lats was 200:1. The first banknotes denominated in lats that were put into circulation on 5 March were five lats notes. Latvian roubles were gradually phased out with the further issuance of lats notes. By June, two-thirds of cash in circulation was already in lats. From July, all prices had to be in lats, and all taxes and duties were also collected in the new currency. Latvian rouble bank accounts were converted into lats although foreign currency accounts remained untouched.

The use of foreign currencies is still permitted. The last Latvian rouble notes were withdrawn from circulation in October 1993.

The Latvian and Russian authorities did not reach a final agreement regarding the Russian roubles that had accumulated in the Latvian central bank in connection with the currency reform. Latvia agreed to keep the roubles in its custody at the central bank. There were some unresolved issues between the countries regarding debts, and Latvia was interested in linking them to the return of the roubles to Russia. As in the Estonian case, the Russian note reform of August 1993 changed this situation. A total of 1.5 billion roubles accumulated in the central bank of Latvia during the currency conversion (Baltic News Service, 9 October 1992). Their value has since been decimated by Russian inflation.

Like Estonia, Latvia also recovered the gold reserves it deposited with Western central banks before 1940. The gold reserves were, in late 1992, estimated to amount to a meagre 7 tonnes (*Financial Times*, 19 December 1992).

Despite heavy domestic criticism, the Bank of Latvia, which enjoys a high degree of independence, remains committed to tight monetary policy. Owing to this, the annual rate of inflation which was 959 per cent in 1992, fell in 1993 to 35 per cent, the same figure as in Estonia. In the run up to the June 1993 parliamentary elections, these achievements were in danger as the Bank of Latvia seemed to be almost the sole domestic defender of stabilization policies. In the end, however, stabilization policies proved perhaps even surprisingly popular in the elections. In May 1993 Latvia was the first transition country to record a fall in consumer prices in spite of the central bank increasing liquidity through currency intervention. On the basis of developments in the first half of 1994, it seems that Latvia has been the most successful among the Baltic countries in bringing down the rate of inflation. During the first six months, consumer prices increased by 15 per cent. For monthly inflation rates see *Figure 3.2*.

3.4.2   Exchange Rate System

The officially announced exchange system in Latvia is very liberal. This could at least be partly owing to incomplete foreign exchange legislation and the undeveloped state of monetary institutions and instruments. On the other hand, the Latvian authorities seem to be strictly committed to the continuation of this liberal regime. The lats is freely convertible as regards both current and capital transactions. Enterprises are not obliged to repatriate foreign currency earned abroad although the state taxes foreign exchange earned by enterprises and individuals. There are no restrictions on the repatriation of either capital or dividends by non-residents.

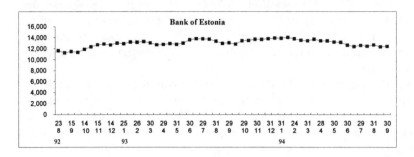

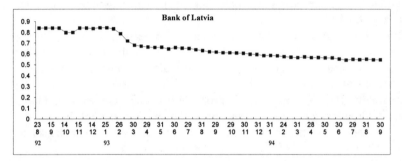

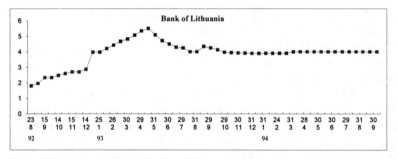

Note: Quotations are shown for the middle and end of each month.
Source: Äripäev, Baltic News Service.

Figure 3.3: Exchange value of the US dollar in the Baltic countries
            (domestic currency / US$)

The exchange rate of the lats floats both against convertible currencies and
the Russian rouble. In principle, exchange rates are determined freely in the
market. A special feature of Latvia is the existence of private foreign
exchange offices, which have been set up in large numbers in a short period
of time. The best known of these is Parex, which controls the major part of

the market. Officially at least, in the beginning neither the banks nor the central bank were very active in controlling the foreign exchange market. This was mainly owing to the undeveloped state of the banking sector and a lack of resources. With time the involvement of the central bank has become more apparent.

Actually it seems that the floating of the Latvian rouble is not clean at all. Originally, the Latvian rouble was clearly undervalued, and the monetary authorities have announced that they consider exchange rates based on purchasing power parity to be the proper ones in the longer term (Repshe, 1993). Therefore the appreciation of the rublis (and later of the lats) against the dollar during the past year is also an intentional consequence of tight monetary policies.

Over the shorter term, developments have also been informative. During the latter half of 1992 the Latvian rouble was notably stable against the dollar (see *Figure 3.3*). After the period of turbulence connected with the introduction of the lats, this stability has continued, particularly against the deutschmark.[7] It is of course most improbable that such stability would have existed without central bank intervention in the currency market. In fact, the Bank of Latvia has rather consistently bought dollars from the banks to soften the appreciation of the rublis. 'De facto pegging, officially called floating in the face of uncertainty concerning the authorities' ability to defend the rate of exchange originally chosen', may be the apt characterisation of actual Latvian policies. The accumulation of dollar reserves by the central bank was also necessary because of the meagre level of initial reserves. In February 1994, the central bank finally introduced an informal peg of the lats to the SDR.

According to a semi-official estimate, the Riga markets for cash roubles and convertible currencies were in 1992 the biggest in the area of the former Soviet Union. Latvia was considered to be the only former Soviet republic where obstacles to the exchange of non-cash roubles for cash and vice versa had in principle been removed. According to the authorities, the size of the rouble–foreign currency market is unknown, nor is any attempt made to determine the origin of the convertible currencies traded on it. Despite efforts to develop Riga into the biggest money market centre in the Baltic region, the complete lack of control that is claimed to exist in the market, especially regarding the origin of the currencies traded on it, could turn out to be a

---

[7]   Or perhaps the implicit pegging has been to the ECU. February was the time of rumours concerning the impending introduction of the lats, and many holders of Russian roubles and other currencies may have wanted to convert their balances into Latvian roubles in case there might be an Estonian-type sudden exchange of (only) Latvian roubles into the lats.

major problem. The authorities may not be sufficiently sensitive to this question.

3.4.3   Impact of the Reform on the Foreign Trade Sector

Prior to the withdrawal from the rouble zone, Latvia held negotiations with Russia on new arrangements for payments and settlements between the two countries. Accounts have been opened in the central banks of both countries, through which payments are made. Latvian commercial banks may open correspondent accounts in Russian banks and transfer companies' payments through these accounts.

Since markets between the roubles – and more recently the various national currencies – of different republics have been somewhat slow to emerge, the central bank quotations regulate the market and divide it into segments according to republics, which can nevertheless be circumvented, in particular through convertible currencies. It seems, however, that this is rarely done, and enterprises trading with the former Soviet Union have therefore to be able to bilaterally balance their transactions with each of the former republics. This is a major impediment to trade. The central bank has emphasized that its quotations are only meant to serve as guidelines for trans-actions between banks and enterprises.

With the aim of protecting its economy against a possible flood of roubles from the former Soviet republics, the Bank of Latvia introduced differentiated exchange rates in August 1992 for non-cash roubles transferred from different republics. According to the first quotation, roubles originating from Ukraine had the lowest value with a buying rate of 0.3 Latvian roubles. The highest rates were for roubles coming from, inter alia, Russia and Lithuania, with a buying rate of 0.9 Latvian roubles (Baltic News Service, 14 August 1992, 16 August 1992). Commercial banks may set their rates freely, as long as buying rates do not exceed the central bank quotations. The Bank of Latvia quotes exchange rates daily on the basis of the balance of trade between Latvia and each republic and the monetary and credit policy pursued in each republic. Thus the rates quoted by the central bank are administra-tively determined.

Latvian enterprises have been highly critical of the central bank's new system as their export earnings were significantly reduced because of the new rates. In early 1993, the Bank of Latvia stopped exchanging CIS currencies for Latvian roubles. It continues to quote their rates of exchange but now wants banks and exchange offices to do the trading. It is understood that this decision was prompted by the accumulation of rouble assets in the central bank.

3.4.4   Latvia: Concluding Remarks

We pointed out above that the underlying specific problem for Estonian monetary policy in coming years will be an orderly transition from the current modified currency reserve arrangement to something closer to ordinary central banking. In the case of Latvia, three specific questions seem to stand over and above others.

First, noble as the general Latvian goals of an independent central bank, zero inflation and purchasing power parity exchange rates may be, low inflation levels have been bought at a very high price. At the beginning of 1994, with monthly inflation averaging 3 per cent, commercial bank yearly lending rates were around 75 per cent for both domestic and foreign currency credits. The central bank's annual refinancing rate was 27 per cent. It is unclear whether these rates merely reflect the inertia of inflationary expectations or whether they are needed for balance of payments purposes, to facilitate a slow convergence of exchange rates towards purchasing power parities. In the latter case, the exchange rate goal should clearly be abandoned. Transition countries generally have exchange rates which are widely depreciated relative to purchasing power parities, and current Latvian interest rates are catastrophic.

Second, the *laissez-faire* attitude of the authorities is not sustainable. The risks involved are evident. The country has already had its share of financial scandals, and much supervision (and possibly also controls) will be needed to make Riga a respectable financial centre.

Finally – and in particular against a Finnish background – one may ask whether the declared libertarian stance is in fact credible, given the possibilities for implicit agreements and backroom deals in any small society. A general clarification of the rules of the game might be in order.

3.5   LITHUANIA: COUPONS AND LITAS

3.5.1   Implementation of the Currency Reform

The Lithuanian parliament passed an act on the introduction of a national currency at the end of 1991. At the same time, a currency reform committee was set up. After that, the introduction of the Lithuanian currency, the litas – divided into 100 centai – was widely expected throughout 1992. As, however, there were diverging views on how this should be done and the appropriate timetable, Lithuania became the last Baltic country to escape from the rouble zone.

After much debate, Lithuania – accepting the views of the central bank – decided to follow Latvia in embarking upon gradual monetary reform. The necessary conditions for a true national currency, including payment agreements with neighbouring countries, were deemed to be absent, and under the pressure of a rouble note shortage, Lithuania introduced an interim currency in May 1992. It had no proper name but was simply called the coupon, 'talonas' in Lithuanian. The coupon was valued at par with the rouble. Initially, 40 per cent of incomes were paid in coupons. They were accepted as payment in the same way as roubles.

Somewhat later, towards the end of September 1992, the authorities began to withdraw roubles from circulation. Rouble notes and bank deposits held by the population were converted into coupons at the rate of 1:1 for one week until 1 October. After that, the use of roubles as a means of payment was forbidden. Convertible currencies could still be used with special permission. Roubles were regarded as foreign currency and could be exchanged in commercial banks at the market rate.

The sudden withdrawal of roubles was motivated by a large inflationary inflow, especially from Ukraine. Declaring coupons the sole legal tender was judged to be the quickest solution. This was contrary to expectations, as the original intention had been for there to be a changeover from roubles to litas. There were also technical, but politically sensitive, problems in printing the litas notes.

In June 1993 the authorities finally announced that the litas would be put into circulation beginning from 25 June at the rate of 1 litas = 100 coupons. On the same date, bank deposits were also converted and all prices had to be given in litas.

The coupon was not accepted as a means of payment after 20 July. The use of convertible currencies was also soon banned, and since 1 August. the litas has been the sole legal tender in country. The conversion seems to have succeeded fairly well, although there may have been difficulties in implementing the prohibition of the use of convertible currencies. Though the litas became the only legal tender, convertible currency deposits held in Lithuanian banks were not converted without the consent of the depositor.

Like Estonia and Latvia, Lithuania also recovered its pre-war gold reserves, a total of 6.3 tonnes, still mostly in gold. The roubles collected in the conversion process were stored and their return was to be negotiated with the rouble-zone countries. As in the cases of Estonia and Latvia, this issue has been further complicated by the Russian rouble note reform in August 1993.

3.5.2   Exchange Rate System and Foreign Trade

Like coupons, litas are convertible for current account purposes. As regards capital account transactions, there are some limitations for convertibility. State companies have faced requirements to surrender their foreign currency earnings, although these requirements were abolished in 1993. Private persons are allowed to maintain foreign currency accounts in domestic banks or abroad, while enterprises need the permission of the central bank to hold accounts abroad.

Lithuania maintained a dual exchange rate system as late as autumn 1993, with an official rate set by the central bank and a market rate. Later on the dual exchange rate system was abandoned, and currently there is only one rate, which is determined by the market and quoted by the central bank. The foreign exchange market is, however, very thin, and the central bank is its major participant.

In 1992, Lithuanian financial policy was basically balanced while monetary policy was lax. Therefore the authorities were unable to bring down inflation rates in the same way as in the other Baltic countries. During 1992, the annual rate of inflation was 1163 per cent. In 1993 it had slowed down to 189 per cent, which was still considerably higher than in Estonia and Latvia. During the first half of 1994, the increase in consumer prices was 23 per cent.

The coupon depreciated considerably against the dollar, from 250 coupons per dollar in early October 1992 to 550 coupons in May 1993. Later, the coupon (and litas after that) appreciated, as monetary policies started to become stricter. Since the autumn of 1993, the central bank kept the rate of the litas practically stable at 3.9 litas per dollar. (See *Figure 3.2* and *Figure 3.3*)

Owing to the problems of strengthening the credibility of Lithuanian monetary policy, there was active discussion in the government during the autumn of 1993 about adopting a currency board arrangement similar to that of Estonia. In March 1994 the parliament adopted a law to that effect, and the new system became effective in April. The rate of the litas was then pegged to the dollar at a rate of 4 litas per dollar.

The decision to introduce a currency board in Lithuania was a controversial one. In particular, the central bank argued against the decision, as it was deemed that the lowering of inflation since mid-1993 showed that the monetary authorities were beginning to master the art of monetary policy under managed exchange rates. The parliament felt, however, that the Estonian experience was a convincing argument for tying the hands of policy-makers. Given recent Lithuanian political traditions, it may however be more difficult there than in Tallinn to endorse the principle of a balanced budget in practice, rather than just in words. Lithuania will provide an interesting example of applying a currency board.

As early as August 1992, Lithuania and Russia reached an agreement in principle concerning payments between the countries, although practical problems remained to be resolved. In the same way as between Lithuania and Russia, payments with other CIS states are supposed to be settled through correspondent accounts held in central banks. Commercial banks may also transfer payments through their correspondent accounts.

3.6 CONCLUDING REMARKS

The withdrawal of the Baltic states from the rouble zone and the introduction by these countries of their own currencies proceeded smoothly and the process was much easier than expected by many foreign experts. The sharp depreciation of the rouble since the summer of 1992 shows that the Baltic countries were correct to detach themselves from the rouble and issue their own currencies. In those countries where economic stability has been given priority in policy making, domestic currencies have facilitated the attainment of that goal. The convertibility of the currencies has been a key to opening up and integrating the countries. At the same time, national currencies are no panacea. A prerequisite for stability is responsible fiscal and monetary policies.

The example of the Baltic countries shows that a national currency and independent monetary policy can be introduced under very different principles and procedures. However, given the fairly sparse information often available, it is sometimes difficult to assess how the systems actually function in practice. Existing evidence however already suggests two further conclusions. First, the size of a country does not determine the credibility of a national currency. Second, far from forming an optimal currency area, the Baltic countries are dissimilar enough to make any ideas of a monetary union totally illusory.

The Baltic countries have successfully passed through the first stage of the introduction of their own currency units, that is, they have left the rouble zone. However, bigger problems lie ahead because these countries will have to secure the long-term viability and stability of their currencies. This calls for responsible monetary and fiscal policies together with the restructuring of the economy, which, initially, will be felt in a declining standard of living. Foreign trade plays a crucial role in the small Baltic economies and the countries' capacity to earn foreign currency through exports is a key factor in terms of the stability of their own currencies. Finally, the availability of international financial support for the changes in these economies will remain important.

3.7   REFERENCES

Bennett, A.G.G. (1992), The Operation of the Estonian Currency Board, *IMF Paper on Policy Analysis and Assessment,* no. 3.

Bofinger, P., E. Svindland and B. Thanner (1993),   Prospects of the Monetary Order in the Republics of the FSU, in *The Economics of New Currencies*, London, pp. 9–33.

Eesti Pank (Bank of Estonia) (1992), *The Monetary Reform in Estonia 1992*, Tallinn.

Fieleke, N.S. (1992), The Quest for Sound Money: Currency Boards to the Rescue?, *New England Economic Review*, November–December, pp. 14–24.

Hanke S.H., L. Jonung and K. Schuler (1992), *Monetary Reform for a Free Estonia*, Stockholm.

Hanke, S.H., L. Jonung and K. Schuler (1993), Estonia: It's not a Currency Board System! *Transition*, no. 1, p. 12.

Hansson, A. (1992a), *Transforming an Economy while building a Nation: the Case of Estonia*, Stockholm Institute of East European Economics Working Paper 62.

Hansson, A. (1992b), *Estonian Currency Reform: Overview*, *Progress Report and Future Policies*, Östekonomiska Institutet, Stockholm, Memorandum, 7 August.

Hansson, A. (1993), The Trouble with the Rouble: Monetary Reform in the Former Soviet Union, in Åslund, A. and R. Layard, eds, *Changing the Economic System in Russia*, London, pp. 163–82.

Hansson, A. and J. Sachs (1992), The Crowning of the Estonian Kroon, *Transition*, no. 9, pp. 1–3.

Hernández-Catá, E. (1992), Introduction of a National Currency, in Gros, D., J. Pisani-Ferry and A. Sapir, eds, *Inter-State Economic Relations in the Former Soviet Union*, CEPS Working Document no. 63, pp. 63–71.

Hernández-Catá, E. (1993), The Introduction of National Currencies in the Former Soviet Union: Options, Policy Requirements and Early Experience, in *The Economics of New Currencies*, London, pp. 53–79.

Kallas, S. and M. Sörg (1993), Estonia's Currency Reform of 1992, *Bank of Finland Bulletin* vol. 67, no. 3, pp.3–7.

Lainela, S. (1993), Currency reforms in the Baltic countries, *Communist Economies and Economic Transformation*, no. 4.

Lainela, S. and P. Sutela (1993), *Escaping from the Rouble: Estonia and Latvia Compared*, a paper presented at the Third EACES Workshop on 'Integration and Disintegration in European Economies: Divergent or Convergent Processes?', Trento, 4–5 March.

Misiunas, R.J. and R. Taagepera (1983), *The Baltic States: Years of Dependence 1940 –1980*, Los Angeles.

Odling-Smee, J. (1992), Letter to the Editor, *Transition*, no. 10, p. 9.

Osband, K. and D. Villeneuva (1992), Independent Currency Authorities: An Analytic Primer, *IMF Working Paper,* 92/50.

Otsason, R. (1992), Eesti krediitturg on täiesti tühi, *Äripäev*, 30 July.

Rajasalu, T. (1992), Rahareformist, valuutakursist ja selle võimalikust järelmõjust, *Äripäev*, 9 July.

Repshe, E. (1993), The Experience with the Latvian Rouble and the Lats, in *The Economics of New Currencies*, London, pp. 197–210.

Van Arkadie, B. and M. Karlsson (1992), *Economic Survey of the Baltic States*, London.

Walters, A. (1987), Currency Boards, in *Money*, Eatwell, J., M. Milgate, P. Newman, eds, The New Palgrave, Macmillan London, vol.1, pp. 740-42.

4. Public Sector Development: Difficulties and Restrictions

Hans Aage

4.1 THE BASIC DILEMMA

The policies of marketization, privatization and liberalization of foreign trade inflict a serious dilemma upon economic policy options in transforming economies. On the one hand, they are the only way forward towards wealth and democracy, or at least the only one perceived and accepted by foreign creditors and the IMF. On the other hand these policies of necessity impose severe strains upon public finances and impair the government budget balance – the restoration of which is a recurring requirement or an explicit quid pro quo from the IMF and other international organizations – in two ways: the demands on public expenditure increase, and public revenues decrease.

The recession during 1990–93, with GNP collapsing by 39 per cent in Estonia, 48 per cent in Latvia and 56 per cent in Lithuania, has bottomed out. Positive real growth rates of 2–5 per cent are expected for 1994 in Estonia and Lithuania and perhaps also in Latvia. This creates an urgent need for government social policy including unemployment allowances, although rates of registered unemployment are still very low by Western European standards, between 3–6 per cent. It is to be hoped that closing down unprofitable production will mean that workers are laid off. Progress in this direction has been slow, although new more restrictive bankruptcy laws, for example in Hungary in 1993, have given rise to a number of improvements. Privatized firms lay off redundant workers and no longer fulfil their former social policy functions, such as providing workers with cheap meals, housing, health care, leisure activities, holidays and income. These benefits had also been extended to non-productive workers. The government must now carry out some of these activities or establish separate insurance schemes for social security.

96

Table 4.1: The composition of tax revenue in various countries (per cent of GDP)

	total	personal	corpo-rate	VAT excises	trade taxes	social security	property
Estonia, 1993	33	8	4	10	1	10	0
Latvia, 1993	34	4	8	7	1	11	3
Lithuania, 1993	25	5	5	7	1	6	1
Denmark	36	13	4	17	0	2	2
USA	18	9	2	1	0	7	0
USSR, 1989	45	4	18	12	6	4	0
Developing countries	18	2	3	5	5	1	1
Industrial countries	31	8	3	9	1	6	1

Notes: Tax structures are for 1987, except for the Baltic countries and the former USSR.

Sources: Tables 2–4, World Bank (1993a, b, c), Hussain and Stern (1993, pp. 68–9), Newbury (1993, p. 246), Andres Saarniit, Eesti Pank (personal communication).

The recession has also eroded the tax base. Tax payments from the remaining state-owned enterprises decline. However, this decline has been partly offset by the elimination of government subsidies. In certain Eastern European countries, they are more than offset, so that net profit taxes have increased after 1990 computed as a percentage of GDP.[1] The sharp drop in output levels nevertheless reduces the tax paying ability of state-owned enterprises. Privatized firms deliberately avoid paying taxes, especially if the

[1]   Barbone and Marchetti (1995, p. 66).

private sector is an unrecorded cash economy. A successful privatization thereby leads to a further erosion of the tax base.

The old system had one important advantage, which is realized now that it has gone: it could collect taxes efficiently. Unfortunately, it did so by means of wage and price controls and the blocking of enterprise 'account money' so that there was little codification of tax rules or administrative procedures which could be carried over into the new system. The former socialist states were owner states rather than tax states, and in 1989 the bulk of tax revenues, 70–85 per cent, was appropriated from state enterprises as residual profits, turnover taxes with a multitude of rates, social security taxes and modest taxes on land and capital assets (see *Table 4.1*). The state bank was the only intermediary between enterprises and between enterprises and the state budget. This made tax collection a relatively simple task. Personal income taxes were small; in the USSR the maximum marginal tax rate was 13 per cent for ordinary wage income, although certain private incomes and foreign income were taxed at much higher, even extreme, rates exceeding 80 per cent. Total government revenues amounted to about 50 per cent of GDP, 5–10 per cent higher than the OECD average.

Expenditure can be roughly divided into purchases of goods and services (on average 35 per cent), subsidies to state enterprises (25 per cent), transfers to households (20 per cent) and other items. In recent years the share of enterprise subsidies declined in several countries, whereas social expenditures including health care and education increased.

Budget deficits should be avoidable or manageable given the vast political powers of government to control prices, wages and enterprise payments. However, for political reasons there was a tendency for real income to increase more than output creating moderate deficits of 2–3 per cent of GDP. In the USSR, budgetary problems were aggravated during Gorbachev's perestroika; one example is the anti-alcohol campaign where a 50 per cent cut in alcohol production in 1985–7 caused a significant drop in government turnover tax revenues, although the impending budgetary dangers were largely neglected, not only by the Gorbachev government but also by Western observers. It was only later, when the deficit reached 9 per cent of GDP in 1989, that the automatic inflationary financing of deficits through the money printing press was seen to contribute seriously to the acute economic crisis.[2]

Thus, the recession inflicts severe limitations upon government expenditure, and the economic transformation necessitates a radical reconstruction of taxation and expenditure. On the other hand, budgetary policies also contribute to the recession because of the macroeconomic

[2]   Gandhi and Mihajlek (1992), Campbell (1995), McKinnon (1992, p. 110).

effects and the need to curb inflation. The policy of trade liberalization, especially currency convertibility requires considerable currency undervaluation in order for domestic producers to be competitive. The resulting inflationary pressure has been curtailed by the otherwise unnecessary restrictive fiscal and monetary policies that have contributed to the severe recession.[3]

It is extremely difficult to see a way of escaping this dilemma, particularly because there are also in addition to macroeconomic conditions and policies, more deep-rooted, long-term causes of the recession related to availablility of resources and global economic prospects.

4.2   RECONSIDERING THE ROLE OF THE STATE

In relation to taxation, the contrast between public and private ownership could easily be too sharp and simplified. Ownership of capital goods is composed of different property rights which may be categorized as follows: 1) the right to manage and utilize property, 2) the right of access to income and profits originating from capital, and 3) the right to trade and dispose of capital values.[4]

Confidence in the right to future incomes from capital is essential for private investment and a well functioning market economy. However, this is not an original, natural state of economic life, it requires instead a complex system of legal, political and social structures that took five centuries to establish in Western Europe, and a further 200 years to cultivate into a civilized, socially acceptable system, as the institutional approach to economic history suggests.[5]

Taxation and regulation are related to these ownership rights. Hence, a 50 per cent profits tax that has full loss offset corresponds to 50 per cent state ownership as far as the right to income is concerned. A tax on capital gains is similarly the equivalent of state ownership of part of the right to the capital value.[6] For taxation purposes, there are strong arguments in favour of partial retention of state ownership.

Private ownership may be restricted in a number of ways, and different types of state interference in economic activity constitute a spectrum of forms of regulation, from the one extreme of complete state ownership and disposition to various intermediate forms such as the specific regulation of branches and enterprises through laws, franchises, leases as well as specific

[3]   Nuti and Portes (1993, p. 11).
[4]   Gregory and Stuart (1989, pp. 10–11).
[5]   North (1990), Gerner et al. (1995).
[6]   Hussain and Stern (1993, pp. 65–66).

taxes and subsidies. At the other end of the spectrum are the very general types of civil and criminal law, common taxes and macroeconomic policies.

To restore government activity, particularly in relation to taxation and public expenditure, and to establish an efficient mix of various forms of government instruments, is crucial for future economic development in general, not only in relation to the public deficit and macroeconomic stabilization. Indeed, according to one study of growth in developing countries 'the single most important explanatory variable is political organization and the administrative competence of government'.[7] Although this does not mean detailed state interference in economic activity, there are in fact increasingly strong reasons for emphasizing the role of active government policy in order to foster the ultimate aim of economic growth. Since this involves expenditures, as state activities usually do, it will also put additional strain on public budgets.

First, in the current situation in the Baltic countries and in other economies in transition, the requirements of restructuring are so overwhelming that they can hardly be fulfilled by the invisible hand of the market, unless it receives some badly needed assistance from a firm and visible government policy.[8] Substantial parts of manufacturing enterprises in Eastern Europe appear to be value subtractors producing negative value added at world market prices – 24 per cent, 19 per cent and 24 per cent in 1991 in Poland, Czechoslovakia and Hungary, respectively, according to the study by Hughes and Hare.[9] Similarly, another study concludes that the Russian output of raw materials in 1992 could have brought in 27 trillion roubles (110 billion dollars) if it had been sold in the world market. This is almost twice the value of Russia's GNP in 1992 of 15 trillion roubles. This paradox reflects an undervaluation of the rouble, but also the fact that 8 per cent of Russian industry actually subtracts value, and 35 per cent is unprofitable in the long term.[10]

Second, state enterprises have shown themselves to be more able to adapt to changes in business conditions and hard budget constraints during the Polish transition than was commonly presumed at the outset of the big bang.[11]

Third, there is a growing scepticism, for both theoretical and empirical reasons, towards unregulated market forces and trade liberalization as means

[7]   Reynolds (1983, p. 976), cf. Stern (1989).
[8]   Taylor (1994).
[9]   Hughes and Hare (1991, pp. 105, 106–108).
[10] Senik-Leygonie and Hughes (1992; *The Economist*, 24 October 1992, p. 69).
[11] Pinto, Belka and Krajewski (1993)

of obtaining benefits for all parties involved, including some leading economic advisers of the Clinton administration.[12]

The empirical evidence suggests that the Asian growth economies such as Japan, South Korea and China are characterized by comprehensive state intervention and at the same time by tough competition between domestic producers.[13] But it must be admitted that 'the sources of sustained growth remain mysterious'.[14] In the 1950s expert economists predicted a gloomy future for South Korea owing to lack of resources, educated labour force and entrepreneurial tradition. What is required, it seems to turn out, is 20–30 years of hard work, low wages, high levels of savings and investment, competent government industrial policy – and a substantial amount of luck concerning external conditions. Argentina, on the contrary, was at the turn of the century a high-growth economy with 5 per cent annual economic growth overall, and 2 per cent per capita in preceding decades, and was expected to become a counterpart to the USA. It turned out quite differently, however, mainly owing to mistaken economic and other policies.

The most relevant experience for transforming economies is probably China, which holds the world record in growth rates 1983–92 at 9.7 per cent. This spectacular success is the result of economic reforms without privatization, convertibility, democracy or Western assistance, that is, without any of the four main ingredients of the universally prescribed transition medicine. However, there is a flourishing private sector, an undervalued yuan to stimulate exports and large foreign investments from Chinese living abroad. Agricultural lands are leased rather than privatized. In conclusion: 'the conditions for a successful piecemeal reform of state enterprises are not so bleak as they seem', and 'it is possible that a big and painful programme of privatization may be unnecessary'.[15]

A distinctive feature of the Chinese reforms is the drop in the share of government revenues in relation to GNP, from 34 per cent in 1978 to 19 per cent in 1989.[16]

The conclusion in relation to taxation and government expenditure is that there are no inescapable adverse effects on growth, which preclude state involvement in the economy if needed for budgetary reasons.

---

[12] Yoffie (1993), Auerbach and Skott (1995), Nove (1995), Åslund (1992), Aage (1994).
[13] Taylor (1994).
[14] Reynolds (1985, p. 102).
[15] Rohwer (1992, pp. 10, 11).
[16] McKinnon (1992, p. 102).

4.3 GOVERNMENT REVENUE

The long-term goal of establishing a Western-type tax system implies the substitution of the former taxation of residual enterprise income with a system of personal and corporate income taxes, social insurance contributions, VAT and excises, trade taxes and property taxes. Industrial countries normally have a larger tax share of GNP and a lower share of import and export duties than developing countries, although there is substantial variation among industrial countries (see *Table 4.1*).

New tax systems were introduced in the Baltic countries in 1991 after the decline of the volume transferred to the USSR in 1990. Before the transition, most revenues were transferred to Moscow and allocated under an all-Union plan. Following economic reform the ties with Moscow were severed, and the economic activities of enterprises were gradually separated from the government budget, whereas social expenditures and other expenditures like defence and security formerly financed from Moscow had to be financed from national revenues. Initially, the discontinuation of payments to the central budget in Moscow contributed to fiscal surpluses of 3–6 per cent in 1991 (see *Tables 4.2–4.4*). However, this does not necessarily imply that the Baltic countries were net contributors to the all-Union budget; if subsidies are taken into account, the Baltic countries, like almost all other Soviet republics, probably received positive net transfers from Russia, mainly in the form of cheap energy. However, the total economic impact of 50 years of Soviet rule is of course a much more complicated question.[17]

Since 1991, the general tendency is a sharp drop in the absolute size of government budgets, in the case of Lithuania even in the budget's share of GNP. Total revenue as a percentage of GDP has declined slightly in Estonia and Latvia and substantially in Lithuania, to a level of 25 per cent compared to 35 per cent in Estonia and Latvia. Taking into account the dramatic decline in real GDP, this means that government revenue in constant prices has decreased since 1991 by some 40–50 per cent in Estonia and Latvia and by 75 per cent in Lithuania. Even if these figures overestimate the decline in real GDP, they do not overestimate the decline of real government revenue.

The composition of government revenue has changed. There has been a decrease in the share of corporate taxes, an increase in payroll and social security taxes, and an increase in taxes on goods and services. This is most pronounced in Estonia and to a lesser extent in Latvia. In Lithuania, however, the taxation structure has hardly changed at all.

---

[17] Van Arkadie and Karlsson (1992), Aage (1991, pp. 150–52), Šmulders (1992).

In Estonia the new tax system introduced a personal income tax with progressive bands with rates ranging from 16 per cent to 33 per cent, which was replaced in 1994 by a flat 26 per cent personal income tax for income exceeding the tax free income of 3 600 kroon. The corporate income tax rate was reduced in 1994 from 35 per cent to 26 per cent, although foreign investors who invest more than a certain minimum amount pay no taxes in the first two years and enjoy a 50 per cent tax reduction for another two years. A value added tax (VAT) of 10 per cent was raised to 18 per cent in 1992; its contribution to total revenue has increased steadily and is expected to become close to 50 per cent in 1995. Indirect taxes also include excise revenues. Payroll taxes have been introduced at a rate of 33 per cent to finance social insurance (20 per cent) and health insurance (13 per cent). Trade taxes have been virtually abolished. The Estonian trade policy is more anti-protectionist than those of Latvia and Lithuania, and this has been a cause of concern in relation to the Baltic Free Trade Agreement between the three Baltic countries which came into effect in 1994.[18]

The share of taxes in GDP has declined slightly to 33 per cent in 1993 and further in 1994, perhaps to 25 per cent of GDP. However, judging from budgetary figures, this trend will be reversed and offset in 1995 and 1996.

Latvia also introduced income taxes on enterprises and on persons. The 1993 profit tax rate was 45 per cent on banking, insurance and trade, 35 per cent on state-owned and partly state-owned enterprises, and 25 per cent on other private companies. In 1994 the 45 per cent rate was lowered to 25 per cent on trading companies, and to 35 per cent on banks and insurance companies. Gambling institutions still pay 45 per cent tax. There are generous tax reductions for foreign investors and tax holidays for new private enterprises.

In January 1994 the personal income flat tax rate of 25 per cent was replaced by a rate of 25 per cent for income below 4 800 lats and 35 per cent for income exceeding this amount. The non-taxable monthly minimum income of 25 lats was lowered to 22.5 lats in May 1994. Personal income taxes are channelled into local government budgets.

Because of the adverse incentive effects of the tax burden on enterprises, the government has increased personal taxes and especially indirect taxes. New tax legislation in 1995 is intended to further shift the tax burden from income to consumption and to replace remaining turnover taxes with the value added tax (VAT) introduced in 1992 at a standard rate of 10 per cent. The VAT rate was increased from 6 per cent to 10 per cent in the autumn of 1993 for agricultural products and from 12 per cent to 18 per cent for other

[18] Taaler (1994), Tang and Nilgo (1994), World Bank (1993a, pp. 21, 250–51), Mygind (1993, p. 18), Nørgaard (1994, p. 136).

products. From June 1994, the general rate has been 18 per cent for almost all types of products. Revenues from excise taxes on cigarettes have declined because of extensive smuggling, although the renewed state monopoly on alcohol has increased excise tax revenues.

The 38 per cent payroll social insurance contributions paid by the employer (37 per cent) and by the employee (1 per cent) are a major contributor to government revenues. Taxes on property and land and trade taxes are negligible, and licensing has been abolished, although certain export taxes and import duties have come into effect in 1992. Farmers request increased duties on imported food products to counteract the effects of the appreciation of the lats in 1993, and agricultural prices were a major issue behind the resignation of the government in the summer of 1994.[19]

In Latvia the share of taxes in GDP declined from 46 per cent in 1990 to 31 per cent in 1992 and then increased to an estimated 37 per cent in 1994. The budget for 1995, however, envisages a severe contraction which will reduce the real size of the budget by some 25 per cent.[20]

Even larger declines in the share of taxes in GDP have occurred in Lithuania, where the share has plummeted to 25 per cent in 1993. In contrast to the personal tax systems of Estonia and Latvia the Lithuanian system is progressive with several marginal rates in the range 18–33 per cent. The profit tax was recently reduced from 24 per cent to 10 per cent, with reductions of 50–70 per cent in the first five to eight years. A VAT was adopted in 1994, at a rate of 18 per cent, which replaced the existing excise tax, originally introduced at 25 per cent and later changed to rates between 18 per cent and 25 per cent. The VAT also applies to all imports including energy. There is a 31 per cent payroll social insurance contribution paid by the employer (30 per cent) and the employee (1 per cent). Lease charges are paid for the use of state-owned agricultural lands at a rate of 3 per cent and for the use of state enterprise assets at a rate of 7 per cent. Trade taxes were small until the introduction of 5–10% import tariffs in July 1993.[21]

All three countries experienced fiscal surpluses in 1991 of 3–6 per cent mainly because of improved terms of trade vis-à-vis the former USSR, the suppression of tax payments to the central government in Moscow, the cut in subsidies expenditures and the delay of some social security expenditures.

[19] World Bank (1993b, p. 10), Paeglis (1994), Dellenbrant and Nørgaard (1994, p. 154).
[20] Vilne (1995), The Economist Intelligence Unit (1995).
[21] Kasperowicz (1995), World Bank (1993c, pp. 39–44), Mygind (1993, p. 25), Nørgaard (1994, p. 137).

Table 4.2: Estonia 1991–1994: composition of government revenue and expenditure

per cent	1991	1992	1993	1994
Total tax and non-tax revenue	100.0	100.0	100.0	100.0
Corporate tax	20.5	17.4	11.9	9.8
Personal income tax	18.0	20.4	23.0	19.3
Payroll social security taxes	21.4	25.6	29.3	31.9
Taxes on goods and services	27.1	25.4	28.3	33.7
International trade taxes	5.5	1.8	1.7	1.6
Other revenue	7.5	9.4	5.8	3.7
Total expenditure	100.0	100.0	100.0	–
Economic sphere	20.8	21.7	17.3	–
Social outlays	20.3	24.5	27.8	–
Pensions	28.5	16.8	16.1	–
Education	15.3	19.2	19.9	–
Science	6.4	1.5	1.4	–
National security	2.4	7.2	8.6	–
Other expenditure	6.3	9.1	8.9	–
Total revenue (% of GDP)	36.4	38.5	32.5	–
Total expenditure (% of GDP)	31.8	36.7	33.9	–
Balance (% of GDP)	4.6	1.8	-1.4	–
Real GDP (1989 equal to 100.0)	81.0	62.1	61.0	63.2

Notes: Figures for 1994 are budget figures or figures for the first nine months.
Sources: Economist Intelligence Unit (1995), Tang and Nilgo (1994, pp. 12–13), EBRD (1994, p. 82), Eesti Pank (1994).

Table 4.3: Latvia 1991–1994: composition of government revenue and expenditure

per cent	1991	1992	1993	1994
Total tax and non-tax revenue	100.0	100.0	100.0	100.0
Corporate tax	19.5	20.2	23.0	12.0
Personal income tax	5.3	10.4	11.0	13.0
Payroll social security taxes	32.9	34.1	32.0	34.0
Taxes on goods and services	27.0	23.4	21.0	30.0
International trade taxes	0.1	3.0	4.0	3.0
Other revenue	15.2	8.9	9.0	8.0
Total expenditure	100.0	100.0	100.0	–
Wages and salaries	14.8	20.9	19.4	–
Supplies and maintenance	18.0	15.9	17.4	–
Transfers to households	36.7	33.7	48.0	–
Interest payments	-	0.5	1.9	–
Investments	9.7	4.6	3.3	–
Other expenditure	20.8	24.4	10.0	–
Total revenue (% of GDP)	37.4	30.5	33.5	37.1
Total expenditure (% of GDP)	31.0	31.9	32.5	39.6
Balance (% of GDP)	6.4	-1.4	1.0	-2.5
Real GDP (1989 equal to 100.0)	88.6	59.4	52.3	53.5

Notes: There are considerable differences between various available estimates. The separate social budget used in 1992 is included in the government budget. Figures for 1994 are budget figures.

Sources: Lainela and Sutela (1994, p. 87); EBDR (1994, pp. 82, 86), Ministry of Finance Bulletin (1995, no.1), Economist Intelligence Unit (1995), Paeglis (1994).

Table 4.4: Lithuania 1991–1994: composition of government revenue and expenditure

per cent	1991	1992	1993	1994
Total tax and non-tax revenue	100.0	100.0	100.0	–
Corporate tax	16.2	19.0	18.7	–
Personal income tax	12.3	15.8	18.3	–
Payroll social security taxes	22.8	23.0	22.3	–
Taxes on goods and services	35.8	34.5	28.7	–
International trade taxes	0.2	0.2	1.9	–
Other revenue	12.7	7.5	10.1	–
Total expenditure	100.0	100.0	100.0	–
Goods and services, wages	15.8	28.8	22.6	–
Social outlays	57.3	56.8	48.5	–
Subsidies	14.0	5.3	4.7	–
Investment	7.2	8.2	8.6	–
Other expenditure	5.7	0.9	15.6	–
Total revenue (% of GDP)	41.1	37.6	25.1	–
Total expenditure (% of GDP)	38.3	35.4	29.7	–
Balance (% of GDP)	2.8	2.2	-4.6	–
Real GDP (1989 equal to 100.0)	80.6	52.4	43.8	44.6

Notes: Classifications of expenditure groups are uncertain.
Sources: EBRD (1994, pp. 82, 86), Economist Intelligence Unit (1995).

As expected, tough expenditure cuts were essential in order to limit budget deficits in 1992 and 1993. In Latvia a tax was used resembling the Polish popiwek with very high tax rates on wage increases exceeding allowed levels, while in Lithuania real wages were cut significantly in 1992. Contrary to most other countries in Eastern Europe where public deficits of 5–10 per cent have been common, during 1992 and 1993 the Baltic countries managed to keep budgets almost in balance. However, since 1991 balances as a percentage of GNP have deteriorated, and the most recent figures show moderate deficits of 1–2 per cent in Estonia and Latvia and 5 per cent in Lithuania (*Table 4.2–4.4*).[22]

4.4   TAX COLLECTION DURING TRANSITION

The new tax systems are ambitious attempts at the rapid introduction of Western-type systems, and they compare reasonably well with generally accepted principles of optimal taxation, which can be briefly summarized as follows:[23]

Indirect taxes: should not be levied on intermediate goods (a VAT fulfils this requirement); high rates should be applied to goods that generate negative externalities and goods that have a high degree of complementarity with leisure; tax rates should be identical for imported and domestic goods.

Direct taxes: the tax base should be global; marginal rates should first rise and then fall (this is not observed in Western tax systems); corporate income should only be taxed as it accrues to persons, unless in the case of monopoly rents, foreign recipients, and, probably, capital gains.

Property taxes: are normally of limited importance in Western countries, although they have attractive characteristics with respect to distribution, efficiency, potential revenue and collection, as supply elasticities of property are low, tax evasion difficult, and the tax base fairly easy to measure and related to wealth.[24]

However, during the period of transition when government revenue is desperately needed and the possibility of collecting takes on an overwhelming priority, there may well be reasons for deviating from these general principles. Adverse changes in the distribution of income may also imply that deviations from the rules of optimal taxation are warranted. Considerable tariffs may well be justified for reasons of collection, distributional effects as well as protection of domestic producers. It may also be justified to impose turnover taxes upon intermediate goods.

In accordance with these rules it is very important to widen the tax base, and there are strong arguments for the payroll tax. A tax on profits is difficult to collect, and adverse incentive effects are an argument for abolishing them altogether.[25] Property taxes, on the other hand, could be an important source

---

[22] Nørgaard (1994, p. 123), *The Baltic Independent* (12–18 March 1994).
[23] Hussain and Stern (1993, pp. 72–76), Atkinson and Stiglitz (1980).
[24] Hussain and Stern (1993, p. 75).
[25] McKinnon (1992, p. 117).

of revenue, and the most efficient means of collecting these taxes is that the government retains ownership rights and leases for example land, buildings and housing to the public. Giving property away for free and thus sacrificing future incomes seems to be very problematic from a taxation point of view.[26]

Establishing efficient systems of tax collection from the private sector poses serious problems in all three countries. Tax administration and control mechanisms are not effective in preventing tax avoidance, especially with respect to new enterprises in the private sector where payments are often made as unrecorded cash payments, partly because efficient payment systems are still lacking. In Estonia tax authorities have recently been given some access to bank accounts in an effort to tax the black economy which is estimated to have increased to a size corresponding to 20 per cent of GNP.[27]

In the public sector, the enterprises are often unable to pay their taxes, and all three countries suffer from substantial tax arrears. It has been estimated that in Latvia in 1993 only 10 per cent of payable excise taxes and 28 per cent of the customs duties were actually paid to the authorities. Other estimates suggest that company tax arrears in Estonia and Latvia amounted to 2–3 per cent of GNP in 1993. In Lithuania an estimated 10 per cent of tax revenues were uncollected in 1994.[28]

4.5   GOVERNMENT EXPENDITURE

Generally, the level of expenditure has decreased dramatically owing to the recession, and the structure has changed, as subsidies were more or less eliminated as part of the introduction of the new systems of taxation. Available information is not very detailed and not readily comparable between countries (see *Table 4.2–4.4*). Detailed comparisons with expenditure structures before 1990 are still more difficult, because of the complex transactions with the all-Union budget in Moscow. Thus, social expenditures as well as all-Union enterprises were financed largely by the central budget.

In Estonia as in the other countries, all public expenditures have been severely cut. However, national security is an exception. The share of social outlays has increased. The shares, and even more so the real value, of pensions and of expenditures on science have decreased sharply. The following distribution of total public expenditures in 1993 is available: central government 36 per cent, local government 28 per cent, social security

---

[26]   Hussain and Stern (1993, pp. 76–80).
[27]   The Economist Intelligence Unit (1995).
[28]   Lainela and Sutela (1994, p. 75), Campbell (1995, p. 84), The Economist Intelligence Unit (1995).

28 per cent, pensions 16 per cent, family benefits 6 per cent, medical insurance 13 per cent. Price subsidies have been abolished, except for energy, and subsidies to inefficient enterprises have been largely eliminated, as is the case in Latvia, but not in Lithuania where some subsidies are still paid and 30 per cent of prices are still regulated.[29] The budget for 1995 envisages substantial increases in public sector salaries as well as increased expenditures on education, civil service, the police, border guards, and on child benefits.

In Latvia the share of social security has increased, and the share of transfers to households was 48 per cent of total government expenditures in 1993, although the absolute level is low owing to difficulties in collecting the 37 per cent payroll social insurance contribution. Pensions constitute 60 per cent of the social insurance budget. However, minimum pensions in 1993 were only 75 per cent of the survival minimum. Expenditure on health care is estimated to be 3 per cent of the shrinking gross national income. There is a confused relationship between new municipal authorities, which are financially incapable of performing even basic services, and a central government without a reliable tax base. The intention now is to improve incentives to pay by linking specific payments to specific types of expenditure and reducing the load on the general taxation system.[30]

For Lithuania there are some details regarding the composition of expenditures. Compared to 1989 the share of expenditures used for subsidies has declined from 33 per cent to 5 per cent. Despite this impressive restructuring, the amount of subsidies are still higher in Lithuania than in the other two countries where subsidies have been cut even more radically. The share of social security has increased to a level of about 50 per cent; the share of health care has declined slightly from 5 per cent to 4 per cent and the share of education drastically and alarmingly from 11 per cent to 4 per cent. Government investments are being postponed. In the budget for 1995 a modest deficit of 1–2 per cent of GNP is planned. Public sector salaries and pensions will increase by 10 per cent, and spending on health care, education, agriculture and security will increase following the budgetary cuts during 1994.[31]

All three countries experienced severe pressure on the shrinking real value of budgets. A major source of pressure is the social expenditure needed for old-age pensions for retired people, who constitute about one-quarter of the population, and for the growing number of unemployed. So far unemployment has been limited partly owing to high redundancy payments which state enterprises cannot afford to pay, but it is likely to increase. The

---

[29] Püss (1994), Andres Saarniit, Eesti Pank (personal communication).
[30] Vilne (1995), Kassalis and Dubra (1993, pp. 4, 6, 19, 31).
[31] Kasperowicz (1995), World Bank (1993c, p. 45), Nørgaard (1994, p. 123).

impression is that expenditure on unemployment allowances, health care, old-age pensions and education are all at a very low level compared to earlier standards and to need. Together with more casual evidence – for example, that payment for health care has been introduced in Latvia, except in part for pensioners who, however, receive very low pensions hardly sufficient to cover normal outlays for winter heating – this gives an impression of the hardships inflicted upon the population by the recession. At the same time the distribution of income and wealth has become very unequal. Poverty is visible in the streets simultaneously with very conspicuous consumption by the newly rich with their imported motor cars.

Similar trends of increasing inequality and poverty, decreasing general welfare and declining public income and expenditure during the process of transition have been documented for other countries in Eastern Europe and the former Soviet Union.[32]

Another source of pressure on government expenditure is the demand for subsidies, from state enterprises where employees press for wage increases, and from farmers, especially in Latvia where food prices and attempts to impose VAT on agricultural products have been a major political issue. In Estonia the new government, approved in April 1995, promised small farmers tax exemption this year as well as additional loans and the freezing of debts of farm companies. Moreover, in Lithuania duties on food imports, including a 30 per cent tariff on meat, were imposed in 1994.

However, heavier pressure on expenditure can be expected in the future, because the stimulation of economic growth requires that the state spends vast sums to improve infrastructure and human capital.

One way of relieving the pressure on public expenditure is to privatize public enterprises and public utilities and to introduce payment for public services, especially health care. Estonia has the most comprehensive privatization programme, and it is planned to sell public utilities, telecommunications, the Tallinn Port, the post office, the state insurance company and hospitals. Privatization may provide an immediate source of revenue; it could save future expenditures, but it could also entail the forgoing of future budgetary incomes. The belief that privatization will improve efficiency is founded on surprisingly weak empirical evidence.[33]

Payment for health care may be unavoidable given the scarcity of public revenues. However, it is a last resort to use a tax on illness. Of course it broadens the tax base, and it overcomes problems of the willingness, although not necessarily the ability, to pay. The tendency towards the imitation of the American health care system is nevertheless surprising, as it

[32] UNICEF (1994).
[33] Aage (1994, pp. 20–25).

has very few, if any, virtues compared to, say, the Canadian or the Scandinavian systems. It is expensive, inefficient and antisocial. In 1987 the cost of health care was 11.2 per cent of GDP in the USA, and since then the share has increased to 14 per cent; it was 6.0 per cent in Denmark and 7.3 per cent in the OECD countries on average.[34] Administration takes up 19–24 per cent of total costs in the USA and 4–6 per cent in Denmark. This means that expenditure on health care administration as a percentage of GDP is eight times higher in the USA than in Denmark, largely owing to costly competition between several parallel insurance schemes.[35] It is a striking contradiction of empirical facts when extreme liberals like Milton Friedman persistently claim that socialized health care always implies high costs.[36] Nevertheless, privatization of health care as well as public utilities is on the agenda, especially in Estonia.

4.6 MACROECONOMIC POLICY

The Baltic states have managed comparatively well to escape 'the fiscal trap' of transition and to balance their budgets to a higher degree than most other transition economies.[37] This is supported by tight institutional arrangements. In Estonia and Lithuania, the currency board system prohibits deficit financing by the central bank, and in Latvia this possibility is also legally restricted.

Balanced budgets are also a necessity, as non-inflationary ways of financing deficits did not exist until recently. However, treasury bills were introduced in Latvia and Lithuania in 1994, and in Latvia about half of the budget deficit in 1994 was financed by the issue of short-term state bonds. In Lithuania, the treasury bill programme has been successful. Highly restrictive fiscal policies have nevertheless been necessary in both countries, and for 1995 severe budgetary cuts are envisaged, particularly in Latvia. In Lithuania, budgetary expenditures were pruned substantially during 1994.

It is of the utmost importance to control inflation, because high levels of inflation jeopardize restructuring and long-term investment. Moreover, they are socially unjust and destroy political support for reform policies and thus threaten production and jobs. The Baltic states have achieved impressive

---

[34]   OECD (1990, p. 10), *The Economist* (24 June 1995, p. 118).
[35]   Pedersen et al. (1992, pp. 99–101), Woolhandler and Himmelstein (1991).
[36]   Friedman and Friedman (1980, pp. 128, 144).
[37]   The detailed figures for the budget deficits differ between various sources: see Lainela and Sutela (1994, p. 74 and Tables 2–4).

stabilizaton, and annual levels of inflation have been reduced to about 40 per cent in 1994 in Estonia and Latvia and 80 per cent in Lithuania.[38]

However, the costs in terms of production decline have been substantial. Policies of external and internal liberalization imply that a major burden of macroeconomic stabilization must be carried by budgetary policy. The scope for taxation is limited, because of the lack of administrative capability and the use of generous tax regulation to stimulate new activity. Therefore, demand has been restricted by expenditure cuts including exceedingly low real wages for state sector employees and low real values of government transfers.

The most important task, for stabilization and for successful reform as well, is to establish effective taxation for the private sector, even if it entails adverse incentive effects for entrepreneurial activity. Otherwise, budget constraints could retard privatization and restructuring and jeopardize its final outcome, because a slowing down of reform policy could be the only alternative way of reducing government social expenditures. External assistance targeted on social expenditures would also contribute to removing perverse pressures to subsidize and maintain the state sector.[39]

4.7 POLICY OPTIONS

The lessons from reform policies so far are that they are difficult to implement, require time, are subject to long-term uncertainties, and cause severe short-term hardships. This paves the way for social disintegration, the withering away of the state, the privatization of tax collection by organized criminals extorting protection money, the impoverishment of large segments of the population, and the disappearance of any confidence in the institutions of society.

Following national independence, budgetary ties with Moscow were severed, revenue and expenditure levels were reduced from about 50 per cent to 35–40 per cent of GDP, enterprise taxes as well as subsidies were cut dramatically and a new budgetary system was gradually established introducing personal and corporate income taxes, social insurance contributions and VAT. Since 1991, the absolute size of the government budget has dropped sharply following the general recession, and the structure of revenue and expenditure has continued to change with a decrease in the share of corporate taxes, an increase in payroll and social security taxes, and an increase in taxes on goods and services. Generally, the share of social expenditures has increased at the expense of investment outlays, with

[38] Lainela and Sutela (1994, pp. 67–9, 74, 83).
[39] Chadha and Coricelli (1994).

Lithuania as an apparent exception. Budgetary balances have shown a tendency towards slight deterioration, although problems of governments deficits are much less acute than in most transforming economies. However, there are pronounced and growing pressures on government budgets.

The policy options available are extremely narrow for any government. Furthermore, the former communist parties, which are gaining increasing popularity, notably in Lithuania, Poland, Hungary and Romania, will experience tremendous difficulties in restoring former economic growth rates. The first priority appears to be some mitigation and redistribution of the hardships of transition.

For this as well as other reasons, it may be concluded that improvements in government administrative capacity are of the utmost importance. Fiscal strength is increasingly necessary to facilitate economic recovery. What is needed is a redefinition and implementation of government institutions rather than a withdrawal of the state from the economy.[40] There are very strong arguments in favour of improved government intervention in the economy:

- the large state enterprises need ownership control which means government control, as it is impossible to privatize all of them rapidly;
- social institutions and law and order must be restored, and particularly, an efficient tax collection is of especial importance;
- restructuring and growth require deliberate industrial policy;
- the management of natural resources and environmental policy is only possible under government guidance.

The dangers of centralized political power have been reduced owing to the improvement of democratic mechanisms and political freedom, which are themselves major achievements. Democratization may not ease the raising of tax levels or the management of deficit problems, as interest groups become organized and able to exert political pressure. But democratization is the only way forward which may ease the establishment of efficient, incorruptible governments.

[40] Campbell (1995, p. 89).

4.8 REFERENCES

Aage, H. (1991), The Baltic Republics, in R. Weichhardt, ed., *The Soviet Economy under Gorbachev*, pp. 146–66 (NATO Colloquium 1991), NATO Economics Directorate, Brussels.

Aage, H. (1994), Sustainable Transition, in Campbell, R.W., ed., *The Postcommunist Economic Transformation, Essays in Honor of Gregory Grossman*, pp. 15–41, Westview Press, Boulder.

Åslund, A. (1992), *Post-Communist Economic Revolutions. How Big a Bang?*, The Center for Strategic and International Studies, Washington DC.

Atkinson, A.B. and J.E. Stiglitz (1980), *Lectures on Public Economics*, McGraw-Hill, London.

Auerbach, P. and P. Skott (1995), Michael Porter's Inquiry into the Nature and Causes of the Wealth of Nations, *Working paper*, University of Aarhus.

Barbone, L. and D. Marchetti (1995), Transition and the Fiscal Crisis in Central Europe, *Economics of Transition* 3 (January, no. 1), pp. 59–74.

Campbell, J.L. (1995), Institutional Theory, State Building and Fiscal Reform in Post-Communist Europe, *EMERGO Journal of Transforming Economies and Societies* 2 (winter, no. 1, Special Issue on Fiscal Policy and Post-Communist States: Comparative East European Perspective), pp. 76–96.

Chadha, B. and F. Coricelli, (1994), *Fiscal Constraints and the Speed of Transition*, Discussion Paper no. 993. Centre for Economic Policy Research, London.

Clague, C. and G.C. Rausser, eds (1992), *The Emergence of Market Economies in Eastern Europe*, Basil Blackwell, Oxford.

Dellenbrant, J.Å. and O. Nørgaard, eds (1994), *The Politics of Transition in the Baltic States*, Research Reports 1994/2, Department of Political Science, Umeå University, Umeå.

Eesti Pank (1994), *Eesti Pank Bulletin*, no. 7.

EIU (Economist Intelligence Unit) (1995), Country Reports, London.

EBRD (European Bank for Reconstruction and Development) (1994), *Transition Report*, October 1994. Economic Transition in Eastern Europe and the former Soviet Union. EBRD, London.

Friedman, M. and R. Friedman (1980), *Free to Choose. A Personal Statement*, Penguin, Harmondsworth.

Gandhi, V.P. and D. Mihaljek (1992), Scope for Reform of Socialist Tax Systems, in Tanzi, V., ed., *Fiscal Policies in Economies in Transition*, pp. 142–265, International Monetary Fund, Washington DC.

Gerner, K., S. Hedlund, and N. Sundström (1995), *Hjärnridån. Det europeiska projektet och det gåtfulla Ryssland*, Fischer & Co., Stockholm.

Gregory, P.R. and R.C. Stuart (1989), *Comparative Economic Systems*, 3rd edn, Houghton Mifflin, Boston.

Hughes, G. and P. Hare (1991), Competitiveness and Industrial Restructuring in Czechoslovakia, Hungary and Poland, *European Economy* (Special edition no. 2), pp. 83–110.

Hussain, A. and N. Stern (1993), The Role of the State, Ownership and Taxation in Transition Economies, *Economics of Transition* 1 (January, no. 1), pp. 61–88.

Kasperowicz, A. (1995), *The Reform of Lithuania's Fiscal System during the General Economic Transformation*. Working Paper no. 12, UCEMET (University Council for Economic and Management Education Transfer), Krakow.

Kassalis, E. and E. Dubra (1993), *Social Welfare in Latvia. A Case Study*, Working paper.

Lainela, S. and P. Sutela (1994), *The Baltic Economies in Transition*, Report A:91, Bank of Finland, Helsinki.

McKinnon, R.I. (1992), Taxation, Money, and Credit in a Liberalizing Socialist Economy. Chap. 7, pp 109–27 in Clague and Rausser, eds, *The Emergence of Market Economies in Eastern Europe*, Basil Blackwell, Oxford.

Ministry of Finance (1995), *Ministry of Finance of the Republic of Latvia Bulletin*, no.1.

Mygind, N. (1993), *A Comparative Analysis of the Economic Transition in the Baltic Countries – Barriers, Strategies, Perspectives*, Institut for Nationaløkonomi, Handelshøjskolen, København.

Newbury, D.M. (1993): Tax and Expenditure Policies in Hungary, *Economics of Transition* 1 (June, no. 2), pp. 245–72.

North, D.C. (1990), *Institutions, Institutional Change and Economic Performance*, Cambridge University Press, Cambridge.

Nove, A. (1995), The Role of the Public Sector: A Critique of Libertarianism, Chap. 2 in Hersh, J. and J.D. Schmidt, eds, *Dilemmas and Choices of Post-Command Societies. Eastern Europe: Between Western Europe and East Asia*, vol. 1, Macmillan, London.

Nuti, D.M. and R. Portes (1993), Central Europe: The Way Forward, in Portes, R., ed., *Economic Transformation in Central Europe*, pp. 1–20, Office for Official Publications of the European Communities, Luxembourg.

Nørgaard, O., ed. (1994), De baltiske lande efter uafhængigheden. Hvorfor så forskellige?, *Politica*, Århus.

OECD (1990), Health Care Systems in Transition. The Search for Efficiency, *OECD Social Policy Studies 7*, OECD, Paris.

Paeglis, I. (1994), *Latvian Fiscal Policy in the First Quarter of 1994*, RFE/RL Research Report 3 (12 August, no. 3), pp. 48–54.

Pedersen, K.M., Ø. Lidegaard, J.P. Steensen, and T. Larsen (1992), *Struktur og finansiering af det danske sundhedsvæsen i 1990'erne*, Lundbeckfondens prisopgave 1990, Jurist- og Økonomforbundets Forlag, København.

Pinto, B., M. Belka, and S. Krajewski, (1993), *Transforming State Enterprises in Poland: Evidence on Adjustment by Manufacturing Firms*. Brookings Papers on Economic Activity (no. 1), pp. 213–70.

Püss, T. (1994), *Social Security in Estonia*. Reform Round Table Working Paper no. 13, Institute of Economics, Estonian Academy of Sciences, Tallinn.

Reynolds, L.G. (1985), *Economic Growth in the Third World, 1850–1980*, Yale University Press, New Haven.

Rohwer, J. (1992), China. Survey, pp. 1–22, *The Economist*, 28 November.

Senik-Leygonie, C. and G. Hughes (1992), Industrial Profitability and Trade among the Former Soviet Republics, *Economic Policy* (October).

Šmulders, M. (1992), The Results of 70 Years of Bilateral Relations between Latvia and the USSR, *Latvijas zinatnu akademijas vestis* (no. 1), pp. 31–8.

Stern, N. (1989), The Economics of Development: A Survey. *Economic Journal* vol. 99 (September, no. 397), pp. 597–685.

Taaler, J. (1994), *Tax Reform in Estonia*, Reform Round Table Working Paper no. 6, Estonian Academy of Sciences, Institute of Economics, Tallinn.

Tang, P. and H. Nilgo (1994), *Budget Reform in Estonia*, Reform Round Table Working Paper no. 7, Estonian Academy of Sciences, Institute of Economics, Tallinn.

Taylor, L. (1994), The Market Met its Match: Lessons for the Future from the Transition's Initial Years, *Journal of Comparative Economics* vol. 19 (August, no. 1), pp. 64–87.

UNICEF (1994), *Crisis in Mortality, Health and Nutrition. Central and Eastern Europe in Transition. Public Policy and Social Condititons* (Regional Monitoring Report, no. 2, August 1994). UNICEF International Child Development Centre, Florence.

Van Arkadie, B. and M. Karlsson, eds (1992), *Economic Survey of The Baltic Republics*, Pinter, London.

Vilne, V. (1995), *Fiscal Reform – on the Way to Market Economy*, UCEMET (University Council for Economic and Management Education Transfer), Working Paper no. 10, Krakow.

Woolhandler, S. and D.U. Himmelstein (1991), The Deteriorating Administrative Efficiency of the U.S. Health Care System, *New England Journal of Medicine* 314, pp. 1253–8.

World Bank (1993a), *Estonia. The Transition to a Market Economy*, A World Bank Country Study, The World Bank, Washington DC.

World Bank (1993b), *Latvia. The Transition to a Market Economy*, A World Bank Country Study, The World Bank, Washington DC.

World Bank (1993c), *Lithuania. The Transition to a Market Economy*, A World Bank Country Study, The World Bank, Washington DC.

Yoffie, D., ed. (1993), *Beyond Free Trade. Firms, Governments, and Global Competition*, Harvard Business School, Boston.

5. The Future Trade Opportunities of the Baltic Republics

Tor Wergeland[*]

5.1 INTRODUCTION

The purpose of this chapter is to try to identify areas of economic activity where the Baltic states could develop high export performance in the future. The first part of the chapter discusses some theories of international trade and their relevance to the Baltic situation. Certain figures relating to the Baltic states are then examined to identify concrete areas of competitiveness. As the data are already outdated and very much influenced by the former Soviet era, they cannot be regarded as reliable nor particularly relevant for future perspectives. Hence, this empirical exercise should not be treated as more than an attempt to apply elements of theory to the Baltic situation. A more realistic analysis could be conducted by Baltic analysts with access to (and insight into) updated statistics. The recommendations that follow from the data should thus be regarded as mere indications of trade opportunities.

5.2 THEORIES OF INTERNATIONAL TRADE

International trade is by definition the difference between domestic consumption and production. If consumption exceeds production, we get imports; if production exceeds consumption, we have exports. A study of the export opportunities of individual countries is therefore very much a question of identifying production areas where the country in question has particular advantages. Production is carried out by individual firms, so the question is really one of identifying commodities or types of production where firms can develop international competitive advantage.

[*] I am indebted to Richard E. Baldwin for giving me access to his detailed calculations on the gravity model and to Robert McCallum for helping me with the compilation of the numerous tables.

Traditional trade theory is based on the concept of comparative advantage, that is, countries will tend to export commodities whose relative costs are lower and import commodities whose relative costs are higher. The source of advantage to individual firms is in this case the cost of input factors. The broad pattern of international trade can to a large extent be explained by such theories. The theory is, however, only a theory of net trade, that is, in the typical Heckscher–Ohlin theory, the countries will either be net importers or net exporters of a commodity. Only a part of world trade can, therefore, convincingly be explained by theories based solely on comparative advantage.[1] A concept like intra-industry trade, where countries exchange fairly similar goods, can only be explained by theories based on imperfect competition.[2] In these cases, the source of advantage is the existence of economies of scale. All traditional trade theories assume that factors of production are immobile and that goods can be freely exchanged across country borders. More recently, theories of the location of production have led to the development of theories of trade with a clear geographical aspect.[3] This is also trade explained by economies of scale in production combined with trade costs, but where the location of production is not necessarily restricted to within countries, but rather within *regions*. One thing is clear – there is no such thing as *one* theory of international trade, to understand the nature of trade one needs a *set* of theories covering different aspects of a complex phenomenon.

Certain general conclusions can, however, be made. For countries that are similar in size, structure and income levels, theories of comparative advantage will generally contribute less to the explanation of trade than will theories explaining intra-industry trade. The more unlike nations are concerning factor endowments and factor costs, the more one should expect theories based on comparative advantage to illuminate trade patterns. For countries belonging to economic unions, like the European Union, where both commodities and input factors can freely cross borders, the aspects of production location will play a more important role in understanding trade patterns.

For countries in transition towards a market economy it is indeed a question of whether *any* theory can shed light on their future trade

---

[1]   See Deardorff (1984) and Balassa and Bauwens (1988) for an empirical examination of this question.
[2]   See Helpman and Krugman (1985) and Helpman (1987) for an overview of the field.
[3]   See Krugman and Venables (1990) for the basic set of tools for understanding this theory, and Krugman (1990 and 1991) which explores this new theoretical angle elegantly.

possibilities. The basic theories of comparative advantage could of course be used to identify broad areas of production that have strong export potential. However, what is really required is a more dynamic approach, that focuses on the dynamics of the elements that determine the competitiveness of individual firms. Some of these essential factors will be examined in the next section.

5.3   THE COMPETITIVE POSITION OF NATIONS

An influential book that has been widely discussed in recent years is Michael E. Porter's *The Competitive Advantage of Nations*.[4] The primary objective of the book is to try and explain why particular countries seem to succeed in particular industries. The book questions established theories of comparative advantage and offers an analytical framework that spans three levels of aggregation: the firm, the industry and the nation. The national environment for the selected industry is characterized with the help of four sets of variables:

- factor conditions;

- demand conditions;

- industry structure and firm strategies;

- the role of related industries.

These interacting determinants are considered to be the main factors that influence a firm's ability to establish and sustain competitive advantage within international markets. The four sets of variables form what Porter has called the 'diamond'. In addition two 'external' determinants are introduced: the influence of chance and the role of the government. Together these factors constitute the analytical framework for understanding the competitive position of a nation. The 'diamond' is illustrated in *Figure 5.1*.

As Porter in many ways offers a systematic approach to the understanding of the many factors contributing to explain international trade, his 'diamond' concept can be used to highlight relevant issues. His contribution does not constitute a new theory, but it is easy to see how the various boxes in *Figure 5.1* can relate to the theories mentioned earlier. Factor conditions are

---

[4]   Porter (1990). Although the book does not live up to its expectations of presenting a new theory of international competition, it offers a systematic discussion of a set of factors contributing to international competitiveness and is thus a very useful framework for discussion.

primarily about production costs, indicating theories of comparative advantage. Demand conditions and market structure are more related to intra-industry trade and imperfect competition, while related industries are associated with industrial clusters, that is, location factors.

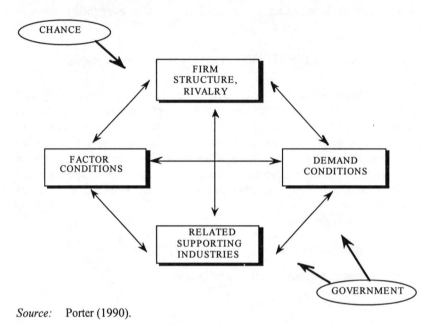

Source: Porter (1990).

Figure 5.1: 'The Diamond' with external influences

5.3.1   Factor Conditions

At the centre of traditional theories of international comparative advantage lie the factors of production. The traditional factors are normally labour and capital. However, land, natural resources, climate, demographic factors and national infrastructure can all be sources of national advantage. It is useful to distinguish between broad categories of factors, such as human, physical, knowledge, capital resources and national infrastructure on the one hand and two aspects of these factors on the other. The first aspect is the degree to which such factors could be called basic or advanced, the second the degree to which they may be called generalized or specialized.

Normally, cheap inputs create cost advantages that give firms export opportunities, and the notion of comparative advantage is closely connected to the identification of cheap production factors. This is sometimes too narrow a viewpoint.

Porter makes several important observations when discussing factor conditions in relation to the competitive position of firms.

First, and most important, it is not the case that endowments of input factors are constant and given, as is the normal assumption in traditional trade theory. Advantageous factors could be created and developed. An example is skilled labour, where a country through special education or training can *create* input factors with particular skills.

Second, the fact that certain input factors may be very expensive in a country does not necessarily give that nation a disadvantage in all production employing this factor intensively. Sometimes high input costs could be a powerful source for innovation, leading to the development of new products or production processes with a cost competitive profile.

In general, it is argued by Porter that the more a competitive position is based only upon large endowments of very basic factors of the generalized type, for example, large endowments of very cheap, unskilled labour or large reserves of crude material input, the more difficult it is to sustain this advantage as the nation develops. On the other hand, a competitive position based on special skills or qualities in the more advanced and specialized factors, for example, particular scientific competence on the part of the workforce, is a position more likely to be defended and upgraded over time. An example could be the competitive position of German firms within optics and chemicals. In both areas, special university programmes have secured a large pool of trained workers and researchers in these fields.

For the Baltic countries, the implication should be that competitive positions based only on the availability of cheap, unskilled labour are difficult to sustain over time. Rather, a nation should strive to develop a pool of skilled labour with a matching educational system to facilitate continuous upgrading of this skill.

5.3.2 Demand Conditions

Porter discusses at length the importance of the home market as a testing ground for internationally competitive commodities. The focus is on the mix and character of home buyer needs, as it is the composition of home market demand that shapes how firms interpret and react to demand signals. If local buyers put pressure on firms to innovate, or if local buyers can give firms either a clearer or an earlier picture of relevant international demand, this is important for the development of internationally competitive commodities. Core qualities of a product are normally always developed in local contexts and will reflect home market needs.

In a trade-theoretical context, the emphasis on the importance of customers has played a minor role in the literature relative to the extensive contribution on supply elements. Some significant contributions[5] do offer insight into the importance of demand factors to explain competition.

This part of the 'diamond' is not very relevant to the Baltic situation as the home market has been totally dominated by the traditional Soviet trade and competitive forces have not existed. It is, however, extremely important that Baltic firms do receive impulses from international demand. This can partly be achieved through joint-ventures with Western firms, and partly where Baltic firms are testing their products on a smaller scale in nearby Western markets in order to get the appropriate market feedback.

5.3.3   Industry Structure, Rivalry and Firm Strategies

Any firm would strive towards becoming monopolists for their product, as this would maximize the profit of the firm. In a competitive environment, however, the existence of substantial monopoly profit would lead to new entries and the development of substitutes. In practice the existence of pure monopolies is limited, and in all countries one will tend to find a whole range of types of competition from pure competition on the one hand to monopolies on the other. The market structure is of vital importance to the strategy options of firms.[6]

The strategies of individual firms, the way firms are organized and managed as well as the nature of domestic rivalry are very important determinants of competitiveness. National advantage results from an appropriate match of the organization of firms and the national sources of competitive advantages.

It is common to simplify matters and talk about American management, Japanese management or Scandinavian management, as if they were distinct and homogeneous types of management. Although variations are large both across and within nations, it is possible to identify certain general

---

[5]   The pioneering work of Linder (1961) attempts to explain trade solely from the demand side. Andersen et al. (1981) lend support to the connection between international specialization and home demand, while Barker (1977) points out that as countries grow richer, demand is more differentiated and the need to become more specialized is evident. Grubel and Lloyd (1975) explain intra-industry trade partially by demand arguments. This is further discussed in chapter 3 of Porter (1990).

[6]   See Krugman (1980), Helpman (1987) and Krugman (1990) for some discussion on this matter.

characteristics. Examples are Italy's small sized and family-dominated firms with a high degree of individualism, the Scandinavian style with democratic labour/owner relationships, the German archetype with a large corporate and hierarchical structure and a top management team of scientists, and the Japanese model of worker participation, strong hierarchical structure with a strong sense of loyalty and a general cooperative attitude. There is no doubt that local choices in relation to the organization of firms will to a large extent determine the competitiveness of an industry. This has to do with the general orientation of leaders, group versus hierarchical style, strength of individual initiative, tools for decision making, nature of relationship with customers, ability to coordinate across functions, attitude towards international activities, relations between labour and management and the relationship between firm and public authorities. This is a particularly important point for Baltic firms, as they tend to be very large and dominated by managers not well versed in Western management thinking.

One of the strongest findings in the studies reported by Porter is the importance of domestic rivalry. Some argue that competition is wasteful and that one should create national *'champions'* instead of having competition. This does not receive support from studies on successful industries. In the German chemical industry, BASF, Hoechst, Bayer and numerous others secure a high level of competition. The same is found in Switzerland for pharmaceuticals, in the USA for computers and in Japan for most export products. Rivalry, more than anything else, emphasizes the need for continuous upgrading and product development. Currently the most popular management topic in the USA is 'benchmarking', that is, measuring in detail your own performance against that of the best competitors.

Again an important implication for the Baltic states should be highlighted: in the process of privatization of state-owned companies, one should strive towards establishing strong domestic rivals within industrial clusters, thus creating a competitive environment with a potential for continuous upgrading and adjustment.

5.3.4   Related Industries

Another main conclusion drawn by Porter is that successful industries seem to be located in places where they not only have one or more rivals, but where internationally competitive firms in *related* industries also exist. Porter introduces the term 'industrial cluster' to characterize a situation where locally one could find many firms of a similar nature, recruiting from a joint pool of specially trained personnel, sharing information and generally creating an environment for active innovation and upgrading products and business practices.

One of the best examples of a large and successful cluster is perhaps the Norwegian maritime industry. Here, we can find examples of internationally competitive firms in all activities related to a Norwegian shipping company (broking, classification, insurance, finance, maritime law, technical appraisals, ship building, repair, ship equipment, and so on). The existence of such a complete cluster is believed to be an important reinforcing factor in making the Norwegian shipping industry globally competitive.[7]

Again the implications must be to look for natural industrial clusters within the Baltic region and to create a total infrastructure for such clusters, facilitating career prospects for specialized workers and the best environment for productivity growth.

5.3.5   The Role of Government and Chance

In the history of most successful industries, unpredictable events play an important role in the development of the industry. Some examples of chance events that could drastically change market conditions and thus create new opportunities might be acts of pure invention, discontinuities in technology (biotechnology) or input cost conditions (oil price shock), exchange rate regime shifts, wars or other dramatic political shifts, where of course the recent developments in Eastern Europe is the best example. There is not much to say about pure chance events, but one point should be stressed: technological innovations are not necessarily as accidental as they may appear. Some industries have developed a favourable environment for research that naturally attracts new researchers and in such an environment new inventions or innovations take place more often than in industries without such an environment. The Silicon Valley in California is one obvious example.

The role of governments is also obvious. In Japan the mighty MITI[8] has played an important role in defining and implementing strategies for the investment and research agendas of Japanese firms, and in most industries secured a satisfactory level of domestic rivalry. Governments can influence the factor conditions of a nation through educational investments and other infrastructure investments.

---

[7] See Wergeland (1993) for a thorough discussion of the Norwegian maritime sector.

[8] The Ministry of International Trade and Industry. The role of MITI is discussed in Porter (1990, pp. 384–421).

The main conclusion regarding the role of government intervention made by Porter is that the most important role for governments is to create favourable conditions for individual firms in terms of supply of specialized and advanced factors, to facilitate innovation and research and to make sure that domestic rivalry exists. Protectionist measures have long-term negative effects and should be avoided. The important message is: governments lack the power to create advantage by themselves, this can only be achieved by individual firms. Governments may influence the odds of success for firms, however, particularly through careful investments in the necessary infrastructure for business, including education at all levels.

5.4   A STATISTICAL LOOK AT THE BALTIC REPUBLICS

Table 5.1 summarizes some statistics for the three Baltic republics. Although small by size, the population density is low compared to the rest of Europe. They have more space than Spain (density of 77), France (102), Poland (122), Germany (221) or UK (234), and, in fact, the density measures are the lowest ones in Europe, except for Russia (8), Norway (14), Finland (15) and Sweden (19).

Living conditions indicate that a social indicator such as life expectancy is on a level with Finland, and only slightly lower than Germany (72.2) and Norway and Sweden (74).

Table 5.1: General statistics for the Baltic republics

	Estonia	Latvia	Lithuania
GDP, 1991(US$ per cap.)	3 830	3 410	2 710
Area (square kilometres)	45 215	64 600	65 200
Population, 1990 (thousands)	1 575	2 670	3 737
Density, 1990 (per square km)	35	40	57
Social indicators			
birth rate	14.2	14.2	15.1
death rate	12.4	13.0	10.6
life expectancy at birth	70.8	70.5	72.0

Sources: World Bank (1993a), World Bank (1993b), World Bank (1993c).

Table 5.2: Composition of trade in world prices, 1989 (million roubles)

	Estonia		Latvia		Lithuania	
	Exp.	Imp.	Exp.	Imp.	Exp.	Imp.
Industry	1 861	3 262	3 995	5 375	4 530	7 608
of which (%):						
Energy	10	17	3	19	24	33
Metallurgy and machinery	33	52	53	54	45	50
Chemical and petroleum	13	13	13	9	7	8
Wood, paper, building materials	6	3	4	4	4	2
Light industry	17	7	7	4	10	4
Food production	18	5	15	7	10	4
Other industries	3	2	4	2	0	0
Agriculture	17	76	47	188	65	197
Other Prod. sectors	190	125	371	78	224	286
Total	**2 068**	**3 462**	**4 413**	**5 640**	**4 819**	**8 091**

Source: World Bank (1993).

The most unreliable figures in *Table 5.1* are, however, the GDP per capita estimates. The numbers are taken from World Bank reports, and the estimates are higher than those reported by CEPR (10–30 per cent higher), but lower than the EFTA estimates (40–50 per cent lower), according to Baldwin 1993. As the estimates vary substantially, the value of the GDP estimates is limited.

Trade figures for the Baltic Republics are no less uncertain than GDP per capita. First, most trade has been with the former Soviet Republics, and trade has taken place at prices different from world market prices. The World Bank has estimated the value of the 1989 trade and converted it to world market prices, as given in *Table 5.2*. Owing to artificially high export prices, a conversion to world market prices indicates an import surplus for all three nations. As these trade figures reflect the situation in the Soviet period and can hardly be regarded as very reliable, one should not put too much emphasis on the data. At the time of writing this is, however, the most complete data that is readily available, and will thus be used to indicate the kind of reasoning one could use to identify possible future trade opportunities.

Even when using a commercial value of roubles as high as 1.75 per US dollar for 1989, the export values are low. The total Baltic exports in 1989

(11 300 million roubles) constitute one third of Norwegian export values and only 3 per cent of German exports for that year. The Baltic republics are, therefore, tiny players in world trade.

The trade figures indicate a high dependency on energy imports. Furthermore, the trade in industrial products indicates that metallurgy and machinery is a dominating sector. Generally the region is a large net exporter of light industry products (fabrics, clothes and leatherware), particularly Estonia. Agricultural products play a minor role in trade.

It is against this background that I will examine a few aspects of what could form the future trade for the Baltic republics.

5.5   THE TRADING POTENTIAL

It is of course quite impossible to estimate future trade potentials for nations that for several decades have been excluded from free participation in world markets. Nevertheless, several such attempts have been made in recent years.[9] The point of departure of these studies is to ask the following question: if the Eastern European nations had been as integrated with the rest of Europe as Western Europe is today, what would the trade pattern have been then? Knowing the complexity of factors that determine world trade, it would seem to be more than foolhardy to try and model these trade flows in a realistic way. Therefore it is better to use simplistic models that at least capture a major part of reality. One such model framework is the gravity model.

5.5.1   The Gravity Model

The gravity model has never been quite accepted by most trade economists until Wang and Winters (1991) brought it back into fashion. The beauty of the model is the combination of its simplicity and the fact that it predicts trade flows well. The model is a single equation of the following type:

$$X_{ij} = \beta_0 + \beta_1(GDP_j/Pop_j) + \beta_2 GDP_j + \beta_3(GDP_i/Pop_i)$$
$$+ \beta_4 GDP_i + \beta_5 Dist_{ij} + \text{dummies},$$

where X_{ij} denotes total exports from country i to country j, *GDP* is the total GDP and *Pop* the total population of the relevant countries, and *Dist* is the physical distance between the countries. In addition a series of dummies is introduced to handle specific features of the countries or the data sets.

[9]   The two most thorough studies are Collins and Rodrik (1991) and Wang and Winters (1991). They are summarized and discussed in Baldwin (1994).

The Transition to a Market Economy

Table 5.3: Estimated potential trade levels for the Baltic republics

Estimated medium-term trade matrix, 1989 (in billion US$ – 1985 prices)								
				Importers				
Exporters	Baltics	NEU	FSR	Nordic	FCPE	EFTA	EU 12	Total
Estonia	0.04	0.11	0.27	0.46	0.43	0.49	0.71	1.63
Latvia	0.08	0.23	0.51	0.40	0.84	0.46	1.28	2.58
Lithuania	0.07	0.33	0.63	0.32	1.07	0.40	1.41	2.88
FCPE	2.27	10.17	15.91	10.81	33.60	33.12	33.12	86.36
EFTA	1.25	7.43	7.16	12.76	18.77	15.72	104.55	139.04
EU 12	3.10	22.64	26.31	47.75	65.45	102.59	778.15	946.18
Total	6.62	40.25	49.39	71.32	117.81	137.95	952.72	1 208.48

| **Potential trade level if partial GDP catch-up by 2010** | | | | | | | | |
(in billion US$ – 1985 prices)								
				Importers				
Exporters	Baltics	NEU	FSR	Nordic	FCPE	EFTA	EU 12	Total
Estonia	0.40	1.00	1.97	2.33	3.42	2.48	3.63	9.53
Latvia	0.77	1.99	3.42	1.87	6.19	2.13	5.96	14.28
Lithuania	0.65	3.11	4.94	1.73	9.23	2.18	7.70	19.11
FCPE	18.55	74.81	105.73	45.58	239.30	70.47	70.47	392.77
EFTA	6.55	33.45	28.22	34.23	81.10	42.18	280.59	403.87
EU 12	16.29	100.91	104.98	128.15	283.46	275.3	2 088.31	2 647.08
Total	41.39	209.17	238.92	207.96	603.86	400.5	2 665.47	3 669.83

Potential trade growth rates per year 1994–2010 (per cent)								
				Importers				
	Baltics	NEU	FSR	Nordic	FCPE	EFTA	EU 12	Total
Estonia	14.2	13.7	12.4	10.2	13.0	10.2	10.2	11.0
Latvia	14.1	13.3	11.9	9.6	12.5	9.6	9.6	10.7
Lithuania	14.4	14.1	12.9	10.6	13.5	10.6	10.6	11.8
FCPE	13.1	12.5	11.8	9.0	12.3	4.7	4.7	9.5
EFTA	10.3	9.4	8.6	6.2	9.1	6.2	6.2	6.7
EU 12	10.4	9.3	8.6	6.2	9.2	6.2	6.2	6.4
Total	11.5	10.3	9.9	6.7	10.2	6.7	6.4	6.9

Source: Baldwin (1994) and own calculations.

Applied to data for Western Europe, the coefficients of the above equation have been estimated using cross section data. The gravity model predicts that trade increases with the economic mass of the countries in question and is reduced by the distance that separates countries. The model can easily be interpreted in a way consistent with models of intra-industry trade[10] and is particularly relevant for trade among developed countries not too distant from each other.

The experiment is to estimate what would be the GDP per capita in Eastern European *countries if they had been fully integrated market economies*, and then estimate bilateral trade flows using the equation above with the estimated coefficients from Western European data. Two experiments have been made, one with a medium-term perspective, the other long term. The first is to ask what the trade potential is based on revised 1989 data and the second is to estimate long-term potential up to 2010, assuming that the Eastern European countries manage to bridge some of the income gap to their Western counterparts.[11]

The calculations have been made on individual country data applying the equation above. The results have, however, for practical purposes been aggregated by summarizing individual country data.

The results for the two scenarios are given in *Table 5.3*. The size and income levels of the Baltic republics would justify export levels of 1.6–2.9 billion US dollars (at 1985 prices) according to the gravity model. Very much dependent on the exchange rates that are used to convert trade figures from 1989, the value of Baltic exports would vary from 0.3 to 3.3 billion US dollars for Estonia, and similar variations for the two other republics. Using commercial exchange rates would produce estimates close to the potential estimated below, indicating that initial trade levels with Russia have been high, although trade with the rest of the world has been negligible. The two most striking features of the results are, however, the changes in trade partners being indicated and the high potential growth figures.

In *Figure 5.2*, the changes in trading partners have been indicated. There are similar patterns for all three countries in the sense that trade with the former Slavic republics (Russia, Belarus and Ukraine) will be dramatically reduced and trade with the EU will increase. In the longer run, however,

---

[10] A formal treatment of the gravity model can be found in Bergstrand (1985) and Bergstrand (1989) and can be seen as a gravity relationship consistent with the simple Krugman model: Krugman (1979) and Krugman (1980). This is discussed further in Baldwin (1994).

[11] More specifically, the assumption is that the Baltic republics will catch up with Spain, implying growth rates of 4 – 5 per cent per year. Population growth is assumed constant.

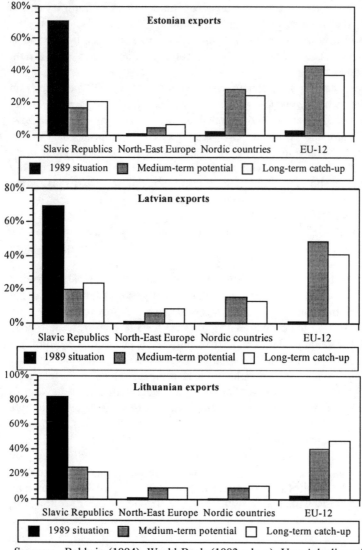

Sources: Baldwin (1994), World Bank (1993a, b, c), Van Arkadie and Karlsson
            (1992) and own calculations.

Figure 5.2: Changes in market shares

market shares for the former Eastern European countries will again increase.
This is only because the scenario assumes higher growth rates in these

economies, thereby implying higher trade as well. It is noteworthy that the trade relations with the Nordic countries show good prospects, particularly for Estonia, because of trade with Finland. This is a development already apparent in recent years. One should, of course, not read too much into these scenarios. They only reflect some of the potential changes that *could* take place if the former Eastern European countries really succeed in transforming their economies quickly into fully integrated market economies. This by no means guaranteed. From a trade perspective, I will thus turn to discuss and hopefully identify some areas where the Baltic republics may concentrate their efforts in order to realize some of the potential indicated by the gravity model scenarios.

5.6   SOURCES OF COMPETITIVE ADVANTAGE

The main source of comparative advantage for the Baltic states is undoubtedly the low wage rates of a highly educated workforce. This makes it tempting to jump to the conclusion that the Baltic republics should concentrate on labour-intensive production, and if possible, production that is intensive in the use of semi-skilled to skilled labour. This would be too easy an argument. During the process of restructuring, wages will no doubt increase fairly rapidly. Consequently, strategies should not be built solely upon wage rate levels. Instead, one needs to identify whether the workforce has special skills in areas that could easily adjust to Western markets.

The region is specialized in producing, among other things, electronics and electrical motors. There is also a large light industry in the three republics which indicates that the workforce has considerable technical experience and special skills. Another obvious source of comparative advantage is arable land as the basis for agricultural production. The farmers of the Baltics were among the most productive in the former Soviet Union.

It could be instructive to look at some evidence of comparative advantage from figures that reflect factor conditions.

5.6.1   Human Capital

There are two distinct features of the labour force in the Baltics. First and foremost, the average level of education is high and fairly comparable to Western standards, particularly within the fields of natural science. Second, the participation rate of the population in the labour force is higher than in the West, particularly for the female part of the population. These facts are presented in *Table 5.4*. According to *Table 5.4*, the perspectives of the basic research infrastructure should be very positive, since a high percentage share

Table 5.4: Human capital and labour force

Enrolment rates					
	Country				
Enrolment rates	Estonia	Latvia	Lithuania	Norway	UK
Primary and secondary	93.2	95.0	–	99.0	100.0
Tertiary	25.3	25.0	–	42.5	25.2

Population participation rates (%) in labour force					
	Estonia	Latvia	Lithuania	Norway	Italy
Male	85	85	83	75	82
Female	77	77	72	62	51
Population	80	83	78	68	66

Indication of potential R&D personnel					
% of labour force	Estonia	Latvia	Lithuania	EU North	EU South
University students	3.0	3.5	4.4	2.9	1.4
Government research dept.	2.6	>0.8	1.0	0.7	0.2

Sources: CEPR (1990), World Bank (1993a, b, c), Statistics Norway (1993).

of the work force has university education. It must be concluded that the Baltic republics have a well-educated labour force and an educational infrastructure with a high potential. The question is, of course, how this infrastructure is used and upgraded. There seems to be a very great need for improvement in business and management related topics, and a lack of qualified teachers in these areas. The few economists that worked in the universities with business related topics have, to a disturbing degree, left the universities to work for financial institutions or gone into politics. This could easily prove to be a major obstacle for restructuring and development in the future.

5.6.2 Agriculture and Natural Resources

The Baltic republics have relatively more agricultural land per capita than most countries, and the quality and productivity of the agricultural sector are on average better than for most former Eastern European countries. Figures in *Table 5.5* illustrate some basic facts in comparison to certain North European countries.

Table 5.5: International comparison of agricultural production

	Estonia	Latvia	Lithuania	Finland	Germany	Poland
Land resources, 1990						
Agricultural land (million ha.)	1.3	2.6	3.5	2.6	30.6	18.8
Arable land (million ha.)	1.0	1.7	2.3	2.4	19.2	14.7
Agricultural land per capita	0.83	0.97	0.94	0.51	0.54	0.49

	Estonia	Latvia	Lithuania	Finland	GDR	Poland
Agricultural productivity, 1989						
Crop Production						
Grain (quintals/ha.)	24.4	23.5	29.1	31.9	44	32.2
Potatoes (quintals/ha.)	166	155	161	219	233.6	185
Sugar Beet (quintals/ha.)	na	294	313	320	302.3	340
Dairy Production						
Milk (kg/cow)	4 230	3 636	3 806	5 246	3 821	3 278
Eggs (units/hen)	250	219	246	na	220	na
Livestock Industry Production						
Feed conversion (pigs)	na	na	6.5	3.2	na	na
Inputs						
Labour/100 ha.	11.4	11.7	14.4	7.9	8.2	na
N/ha.	83.3	101.1	137	100	141.3	na
P/ha.	61.9	65.9	83	30	56.4	na
K/ha.	103.2	101.1	132	56	94.4	na

Notes: ha.=hectare; kg=kilogram; N=nitrogen; P=phosphorus; K=potassium
Sources: World Bank (1993a,b,c) and Statistics Norway (1993).

Although the Baltic republics have more agricultural land per capita than most other European countries, agricultural exports have not played a major role in their exports. Successful restructuring of the agricultural sector and a further development of fertile land could be a source for both direct exports and for food production. The main obstacle is, of course, the Common Agricultural Policy of the EU and the restrictions such trade meets at the moment. Further progress within the GATT framework and more bilateral trade arrangements with former Soviet republics might allow agricultural products to become important export commodities in the future.

The Baltic republics have limited endowments of natural resources which might have been a potential source of comparative advantage.

Estonia has some deposits of oil shale, *kukersite* (reserves of 6 000 million tonnes), phosphorite (reserves of 700 million tonnes), limestone and Cambrian blue clay. There is also a considerable quantity of peat in the country (around 4 000 million tonnes in reserves). Woodland covers approximately 40 per cent of Estonian territory. This implies a limited basis for local supplies of energy resources and building materials.

Latvia has deposits of peat (530 million tonnes), dolomite (137 million tonnes), limestone (82 million tonnes), gypsum (55 million tonnes) and clay (85 million tonnes). Woodland covers 41 per cent of Latvian territory. Again building materials are the main product group that can be produced from these resources.

There are possibly oil reserves in the western part of Lithuania and in the Baltic Shelf. Small deposits of iron ore, limestone, clay, dolomite and gypsum are also available. Woodland covers 27.9 per cent of Lithuanian territory. Lithuania is thus the only one of the Baltic countries that has potential energy resources to be developed. However, the expected reserves are too small to make Lithuania a net exporter of energy.

The conclusion must be that it is hard to see how this could be an important source of competitive advantage for any large-scale industrial activity, except perhaps for building materials. This will, however, normally be trade that is limited by distance and implies eventual export to neighbouring countries.

5.6.3   Potential Industrial Clusters

It is more likely, therefore, that it is within the industrial sector that the Baltic nations must try to identify areas of competitive advantage.

Table 5.6 indicates the structure of industrial production as well as the number of firms and their average size. There are two major observations to be made from these figures. First, there are two main industrial segments where the Baltic republics are particularly strong, that is, engineering products and light industry. Second, the average size of firms is very high, as in the rest of Eastern Europe. In Western economies, average firm sizes vary

Table 5.6: The industrial structure of the Baltic republics

Industrial subsector	% of industrial output	No. of enterprises	Av. no. of employees
Estonia			
Food industry	14	52	553
Light industry	21	45	962
Engineering	29	46	1 265
(Of which electronics)	–	–	–
Forest industries	14	48	583
Chemicals	8	17	953
Building materials	7	21	681
Metallurgy	0		
Other	7	28	521
Total	100	256	792
Latvia			
Food industry	7	89	417
Light industry	20	74	859
Engineering	42	82	973
(Of which electronics)	–	5	7 809
Forest industries	10	55	445
Chemicals	7	15	1 279
Building materials	5	30	442
Metallurgy	1	4	821
Other	7	55	580
Total	100	407	763
Lithuania			
Food industry	10	142	465
Light industry	20	106	919
Engineering	40	–	–
(Of which electronics)	–	–	–
Forest industries	9	59	702
Chemicals	4	27	850
Building materials	8	64	606
Metallurgy	1	139	1 390
Other	9	47	702
Total	100	584	843

Sources: World Bank (1993a, b, c), Van Arkadie and Karlsson (1992).

from 30– 50[12] in most industries, that is, the typical Baltic firm is ten times larger than their Western counterparts. This is a major problem since most of these firms are overmanned and are managed by people unused to operating under competitive conditions. According to Porter, one of the main challenges would be to break up these large firms, particularly those with several thousand employees, and try to establish a set of smaller, more specialized firms creating environments of local rivalry and constant pressure for productivity improvements.

Although Baltic firms have had little experience with international exports, some sectors do export a relatively high percentage of their total production. In Porter's study a measurement of revealed export performance is used. One calculates first the overall share of world trade for the country in question, then for each sector where the country is a net exporter, one calculates the share of world trade for that particular commodity group. Whenever the share of world exports for a specific commodity is higher than the average share of the country in world trade, the country could be said to have a revealed competitive advantage in that particular commodity. On the basis of data from the World Bank (1993), *Table 5.7* summarizes the findings from 1989 trade figures for the Baltic republics.

The main export products seem to fall into four main categories:

- Textile, leather and related products;
- Building and construction materials, machinery and equipment;
- Fish and dairy products;
- Tools and dies.

---

[12] The problem of large-sized firms and competition is discussed in greater detail in Newbery and Kattuman (1992).

Table 5.7: Revealed advantages in Baltic exports

Product groups	Relative share of world exports (%)	Market share relative to total share of trade
Estonia		
Cooking products	0.72	20.9
Flax products	0.11	3.2
Pre-cast concrete	0.09	2.7
Tools and dies	0.09	2.6
Cotton products	0.06	1.7
Fish products	0.05	1.6
Dairy products	0.05	1.4
Leather	0.05	1.4
Transport expenses	0.05	1.4
Combustible shales	0.05	1.4
Confections	0.04	1.1
Latvia		
Perfume oils	0.69	9.4
Tractors and agr. equip.	0.14	1.9
Chemical fibres	0.11	1.5
Flax products	0.10	1.3
Fish products	0.08	1.1
Lithuania		
Leather	0.47	5.8
Construction M&E	0.36	4.5
Tools and dies	0.17	2.1
Flax products	0.12	1.5
Pre-cast concrete	0.10	1.2

Note: Let *MST* be defined as the overall market share for the country in world exports and let MS_i be the market share for commodity group i in world exports. The numbers are then defined as $RMS_i = MS_i/MST$.

Source: World Bank (1993a, b, c).

In addition, particular commodities like perfume oil and cooking products stand out as important export products. These do not seem to be part of a broader industrial cluster and it is hard to see that the Baltic states should have any particular advantage in the production of these two specific commodities, or that they are large enough to be of any interest. Instead, the broader groups mentioned above have a potential for being developed into industrial clusters of the nature recommended by Porter. This means production areas where local rivalry will foster productivity improvements, where related production activities will help to maintain a pool of competent labour, where local demand will gradually make the producers more sophisticated and where an active government policy will facilitate investments and secure relevant education of the labour force.

These observations are, however, made solely on data from the end of the Soviet period. If the Baltic countries are to form concrete strategies for the future, a more detailed study based on whatever reliable newer information is obtainable, should be conducted.

5.7   TRADE RELATIONS WITH FORMER AND NEW TRADING PARTNERS

The close links to the former Soviet Union represent an obstacle to market transformation that is a major challenge to the Baltic republics. *Table 5.8* indicates some areas where the Baltic states have been totally dominating exporters or were totally dependent on imports from the Soviet Union.

The export products list confirms the above conclusion that the Baltic republics have production skills within electronic equipment, tools and dies, and the list also indicates that they have experience in component production. Some of the products (like diesel pumps, chain belts, drills and spare parts) indicate that a potential strategy is to develop joint-ventures with foreign firms where the Baltic producers could deliver components, using their base of skilled workers to supply internationally competitive firms with essential parts. This would be the best learning ground for product development, production adjustment and productivity upgrading.

Table 5.8: Integration with the former Soviet Union markets

Export products	Nation	Share of Soviet market, %
High speed, high precision drills	Lithuania	100
TV tuners	Lithuania	90
Bus and large car compressors	Lithuania	80
Fuel diesel pumps	Lithuania	85
Passenger minibuses	Latvia	100
Milking equipment	Latvia	100
Chain belts for bicycles, motorcycles and agricultural combines	Latvia	100
Spare parts for metal-cutting machines	Latvia	100
Electrical equipment for electric trains	Latvia	100
Automatic telephone switchboards	Latvia	100
Zinc white pigment	Latvia	100
Telephone sets	Latvia	>50
Import products		
Metals	Latvia	100
Bulldozers, tractors and excavators	Latvia	100
Cardboard	Latvia	95
Mineral fertilizers	Latvia	77
Paper	Latvia	>60

Source: World Bank (1993).

At any rate, monopoly positions must be broken down, as monopolistic positions tend to give the wrong incentive structures. Monopolies should be broken down into smaller units, creating local rivalry to spur the competitive spirit.

Regarding trade policies, the Baltic states have slightly different strategies, although the overall tendency is to move towards as much free trade as possible. Free trade agreements with the Nordic countries and lately new trade arrangements with the EU are important steps in this direction. There have been local debates about using trade policies to protect and control economic development, but all experience shows that this is not a wise strategy. Once protectionist measures are in place, strong forces will try to resist their removal.

5.8   THE ENERGY OPTIONS

The Baltic states have no large endowments of energy resources within their borders. This means that they are totally dependent on imports of energy from abroad. Previously energy was supplied from the Soviet republics at prices much lower than world market prices. The new situation implies that enormous resources will have to be spent on energy imports, and this makes it even more important that these nations should develop competitive export industries to finance this energy import.

Table 5.9 indicates that the Baltic republics are very energy-intensive nations. This is obviously a result of the supply of cheap energy, but it also reflects a potential for energy savings.

Table 5.9: The energy intensity of selected nations

	GDP/Cap. ($US)	Koe/Cap.	Koe/GDP ($1 000 US)
Estonia	4 000	5 732	896
Latvia	3 410	3 668	1 091
Lithuania	2 000	4 134	2 067
UK	12 550	3 756	299
Finland	20 172	5 547	275
Sweden	19 591	6 228	318

Note: Koe = kilogram oil equivalents.
Source: Lunde (1994).

Estonia is the only nation with some indigenous production (mainly oil shale (90 per cent) and some peat and wood), while Latvia imports a lot of energy for re-export mainly through the port of Ventspils.

In a detailed study (Lunde, 1994) of the energy options for the Baltic states, scenarios for energy use and supply have been made for the period up to year 2010. Here the potential for energy savings is estimated, and the possible use of alternative sources of energy is investigated. In one scenario which is rather optimistic regarding economic growth, the energy balances are as given in *Table 5.10*. The profile of the scenario is that energy savings are realized in the ten-year period from 1990 to 2000, reducing the overall energy intensity of the Baltic republics to a level comparable to Western economies. After this period energy demand is directly linked to economic growth which by that time is assumed to be very high. At the same time energy prices in real terms in world markets are assumed to be slightly higher than the level prevailing at the beginning of the 1990s. The result is that the energy needs of the Baltic republics will increase dramatically from the year 2000 to 2010.

Table 5.10: Energy balances up to 2010

Year	Energy expenses/GNP (%)	Total energy consumption (PJ)	Share of energy demand covered by (%)			
			Oil	Natural gas	Nuclear	Others
Estonia						
1990	14.9	342	34.4	14.2	0.0	51.4
2000	47.9	290	74.6	11.4	0.0	14.0
2010	56.7	536	82.8	12.0	0.0	5.2
Latvia						
1990	6.4	300	23.6	34.9	0.0	41.5
2000	18.0	157	49.6	24.0	0.0	79.1
2010	24.9	269	59.7	25.1	0.0	11.9
Lithuania						
1990	6.0	648	55.7	27.6	6.1	10.6
2000	38.9	396	39.0	29.2	10.0	21.8
2010	54.8	681	41.6	35.4	5.8	17.2

Source: Lunde (1994).

The figures are not meant to be forecasts of Baltic energy development, but rather to emphasize the potential burden involved in a switch from cheap access to energy supplies towards paying world market prices for energy.

The recommendations implicit in the scenario could be briefly summarized as follows:

- High investments in energy-saving appliances and processes are necessary;
- Using the Baltic ports for transit oil in the short run in return for Russian supplies;
- Investing in port and pipeline development for oil imports from non-Russian sources;
- Developing gas import opportunities from sources other than Russia;
- Continue, but gradually fade out, oil shale production in Estonia and the nuclear production at Ignalina.

In this scenario, the dramatic increase in energy expenditures per unit of GNP is obvious and will remain the main problem of the Baltic nations in the years to come. This emphasizes the need for the development of competitive export industries to finance this essential import.

5.9   THE TRADING INFRASTRUCTURE

The Baltic states have a well-developed transport infrastructure. In the former Soviet Union, the Baltic ports played a dominant role in the export and import of commodities. After the break-up of the Soviet Union, Russia's only remaining ports in the South and West are those of Odessa and St. Petersburg. The transport infrastructure will no doubt play a dominant role in the economic development of the Baltic states, both as a means of bringing imports and exports to the respective markets, but also as a gateway of transit trade to and from Russia.

5.9.1   Railways and Pipelines

From the ports of Riga, Ventspils and Klaipeda, primary railways have a direct connection with Moscow. From the port of Tallinn, there are similar direct connections with St Petersburg. In addition, the Latvian port of Liepaja is linked to this rail network by a secondary railway.

There is also an extensive internal network of railways linking the main cities of the Baltic republics.

There is an oil pipeline from the St Petersburg area to Tallinn and from Pskov to both Tallinn and Riga. Riga, Klaipeda and Kaunas are further linked to the Belorussian oil pipeline system southwards towards Kiev.

Ventspils is in addition linked to the former Soviet natural gas pipeline system, which gives the Baltic ports an excellent strategic position in bringing eventual future oil and gas exports from the former Soviet republics to the world market.

5.9.2   Ports

All three Baltic republics have good port facilities, all of which have been busy mainly with Russian transit trade.

The two ports of Tallinn, the city port and the deep water port at Muuga 13 kilometres from the centre, are the main shipping centres in Estonia. Muuga can handle vessels up to 150 000 deadweight and has a depth of 18 metres. This port has played a major role in handling Russian wheat imports and has direct rail links to St Petersburg. Ninety-five per cent of all freight passing through Estonian ports has traditionally been transit freight from Russia. Coal from the Donets basin has been shipped from Tallinn, but also cars and other four wheel drives for export to South America. Tallinn has direct ferry links with Helsinki and Stockholm, and the Helsinki link in particular is very important for the development of export industries in Estonia.

Latvia has three ports: Riga, Ventspils and Liepaja. Riga is a well-diversified port handling many different commodities, while Ventspils is a specialized oil products port that used to handle around 30 million tons of products per year. Ventspils could relatively easily be modified to handle all sorts of oil and chemicals, but this will require substantial investments.

In Lithuania, the only main port is Klaipeda. It can also handle many different types of commodities and is currently being modified to handle imports of crude oil to relieve the dependence on Russian supplies. Klaipeda has also established regular ferry services with Germany.

5.9.3   Shipping Companies

During the Soviet regime, all shipping fleets were under the control of the Ministry of the Merchant Marine (Minmorflot), although the 17 individual shipping companies were responsible for the management of their fleets (as well as ports and ship repair facilities). In 1989, the Soviet fleet consisted of as many as 2 827 vessels, totalling about 23 million deadweight, which indicates that the average Soviet vessel is a small vessel (around 8 000 deadweight).

After the break-up of the Soviet Union, fleets were transferred to the individual shipping companies, which, however, still remained under government control. In the Baltic, Latvia has the largest fleet, followed by Estonia and Lithuania.

The Latvian fleet is composed of about 100 vessels with a total deadweight of 1.1 million, of which the Latvian Shipping Company (Latvijas Kugnieciba) controls about 80 ships. About half the Latvian fleet consists of tankers and about one-third is general cargo vessels with refrigerating capabilities. Some of the ships have ice class and lately the Latvian Shipping Company has bought fairly modern tankers from Western shipowners. The near monopoly situation of the Latvian Shipping Company has been marginally modified by the recent establishment (1992) of Latvijas Zvejnieku Savieniba, but this small company (two vessels) is also controlled by the government.

The Estonian fleet has no tankers at all, but consists mainly of dry bulk carriers and general cargo ships, mostly Ro-Ro vessels.[13] In total the Estonian fleet consists of about 90 vessels, of which the majority belong to the Estonian Shipping Company (Eesti Merelaevandus). This company is also controlled by the government.

The Lithuanian fleet consists of about 55 vessels, of which the majority are general cargo and Ro-Ro vessels and about 20 per cent are dry bulkers. The dry bulk vessels are larger, however, and constitute some 50 per cent of the total deadweight. Again the dominating owner is the Lithuanian Shipping Company (Lietuvos Juru Laivininkyste), which is also controlled by the government.

5.9.4   Trading Activities

The Baltic republics are undoubtedly in a most favourable position regarding the transport network to handle not only their own imports and exports, but also transshipment and trading activities.

It is interesting that Estonia became the sixth largest exporter of non-ferrous metals in the world in 1992, owing to large volumes of illegal raw materials from Russia. Huge volumes of illegal nickel, copper and other metals are being smuggled out of Russia and then re-exported from Estonia. One famous celebrity is the 'Metals Queen' of Tallinn, Tiiu Silves, a former school teacher, who admitted that her company had exported at least US$155 million of metals in the first half of 1992 (Forbes, 1992). Similarly, cotton became the largest export item in August 1992, although Estonia does not produce cotton at all. The explanation is a barter deal with Tajikistan and Turkmenistan where Estonia received 10 000 tonnes of cotton in exchange for clothing and food (BEE, 29 June 1992).

Trading activities could prove to be an essential element in building the capitalistic mentality needed by Baltic managers. At the same time, the shipping companies are ideal partners regarding cooperation with Western companies. Successful privatization of these companies, which can use the vessels as perfect collateral for refinancing, together with successful upgrading and investments in the Baltic ports, should be high priority tasks for the Baltic governments.

---

[13] Ro-Ro is an abbreviation for Roll-on, Roll-off, which indicates that the ship can lower ramps to the quay so that cars and trucks can drive directly into the hull of the vessel.

5.10 SOME CONCLUSIONS

The Baltic republics have developed special skills within some engineering products, textiles and clothing, fish and dairy products. These areas could be developed into truly industrial clusters with many smaller firms specializing in narrow segments. Joint-ventures with foreign firms are the fastest way of learning Western mentalities and providing motivation for product development, international marketing and in general for upgrading of productivity. The high skills of workers, combined with their very low wages could give the Baltic region a competitive advantage that may be sustained. The large conglomerates must, however, be fundamentally restructured. The creation of smaller production units, the adoption of Western business mentalities and the provision of local rivalries among privately owned firms are all necessities for the development of international competitive businesses. The role of the governments should be to facilitate this process, to invest in educational and other infrastructure (telecommunications, ports, roads, and so on) and not to try to be owners of companies themselves.

Trading activities should be allowed to flourish and investments should be made to take full advantage of their strategic position as a gateway to former Soviet markets. The shipping and port sectors of the Baltic republics are ideally suited to cooperation with Western interests.

5.11 REFERENCES

Andersen, E.S., B. Dalum and G. Villumsen (1981), *International Specialization and the Home Market: An Empirical Analysis*, Institut for Produktion, Aalborg Universitetscenter, Aalborg.

Balassa, B. and L. Bauwens (1988), *Changing Trade Patterns in Manufactured Goods – An Econometric Investigation*, North-Holland, Amsterdam.

Baldwin, R.E. (1993), *The Potential for Trade between the Countries of EFTA and Central and Eastern Europe*, EFTA, Geneva, Occasional Paper 44.

Baldwin, R.E. (1994), *Towards an Integrated Europe*, CEPR Press, London.

Barker, T.S. (1977), International Trade and Economic Growth: An Alternative to the Neo-Classical Approach, *Cambridge Journal of Economics*, vol. 1, pp. 153–72.

BEE (Business Eastern Europe) (1992), London.

Bergstrand, J. H. (1985), The Gravity Equation in International Trade – Some Microeconomic Foundations and Empiricial Evidence, *Review of Economics and Statistics*, vol. 67, pp. 474–81.

Bergstrand, J.H. (1989), The Generalized Gravity Equation, Monopolistic Competition, and the Factor Proportions Theory in International Trade, *Review of Economics and Statistics*, ol. 71, pp. 143–53.

CEPR (1990), *Monitoring European Integration, The Impact of Eastern Europe*, CEPR, London, A CEPR Annual Report.

Collins, S.M. and D. Rodrik (1991), *Eastern Europe and Soviet Union in the World Economy*, Institute for International Economics, Washington DC.

Deardorff, A.V. (1992), Testing Trade Theories and Predicting Trade Flows, in Jones, Ronald W., Kenen, Peter B., eds, *Handbook of International Economics*, North-Holland, Amsterdam.

Forbes (1992), 21 December.

Grubel, H.G. and P.J. Lloyd (1975), *Intra-Industry Trade: The Theory and Measurement of International Trade in Differentiated Products*, Macmillan, London.

Helpman, E. (1987), Imperfect Competition and International Trade: Evidence from Fourteen Industrial Countries, *Journal of the Japanese and International Economies*, vol. 1, pp. 62–81.

Helpman, E. and P.R. Krugman (1985), *Market Structure and Foreign Trade: Increasing Returns, Imperfect Competition, and the International Economy*, MIT Press, Cambridge, Mass.

Krugman, P.R. (1979), Increasing Returns, Monopolistic Competition and International Trade, *Journal of International Economics*, vol. 9, pp. 469–79.

Krugman, P.R. (1980), Scale Economies, Product Differentiation and the Pattern of Trade, *American Economic Review*, vol. 50, no. 5, pp. 950–59.

Krugman, P.R. (1990), Endogenous Innovation, International Trade and Growth, in Krugman, P., ed., *Rethinking International Trade*, MIT Press, Cambridge, Mass.

Krugman, P.R. and A. Venables (1990), Integration and Competitiveness of Peripheral Industry, in Bliss, C., Macedo, J. Braga de, eds, *Unity with Diversity in the European Community*, Cambridge University Press, Cambridge, UK.

Krugman, P.R. (1991), *Geography and Trade*, MIT Press, Cambridge, Mass.

Linder, S. (1961), *An Essay on Trade and Transformation*, John Wiley, New York.

Lunde, L.A. (1994), Energy Options for the Baltic States, NHH, Bergen, HA-Thesis.

Newbery, D.M. and P. Kattuman (1992), Market Concentration and Competition in Eastern Europe, *World Economy*, vol. 15.

Porter, M.E. (1990), *The Competitive Advantage of Nations*, Macmillan, London.

Statistics Norway (1993), *Statistical Yearbook 1993*, Official Statistics of Norway, Oslo.

Van Arkadie, B. and M. Karlsson (1992), *Economic Survey of the Baltic States,* Pinter Publishers, London.

Wang, Z.K. and A. Winters (1991), *The Trading Potential of Eastern Europe*, CEPR, London, Discussion Paper no. 610.

Wergeland, T. (1992), *Norsk skipsfarts konkurranseevne*, SNF-Rapport 50/92, Foundation for Research in Economics and Business Administration, NHH, Bergen.

World Bank (1993a), *Estonia – The Transition of a Market Economy*, World Bank, Washington DC.

World Bank (1993b), *Latvia – The Transition to a Market Economy*, World Bank, Washington DC.

World Bank (1993c), *Lithuania – The Transition to a Market Economy*, World Bank, Washington DC.

6. State-Owned Enterprises after Socialism: Why and How to Privatize Them Rapidly

Pavel Pelikan

6.1 INTRODUCTION

There is still much disagreement about how to transform and redress the economies impoverished by several decades of real socialism. Perhaps the greatest disagreement is about the privatization issue. While virtually everyone now seems to agree that markets are superior to central planning and that macroeconomic stabilization is necessary, opinions differ widely on what to do about the ownership of the large number of state-owned firms. Although in several of these economies, different programmes for transferring these firms into private hands are already at work, the programmes result more from ad hoc political decisions than from systematic economic analysis. On the other hand, there are also post-socialist economies where the majority of such firms still remain in state ownership, with no concrete decision on their privatization in sight.

The fundamental cause of this disagreement, I contend, is the lack of a clear and generally recognized theoretical reason why firms should be owned privately. Many theoretical economists still doubt whether privatization is at all necessary. Some even argue that reasonable efficiency can be achieved with an improved form of state, communal, or employee ownership of firms, and thus revive hopes that some kind of real market socialism might still be feasible.[1] It is also common to see privatization as a purely ideological issue.

---

[1] An interesting recent design for real market socialism is in Bardham and Roemer (1992) and its refutation is in Pelikan (1993). The adjective 'real' is used to distinguish market socialism which uses real markets, without any central planner, from socialist planning that imitates markets along the lines suggested by Oscar Lange, sometimes also called 'market socialism'. Whereas the latter was refuted by Friedrich Hayek and no one now seems to take it seriously, real market

150

Of course, without knowledge of how privatization could be justified economically, the only visible reasons for it must be ideological. The political demand for privatization that can be observed in many post-socialist countries is then seen as an emotional reaction by local populations to the many years of painful experiments with the wrong kinds of socialism. In consequence, many theoretical economists respect this demand as good democrats, but not as economists.

The lack of clarity about the reasons for privatization cannot but cause disagreement about the extent, the speed, and the methods of privatization. For example, inspired by the Chinese reform, some economists argue that the private sector should be allowed to grow, but that existing state-owned firms should not be privatized.[2] Those who do agree that these firms should be privatized disagree on other questions – such as how fast this should be done; whether privatizing should precede or follow restructuring; how much, if anything, should be privatized by means of freely distributed investment vouchers; and how much reliance should be placed upon emerging financial markets as opposed to large banks and institutional investors. There are even sophisticated mathematical models, based on the assumption that the only reason for privatization is political demand, which show that to meet this demand optimally, privatization should not proceed fast.[3]

The main purpose of this paper is to show that there is a strong economic argument for rapid privatization, which moreover throws new light on alternative privatization methods. The argument is based on my earlier study

socialism is more difficult to refute and still appears to have enthusiastic supporters.

[2] An example of this argument is in Nolan (1993). It is easy to see why this argument is of little general interest. State-owned enterprises in China are about as mismanaged and wasteful as in other socialist economies. The subsidies they require substantially contribute to the high Chinese inflation. The only advantage of China is to have relatively few of them. It is because of their relatively low share in the Chinese economy that they can be tolerated, as a residue of socialist waste in the midst of growing capitalist production. But this is clearly not the case of the highly but wrongly developed post-socialist economies in Europe, where state-owned firms had virtually all of the available scarce resources under their control.

[3] An amazing example of this kind of exercise is in Katz and Owen (1993). Their basic assumption is that privatized firms do not perform better than state-owned firms, but cause unemployment. Their model then tries to find an optimum path between the negative political effects of this unemployment and the positive political demand for privatization (which, according to the assumption, must be considered entirely irrational). The result is an astonishing curve in which the optimal speed of privatization varies in an intricate fashion.

of the role of scarce economic competence in the evolution of firms and industries.[4] Among other things, the argument explains why privatization should precede restructuring, and brings strong support to a certain type of privatization by investment vouchers, which theoretical economists usually reject.

The paper is organized as follows. Section 6.2 recalls the definition of scarce economic competence and exposes its most important properties. Section 6.3 explains why careful examination of the economic competence involved is essential for a good understanding of the privatization issue. Section 6.4 summarizes the competence argument for private and tradeable ownership of firms. Section 6.5 shows what this argument implies for the speed and the sequencing of post-socialist privatization, and Section 6.6 examines the choice of the privatization method. Section 6.7 consists of concluding comments.

6.2   ECONOMIC COMPETENCE AS A SCARCE RESOURCE

The starting point is a simple observation. An economic agent depends not only on his incentives and available information, 'data', but also on his competence, 'rationality', to use the information in responding to the incentives. While the incentives and the information have been frequently analysed, the problem of competence has mostly been neglected. Much of this problem is indeed hidden by the standard assumption of perfect rationality, which postulates that each agent uses the available information optimally (the Optimization Postulate). To understand the competence problem in its entirety, it is indeed necessary to drop the assumption of perfect rationality. The direction to follow is indicated by Simon (1978), who argued that human rationality is bounded, and by Heiner (1983), who considered such bounds in relation to the difficulty of the problem to be solved, and introduced the notion of competence-difficulty gaps. To see also the social dimension of the competence problem, however, we must go even further. Whereas Simon and Heiner are concerned with competence constraints on one-person problem-solving (decision-making) in general, the study of resource allocation in society must consider such competence as an agent-specific scarce resource, of which different agents may possess different quantities and qualities. This makes it necessary to admit, in

---

[4]   For the main results, see Pelikan (1992, 1993). The ones relevant to the privatization issue will be recapitulated here, to allow independent reading of the present paper.

Simon's terms, that the rationality of different agents may be bounded in different ways and degrees, or in Heiner's terms, that for a decision problem of given difficulty, different agents may suffer from competence-difficulty gaps, that vary with respect to size and shape.

This resource, which may be termed 'economic competence' (EC), denotes the competence of economic agents to recognize and use relevant information to solve economic problems and take economic decisions. In other words, EC refers to what is often called 'optimization abilities' or 'rationality'. Much like any other scarce resource, EC raises the problem of its efficient allocation in society. For EC, however, this problem turns out to be more intricate than for any other scarce resource. Although EC has some common features with economic information and human capital – scarce resources whose allocation has been fruitfully studied by standard means – it differs from both in ways that make standard analysis of its allocation impossible. Whereas economic information is assumed to be (possibly at a cost) communicable, economic competence is a kind of tacit knowledge which for each agent can have only two sources: initial endowment and learning, which in turn must be based on the individual's own initial endowment with learning competence, 'talent'. Although this makes economic competence resemble human capital, the crucial difference is that the human capital that standard theory admits to be scarce includes competence in all domains, but not in economic decision-making itself. To admit that even this competence may be scarce leads to a paradox which breaks the theory.[5]

EC resembles human capital in another aspect – namely, in its heterogeneity. It can be classified into many different categories according to the type of decision problems for which it can be used. Different agents may be endowed with different amounts of EC of different categories, so that a simple ranking of agents according to their quantity of EC is not always

---

[5] The paradox is discussed in Pelikan (1989, p. 284). To see it, consider an imperfectly competent investor who wishes to make an optimal investment in the further study of the economics of investment in order to become a better investor. The paradox is that in order to make an optimal investment decision during the current period, he would need the competence which he is seeking to acquire in the future. It is instructive to note that no such paradox arises for other kinds of competence. For example, an imperfect engineer who invests in further study of engineering may very well do so in an optimal manner. All he needs is to be a perfect investor – which is indeed what the human capital theory assumes him to be as a corollary of the Optimization Postulate on which the theory is built. The economic competence of investors is a singular resource: to admit its scarcity breaks the theory.

possible. For example, one agent may have more EC for accounting under certainty, another may have more EC for estimating probability distributions under risk, while a third may be particularly competent at complex problem-solving under uncertainty. EC is thus not only agent-specific, but also problem-specific. If the assignment of a certain problem to a certain agent causes a very large competence-difficulty gap, the implication need not be that the agent is incompetent; his competence might still be substantial, but, from the point of view of the problem, of the wrong kind.

For present purposes, as will be explained below, it will be of particular importance to distinguish EC for managing (sometimes called 'managerial talent') from EC for owning, which includes the competence for recognizing and employing competent managers, but not necessarily the competence for managing itself. Moreover, it will be important to distinguish both these kinds of EC from the politico-administrative competence needed for a successful career within the state and/or party bureaucracy.

Before considering these types of EC in more detail, it is important to note a few general properties of EC-allocation. First, it is upon this allocation that the efficiency of the allocation of all other scarce resources crucially depends. This expresses the rather obvious but in standard analysis neglected truth that the performance of an economy crucially depends on the competence of the agents who assume the key decision tasks – in particular those concerning production investment, industrial strategies, organization and management of firms, and economic policies.

Clearly, incentives lose nothing of their importance. Efficient EC-allocation alone, without appropriate incentives that would make relevant competence work in socially efficient ways, would clearly be insufficient. The point made here is simply that the best incentives would be insufficient if unaccompanied by efficiently allocated EC. Enormous social losses are often caused by correctly motivated agents who are incompetent, or competent about the wrong things.

Second, because of the tacit nature of EC (incommunicability), EC-allocation requires changes in the organizational structure of the economy (restructuring). Hence, EC-allocation is closely associated with the evolution of this structure (including entry, exit and reorganization of firms and industries) and organizing processes in general. It is by creating, modifying, or abolishing decision tasks and/or by replacing the agents that perform them that this allocation proceeds. EC-allocation thus raises the double problem of both organizational design and job assignment, with the further complication – and this is what makes it so intricate – that neither the designers nor the assigners are a priori given. Consequently, their jobs must be endogenously designed and assigned as part of this special allocation process. This introduces into EC-allocation elements of path-dependency and the appearance of infinite regression.

Finally, what further complicates the problem of EC-allocation is that there is no easy way of measuring EC – other than by its actual performance, which usually becomes known only after a long delay, when costly errors may already have been committed. To assess in advance an agent's EC, including one's own, and find for it a suitably difficult and useful decision task is itself a difficult decision task, which requires much EC if costly errors are to be avoided. In other words, EC is also needed for assessing and allocating EC, which introduces into EC-allocation elements of self reference.[6]

Given all these complications, it is understandable why EC-allocation has not become a popular subject of economic analysis. Western theoretical economists have moreover a good excuse for neglecting it. In their domestic economies, although unnoticed by standard static analysis, market selection has made a reasonably good job of correcting the most serious cases of EC-misallocation, thereby making them difficult to observe. In consequence, Western economists have had hardly any reason to believe that this problem was important. Friedman (1953), in his famous justification of the Optimization Postulate, explicitly refers to market selection as a means of making all surviving agents, in the long run, reasonably respectful of the Postulate.

In the study of socialist and post-socialist economies, however, this excuse is no longer valid. There, market selection has been absent for a long time, which allowed even gross EC-misallocation to last. All socialist economies – and, for that matter also, the state-owned firms within mixed economies – suffer from tendencies to allocate inadequate EC to over-ambitious economic decisions, and allow such misallocation to last without effective corrections. The post-socialist economies, which could only inherit these misallocations, were obliged to start with many top economic positions wrongly designed and occupied by inadequately competent people.[7] The success of the entire

---

[6] It should be noted that correct assessment of own EC also requires high EC. While competence differences begin to be studied, it has become common, because of mathematical convenience, to assume that each agent knows at least his or her own competence. It is well known, however, that people often misjudge their own capacities, and incompetent people in particular are often unable to see how incompetent they are. This is indeed an instructive example of how mathematical convenience can make analysis blind in theory to what may cause important social losses in practice.

[7] To avoid misunderstanding, let me emphasize that this does not mean that these people are incompetent in general. They must be highly competent, for otherwise

post-socialist transformation now depends on how fast and how well these misallocations can be corrected. What is thus urgently needed is to start an effective process for making such corrections and for preventing further misallocation of economic competence from occurring and lasting. It is by examining alternative forms of ownership of firms for their role in this process that it will be possible to reach some strong conclusions about post-socialist privatization.

The emphasis on 'process' and 'lasting' deserves a comment. It is important to realize, as will be discussed in more detail below, that in the short run, no form of ownership can prevent EC-misallocation from occurring. No privatization method can guarantee that the right owners will be immediately found. To ignore this leads to disappointment and can be used for demagogic arguments against privatization. An important point in the present argument is that forms of ownership must be regarded as institutional frameworks which allow more or less powerful correction processes to take place. It is in preventing EC-misallocation from lasting, rather than from occurring, that alternative forms of ownership will be found to differ the most.

6.3   SCARCITY OF ECONOMIC COMPETENCE AND THE PRIVATIZATION ISSUE

Let me first clarify why the privatization issue cannot be settled by analysis of incentives alone. At first sight, when interpreted by already convinced believers in private enterprise, such analysis may indeed appear to clearly support private ownership of firms. The popular argument is that non-owners have weaker incentives than owners to organize and manage a firm efficiently. This means that they must be expected to work less hard and misuse the firm's assets for their personal rent-seeking (see, for example, Buchanan et al. (1980) and, in the context of post-socialist economies, Winiecki, (1991)).

Upon closer examination, however, this argument proves to have several weaknesses, which can strengthen the case against privatization. To begin with, it can be pointed out that in a modern capitalist economy, most of the important decisions within large firms are taken by non-owners, while the owners remain passive. Following Jensen and Meckling (1976) and Fama

they would not have been so successful. I only claim, as will be explained in more detail below, that from the point of view of social efficiency, their competence is likely to be about the wrong things. They are certainly competent in terms of their career in the party or state administration, but not necessarily in relation to organizing and managing firms, or deciding on industrial strategies.

(1980), the assumption of passive owners is indeed central to most of the modern literature on corporate control. An opponent of privatization can then successfully argue that it is the quality of management rather than the ownership of firms that is the significant question.

Analysis of incentives can also be used to strengthen the case for government ownership of firms by two theoretically interesting arguments. One consists of the well-known incentive-compatible schemes which, under standard assumptions, can also motivate non-owners to signal truthfully and act efficiently. For example, a variant of this argument is now used by opponents of privatization in Poland, who claim that state-owned firms can be made efficient by means of suitable incentive-compatible contracts between the state and managers. Under the standard Optimization Postulate, which assumes that all the state administrators involved are perfectly competent to choose the right managers and to design, conclude, and monitor such contracts, this claim can hardly be refuted.

The second argument combines agency theory with an analysis of rational political voting. The theory exposes the difficulties in achieving efficiency in private firms where ownership is separated from management – as is the case for most large firms in modern capitalist economies. The analysis then shows that a firm owned by a democratic government, where assumedly rational voters play the roles of assumedly rational stockholders and where the Board of Directors consists of politicians submitted to regular re-elections, can cope with these difficulties at least as well as a private corporation (Wintrobe, 1985). More fundamentally, the importance of economic incentives themselves may be put in doubt by pointing to cases of successful cooperation in teams – such as a kibbutz, a university, or an army – where solidarity and loyalty appear more important. Hence, it is evident that the privatization issue cannot be settled solely by analysis of incentives.

When admitting the scarcity of economic competence into the study of privatization, it is sufficient to consider only a few kinds of the most important decision tasks (positions) on the supply side – in particular those of managers and owners of firms (including banks) and government policy makers – and the corresponding kinds of EC. A necessary condition for efficient EC-allocation – which, as noted, is the key to the efficiency of the entire economy – requires that these positions are suitably difficult and provided with adequate EC. More precisely, these positions must neither cause socially costly competence-difficulty gaps – by being allowed to grow too difficult and/or remain assigned to inadequately competent agents – nor waste scarce high EC by being kept too simple, and thus forgoing economies of scale and other advantages of modern industrial organization.

The study by Lucas (1978) of the relationship between managerial talents and the sizes of firms is a convenient point of departure. To recall, Lucas develops a simple formal model of the idea, due to Manne (1965), that a firm's performance depends on the talent of its manager, and that this talent is scarce and unequally distributed in the population. Assuming a simple production function in which the manager's talent is a parameter, Lucas shows that a given distribution of managerial talent implies an optimal size distribution of firms that maximizes the total output from given labour and capital. The obvious necessary condition is that the firms of different sizes are correctly matched with managers of corresponding talents: the most talented manager must lead the correspondingly largest firm, the next best manager, the second largest firm, and so on, until the last marginally talented manager, leading the smallest firm, fills up the production capacity; those who are even less talented for management than this last manager are employed as labour in one of these firms. It is easy to see that the model is about a case of EC-allocation. The decision tasks to be designed and assigned are those of the managers (chief executives) of firms, the difficulty of which depends on the firm's size, while the competence with which it is performed depends on the talent of the appointed manager.

Of course, the problem studied by Lucas is extremely simplified, in order to allow for a mathematical solution. But in each real economy, this problem arises in a non-simplified form, for which it is necessary to find a real solution. The sizes of all firms – taking into account not only the volume of their production, but also their complexity, and the complexity and the variability of their environments – must somehow be determined and their managers somehow selected and appointed. This is, in the present terms, the problem of EC-allocation to management. As noted previously, there is a double problem here. First, the question of how to design the managerial jobs – which depend, among other things, on how large and how complex the firm is allowed to grow. Second, how to assign these jobs to specific managers.[8] The fundamental point, on which the entire present argument rests, is that the performance of the entire economy crucially depends on how well, or how

---

[8]   A truncated version of this problem is addressed by Sah and Stiglitz (1985). They assume that all the managerial jobs are already designed (which presupposes a fixed population of firms of fixed dimensions) and assigned to managers of a first generation. Their study is limited to how these managers should select their successors, assuming the owners away. It is of course true that incumbent managers sometimes succeed in extending their jobs to decisions on both the growth of firms and the choice of their successors. But, as will become clear in a moment, this can only happen if the owners allow it to happen.

poorly, this double problem is solved. As this fundamental point is seldom properly seen by theoretical economists, additional comments are in order. In standard economics – and this is why this point is so rarely seen – the double problem of EC-allocation is simply assumed to be already optimally solved. The common assumption in most theoretical analysis of both markets and planning is indeed that all the firms involved are productively efficient and always able to optimize, irrespective of whether the firms are capitalist or socialist and whether the optimized variables are profits or plan indicators. Obviously, an implicit part of this assumption must be that all firms are of the right dimensions and are managed by perfectly competent managers. Whatever inefficiencies might plague the economy, their only causes must be in the inter-firm allocation mechanisms, which can fail to make such perfect firms efficiently coordinate their activities. The only policy advice then is to change the allocation mechanism. When all efforts to make socialist planning reasonably efficient fail – as happened in all real socialist economies – the only policy problem that can be seen is how to replace planning by competitive markets, which are now recognized to provide for superior resource allocation. But the form of ownership of firms seems not to matter: if all firms are perfectly organized and managed, social efficiency cannot depend on how they are owned. If equity is valued, avoiding private ownership may even appear advantageous.

However, as close observation of post-socialist economies disclosed in practice, and as the present argument explains in theory, this assumption is grossly false and believing in it leads to costly policy errors. Of course, it is important to note that all forms of socialist planning are highly inefficient as allocation mechanisms. However, this is not the whole truth. The abolition of private ownership of firms distorts also substantially the evolutionary process on which the properties of incumbent firms crucially depend. This leads to a serious and lasting misallocation of EC, as the abolition also dismantles all the effective feedback by which such misallocation could be corrected. Numerous empirical observations confirm that under the influence of politicians and government planners, real socialist firms are normally oversized and managed by mostly mediocre managers, selected for their competence to make a political career within the state and/or party bureaucracy, rather than for their EC relevant to industrial organization and management. To replace planning by markets, although necessary, is thus clearly insufficient. The transformation process must also include deep industrial restructuring and regeneration of the population of firms, in order to encourage the growth of high performance firms that have solved the EC-allocation problem on a reasonably efficient basis. It is as an instrument of such restructuring and regeneration that massive and rapid privatization is shown here to be indispensable. To avoid misunderstanding and false expectations, it should be emphasized that EC-allocation is a long-term ('evolutionary') process, which cannot avoid trials and errors. As noted, not all privatized firms can be expected to find the right owners at once, but many subsequent ownership changes may be required. That privatization may not always bring immediate improvement to individual firms, however, is no reason for slowing it down. Industrial recovery may take a long time, but in the absence of privatization, no systematic recovery process can start.

Much of the old criticism of markets was based on the illusion of an omniscient planner, who could easily avoid all market imperfections. Much of today's criticism of post-socialist privatization seems to be based on the illusion of an omniscient state property agency, which can easily see who has the right competence and capital to take care of its firms, and thus avoid the long and costly search for the right owners through market privatization and secondary trading. Without realizing that the second illusion is as absurd as the first, the privatization issue cannot be properly understood.

To see why privatization is so important for long-term industrial performance, we must first find out what the owners of firms have to do regarding the allocation of EC to the firms' managers. The clue is the question, how can this allocation problem be solved? It is the search for the answer that ultimately leads to the owners of firms – be they private persons, organizations, cooperatives or governments. Indeed the allocation of EC to the firm managers depends ultimately on the owners. Here, as the reader will recall, we are principally concerned with selection, contracting and monitoring of managers as well as seeking to ensure that the size of firms is maintained within the limit that does not overtax the competence of managers.

This is true even in cases in which the owners appear passive, having delegated the decisions on the management and the size of their firms to other agents – such as boards of directors, investment funds or the managers themselves. The reason is, in essence, that all such delegates are subject to the owners' choice, or at least approval.[9] Hence, even if the owners do not decide on the size and management of their firms themselves, they still bear the ultimate responsibility for how these decisions are taken. These are the principals that are responsible for both the competence of the agents who take these decisions in their stead and the incentives by which these agents are motivated to take the right decisions.

The need for competence and adequate motivation among the delegated agents, managers included, deserves emphasis. The competence problem should not make us forget the incentive problem: both of them must be

[9]   A detailed explanation is in Pelikan (1993).

provided with adequate solutions. But this has also an important implication for the role of owners and the competence they are required to have. As both these problems are difficult and as it is the owners who are responsible for how they are solved, the implication is that the owners also face important and difficult decision tasks, for which adequate EC is scarce.

This means that the double problem of EC-allocation, which we just discussed for management, now also reappears for owners. While there are many similarities between the two variants of this problem, there is also an important difference. For management, the solution to the problem ultimately depends on specific agents at a higher level: the owners. For owners, in contrast, there are no specific higher-level agents who could be said to solve this problem. How owners' tasks are dimensioned and specific owners are appointed ultimately depends on the institutional rules (such as property rights) that determine who is allowed to own firms – for example, which kinds of firms may or must be owned by government, and which kinds of firms may or must be owned privately – and define the processes by which the ownership of firms can change hands.

The argument proposed by the opponents of privatization which states that it is the quality of management rather than the ownership of firms that matters may now be properly qualified. While it is true that efficiency and social welfare strongly depend on the quality of management of firms, this is far from the end of the story. What was just made clear is – and this is the crucial point – that the quality of management in turn strongly depends on the competence of the owners: without highly competent owners, it is unlikely that a high quality of management will be obtained and maintained. The question is now: which form of ownership of firms makes it most likely that firms will be owned by adequately competent agents, and protected from the inadequately competent ones? It is the study of this question that results in a strong efficiency reason for privatization, and moreover throws new light on the pace, sequence and methods to be employed.

6.4   WHY PRIVATE OWNERSHIP OF FIRMS?[10]

When considered in detail, there are many alternative forms of ownership of firms, which may differ from each other in many ways. For example, forms of private ownership may differ in details of corporate law, bankruptcy and antitrust law, whereas forms of government ownership may differ in ways in which the ownership function is divided between the central and local governments, or between elected and administratively appointed bodies. For

---

[10]   This section summarizes an argument that is elaborated in detail in Pelikan (1993).

present purposes, however, it will suffice to consider only two large classes of ownership forms:

(1)   private and tradeable ownership;

(2)   government or employee ownership, by definition non-tradeable.

The main proposition to be justified is that (1) is superior to (2) in terms of efficiency and social welfare, largely regardless of the kind of welfare this is chosen to be – for example, whether or not income inequalities are to be limited and whether or not consumption of public and merit goods is to be encouraged.

Two points call for clarification. First, when classes of objects are compared, it is important to distinguish what is true about an entire class from what is true only about some of its members. The present proposition about the superiority of (1) should therefore be clarified as follows: some members of (1) are superior to all members of (2). In other words, it is admitted that (1) may also contain some inferior members – such as inefficient forms of private ownership of firms which prevent financial markets from developing and/or lack properly designed and effectively enforced bankruptcy and antitrust laws – and that difficult problems of detailed institutional design may be involved in the search for the superior ones. The essential point of the proposition is that this search should be limited to (1), as only inferior forms of ownership can be found in (2).

The second point to be clarified is the relationship to final demand and to different criteria of social welfare. It has often been claimed that different welfare criteria require different forms of ownership of firms. More precisely, private ownership of firms has been claimed to be compatible only with high income inequalities and low consumption of merit and public goods, whereas low inequalities and high consumption of merit and public goods have been seen to require government and/or employee-owned firms. These claims, however, turn out to be mistaken. As will be made clear in a moment, the study of economic competence implies that suitable forms of private and tradeable ownership of firms are superior to all forms of government and employee ownership, regardless of the adopted criteria of social welfare. The influence of the criteria upon economic performance certainly cannot be denied. For example, it must be admitted that the severe limitations of inequality damage incentives and thus diminish performance. However, as the history of Stalinist Soviet Union and Maoist China amply illustrates, this happens regardless of the form of ownership of firms. The competence argument shows that even in such cases, a suitable form of private and tradeable ownership of firms maintains its comparative advantage. In general, this argument is more hospitable to income redistribution than the standard incentive argument: it can be used to show that a mild and suitably designed income redistribution often has positive performance effects (Pelikan, 1993, pp. 388–90).

The main proposition can now be justified with the help of two elementary questions :

- Which form of ownership of firms makes it more likely that agents of high competence for owning firms will actually own firms?
- Which form of ownership of firms makes it more likely that insufficiently competent owners of firms will be demoted from this role, and thus prevented from causing unnecessary social losses?

It is easy to show that private and tradeable ownership of firms – or at least a suitable form of it – wins on both accounts. One reason clearly appears when we consider the roles that alternative forms of ownership of firms allow product markets to play. Potentially, there are two such roles. One is in determining the prices and the quantities of products of incumbent firms. The second role is in selecting the firms themselves, by setting capital availability constraints on their growth and survival. Whereas standard economics is preoccupied with the first role, it is the second role – the one pointed out by Schumpeter (1942), Alchian (1950) and Winter (1971) – that is relevant to the promoting and demoting of owners.

The important point is that product markets can always play the first role, whatever the form of ownership of firms – and thus also in market socialism – but not necessarily the second. It is for the second role, which is much more important in the long run than the first, that private and tradeable ownership of firms is essential.[11] It is only with this form of ownership that the most competent owners, who are most likely to obtain and maintain high quality of management, are also most likely to increase their capital and thus be promoted, while less competent owners, who more often tolerate incompetent or disloyal managers, are more likely to lose their capital, and thus be demoted.

It is easy to show that government ownership of firms is inferior in this respect irrespective of whether the government is democratic or authoritarian.

---

[11] A beautiful discussion of why the second role is so much more important than the first is in Schumpeter (1942), in the chapter on capitalist 'creative destruction'. Somewhat surprisingly, however, Schumpeter omitted to examine what happens with creative destruction in socialism. This make him overlook the social value of private ownership of frms and allowed him to arrive at his provocative but mistaken conclusion that socialism could succeed (cf. Pelikan 1987, 1992).

The crucial handicap of democracy is that the owners of firms are all citizens, who can be neither promoted nor demoted. Each of them has exactly one vote, corresponding to one share in each of the firms, regardless of his or her relevant competence. In other words, the entire EC-allocation for ownership of firms is blocked and cannot be improved.

Wintrobe's (1985) argument that a democratic government can be as efficient an owner of firms as a collective of private shareholders is thus clearly refuted. Although in such a collective, the allocation of owners' competence may be far from perfect, market selection can nevertheless be expected to increase the voting power of the more competent shareholders – because of their own intervention in the firm's affairs or because of their choice of competent delegates – and decrease the voting power of the less competent ones. Hence in the long run, ownership by private shareholders is likely to result in more competent ownership, and therefore more competent management, and therefore better performing firms, than ownership by a democratic government.

Note that only giving the more competent voters more voice to advise the less competent voters, rather than more real voting power, would not help. This follows from the above-mentioned fact that economic competence is also needed to recognize and efficiently use economic competence. Certain voters with little competence may simply lack the insight into the limitations of their competence and refuse to listen to any advice. Others, who are willing to listen, may lack the competence to recognize competent advice among all the incompetent advice that is also likely to be offered.

From this point of view, ownership of firms by an authoritarian or technocratic government appears more hopeful. The top government agents who play the roles of effective owners can be promoted or demoted in politico-administrative ways, which means that some EC-allocation at the ownership level can take place. The problem, however, is that this EC-allocation is not very likely to be efficient – significantly less likely than the one implied by private and tradeable ownership of firms and market selection. Politico-administrative selection proves less suitable than market selection for promoting economic competence and, perhaps even more so, for demoting economic incompetence. The reason is, in essence, that these two selections – much like tournaments in two different sports – favour different kinds of competence (Pelikan 1987, 1988).

The competence that the politico-administrative selection favors most is the one for pleasing political leaders, influential administrators or strong interest groups, rather than the one for organizing efficient production units and recognizing competent managers. In the absence of private and tradeable ownership of capital, no automatic, impersonal feedback from economic results to the size of the capital controlled can exist. Consequently, errors in the owners' decisions do not automatically cause this size to diminish. Instead, all promotions and demotions must be determined by decisions of specific agents in specific positions within a corresponding politico-administrative hierarchy – such as a ministry, a government bank or, in a centrally planned economy, the Planning Board. As these agents have also been selected in politico-administrative ways, their competence for correcting economic errors is also likely to be low, and their appointment to such positions is itself likely to be an error. Even gross errors may thus remain uncorrected and their authors may not be demoted for a long time, possibly not until they cause the entire economy to fall into a deep crisis.[12]

At this point, however, some hope may still be maintained for employee ownership of firms, as this need not entirely prevent the product markets from playing the important second role. Employee-owned firms can indeed be exposed to market selection and thus made subject to market-determined capital availability constraints on their growth and survival. To show that this form of ownership is also inferior requires a separate argument. Let us extend the study of market selection from the familiar cases of product markets to the still largely unexplored cases of capital markets, including the market for corporate control.[13]

First, it should be made clear that the argument is about the general institution of employee ownership imposed upon an entire economy, rather than about particular firms voluntarily owned by their employees on market terms within a capitalist economy; there can be no objection to the existence of such firms, as long as they are able to cope with their handicap of not being tradeable and are sufficiently efficient to survive market competition with privately owned firms.

The starting point of the argument is to recognize that selection by product markets – in spite of its superiority over its politico-administrative alternatives – is imperfect. Among other imperfections, such selection works only by a combination of complete bankruptcies and waiting for starts from zero by new firms – both of which may take a long time and cause high social losses.

---

[12] A possible objection is that government could appoint some highly competent winners of market competition to take care of government ownership. The hurdle is that market competition is a continuing process open to entry of new talents and forcing the exit of declining old winners. As government appointments interrupt this process, the competence of the appointed winners might soon relatively or absolutely decline, without triggering effective corrections.

[13] An attempt of mine to understand this kind of selection is in Pelikan (1989). The following discussion recapitulates the main points of this attempt.

It is by examining how this time and these losses can be diminished that an important drawback of employee ownership of firms and the decisive advantage of private and tradeable ownership of firms can be discovered. While bankruptcies and starts from zero remain important as error-correction of last resort, it is selection by capital markets, including the market for corporate control, that adds another powerful process which may make the correction both smoother and cheaper. In this process, the agents to be selected are the exceptionally competent owners of capital, who are able to perform the socially valuable function of distinguishing future winners from future losers.[14] They can then make the selection of firms both faster and cheaper by providing the necessary competence and capital to the former, and accelerating the exit of the latter. It is important to note that the process must allow for changes of ownership – for example, through buy-outs or take-overs. It is these changes that form a significant additional channel for error-correction. Thanks to them, not all declining firms need go entirely bankrupt; at least some may be saved in time, when efficient reorganization is still possible.

In this respect, employee ownership of firms proves inferior for two reasons. First, it only allows for the slower and costlier selection by product markets, and not the one by capital markets. This decreases the probability of selecting agents of the right competence for the highly difficult task of capital owners. This task must be assumed by government banks or industrial policy-makers, whose handicap is their origin in a politico-administrative selection. Their relevant competence is thus likely to be low and the social costs of the errors they will commit – for example, by mistaking future losers for future winners – is likely to be high. Second, as employee ownership of firms is not tradeable, the additional channel for error-correction by changes of ownership is blocked. It is on these two points that private and tradeable ownership of firms proves to have the decisive comparative advantage.

This clarifies, at least on the main points, the decisive support that the competence argument provides for the proposition that private and tradeable ownership of firms is superior to both government and obligatory employee ownership.

---

[14] The high social value of this function leads some economists to advocate selective industrial policy as a means of ensuring that this function would be performed on a socially optimal scale. The spectacular failures of this kind of policy in practice clearly showed what the present argument claims in theory: public policy-makers are unlikely to have the exceptional competence required. As a consequence, they more often than not fail to recognize future winners, and instead waste valuable resources on temporarily bailing out future losers.

To avoid misunderstanding, however, we must keep in mind that this proposition is about institutionally defined forms of ownership, and not about individual firms. Emphatically not all government or employee-owned firms are claimed to be inferior to their privately owned alternatives. The proposition only says that the entire population of firms will evolve towards a socially more favourable state if ownership of firms is private and tradeable than if firms are owned by government or employees – simply because the latter forms of ownership hinder or block important parts of EC-allocation. It is admitted that the populations of firms may have tails where exceptions can be found, for example, efficient state-owned firms or efficient cooperatives. However, it is important to remember that these are and must remain exceptions.

6.5   THE SPEED AND SEQUENCING OF POST-SOCIALIST PRIVATIZATION

What the previous section shows is that, regardless of ideologies and political demands, there is a strong economic reason why ownership of firms should be private and tradeable. The question now is, what can be done, in terms of specific policies, to institutionalize a suitable form of such ownership in a post-socialist economy, where a very large number of firms are owned by the state. Let me divide this question into two parts: the first concerning the speed and the sequencing of privatization programmes, to be discussed in this section, and the other about privatization methods, to be discussed in the following section.

To avoid confusion, policy analysis must clearly distinguish between two phases of the privatization process. One is privatization as institutional change – meaning legislation of a suitable framework of institutional rules within which private enterprise can successfully operate, such as property rights, business law, corporate law, antitrust law and laws allowing capital markets to form and develop. The other stage is privatization as structural change – meaning actual transfer of the existing government or employee-owned firms into the hands of new private owners. Let me refer to these phases as R-privatization and S-privatization, respectively.

This distinction makes it possible to clearly realize the most important differences between post-socialist privatization and privatization in a Western-type mixed economy. In a Western economy, little, if anything, need be done in terms of R-privatization, as virtually all the institutional rules required by private enterprise are already in place. In a post-socialist economy, in contrast, the framework of institutional rules must be built from the very beginning. Whereas in a Western economy, S-privatization may concern only a few state-owned firms and can substantially be helped by already developed capital markets, a post-socialist economy needs to find new owners for virtually all of its industry, while capital markets are seriously underdeveloped or entirely missing.[15]

The first observation is that R-privatization can and must be accomplished faster than S-privatization. The framework of suitable institutional rules is clearly a prerequisite for any meaningful transfer of specific firms to new owners. In principle, there are no economic constraints on the speed with which R-privatization can proceed. In the extreme, the formal institutional rules can be imported overnight, as was done in East Germany. In practice, however, R-privatization is not entirely without obstacles. What may confuse and slow down this process is that legislators may dislike importing foreign laws, while lacking the competence to choose efficient institutional rules themselves. Moreover, formal legislation is not the only source of effective institutional rules, for many of them consist of culturally evolved informal norms (North, 1990). The problem is that after several decades of life in an inefficient socialist economy, accompanied by socialist indoctrination, many of the norms have evolved in the wrong direction – for example, decreasing respect for property, unreliability in observation of contracts, and low working morale. As informal norms can hardly be changed overnight, but require a more or less lengthy process of social learning, effective R-privatization may thus be delayed.

This delay, however, is no reason for slowing down the legislation process and efforts to have the new institutional rules respected. This should still be done as fast as possible. Moreover, policy can also help in accelerating the necessary social learning by investing in extensive educational campaigns, explaining the principles of the working of markets and private enterprise to

---

[15] An interesting exposition of these differences is in Ferguson (1992). While Ferguson correctly argues that Western experience is largely irrelevant for post-socialist privatization, he cannot resist the temptation to use his own Western view for giving policy advice, which in the light of the present argument is absurd. His advice is to retain, 'at least for the time being', firms in state ownership and hire Western management teams to operate them, or to teach the local managers to operate them efficiently. He completely ignores the enormous agency problem that such a solution would create, given the low competence and high propensity to corruption of the state administration by which the Western teams would have to be selected and monitored. Moreover, given the poor average performance of Western state-owned firms (see, for example, Vining and Boardman, 1992) – which is the main reason why they are now being so diligently privatized – it is preposterous to suggest that efficient management of state-owned firms is something that the West can teach the East.

both the legislators and the citizens at large. The scarcity of economic educators, however, may be a serious binding constraint on this policy.[16]

In spite of these difficulties with R-privatization, it is S-privatization that is bound to take more time – although again, this is no reason for slowing it down or postponing it. The reason is that it cannot avoid time-consuming steps, during which specific measures concerning each of the state-owned firms must be elaborated and implemented. The first step is relatively easy and hardly controversial. It was indeed taken without much hesitation in most post-socialist economies. Often denoted 'commercialization', it consists of transforming all such firms into independent commercial units. This involves cutting off their automatic access to the state budget, which made any further subsidies a matter of case-to-case policy decisions.

The best policy which only a few post-socialist economies, however, had the economic wisdom and the political courage to adopt is a rapid phasing out of all further industrial subsidies. A prerequisite for this policy which implies another timing constraint on S-privatization is the liberalization of prices, convertibility of currency, opening of access to foreign markets for both imports and exports, as well as readiness to admit bankruptcies.

A comment on the usual objections to this policy is useful. They are the natural instruments of the incumbent 'nomenclature', whose vested interests the policy seriously threatens. As some of them cannot be refuted without a certain minimum of economic competence, which is not always available, they may be listened to and cause high social losses by slowing down or even interrupting the entire transformation process, while the economy continues to deteriorate.[17] Two objections appear particularly difficult to refute: (i) the objection to price liberalization which points out that even promising firms cannot rapidly adapt to an entirely different price structures of their inputs and outputs; and (ii) the objection to the phasing out of industrial subsidies which points out the high social and individual costs of the unemployment that would be caused by closing down all those firms that cannot become

---

[16] It seems that much of the relative success of the Czech transformation process is due to such campaigns. While the policy measures actually adapted were about the same as in many other post-socialist economies, the effort spent on explaining how markets work and why the measures were taken was unique. This, I believe, is an important factor which allowed the relatively radical Czech transformation policies to obtain and maintain broad political support, without any serious relapse into old socialist illusions.

[17] Ukraine is perhaps the most spectacular example of a rapidly worsening economic situation owing to the absence of radical reforms. Radical reforms certainly have their social costs and difficulties. However, Ukraine clearly shows that the costs and difficulties caused by their absence are substantially higher.

rapidly profitable.   The vested interests of the 'nomenclature', that these objections serve, are clear.[18] The artificially low prices of energy and raw materials, which objection (i) tries to maintain, are sources of enormous rents for all those administrators that can arrange for some private exports at world prices. The industrial subsidies that objection (ii) tries to maintain in the name of the employees of wasteful firms help above all the incumbent and often inadequately competent managers of those firms.

Without entering into detail, let me just point out the most important principles of the answers to these objections. Concerning (i), firms can be given time to adapt to efficient prices without delaying price liberalization. The principle to follow is a (temporary) transfer of the subsidies hidden in inefficient input prices to open subsidies to the consumers of these inputs.[19] This leaves both these consumers and the state finances initially in the same static position, but gives the consumers – and this is the crucial difference – a strong incentive to start economizing on these inputs. Concerning (ii), the principle to follow is that after a strictly limited period of decreasingly subsidized opportunities for efficient restructuring, the only efficient way for softening the negative social impact of radical transformation policies is helping persons – both materially and educationally – rather than loss-making firms. Each day during which such a firm is prevented from wasting valuable inputs on the production of less valuable and sometimes entirely useless outputs is a net saving to society.

Note that this principle is true even in the borderline cases, in which the sum of personal subsidies to the employees is larger than the sum of the required subsidies to the firm. In such cases, the productivity of the firm is positive if labour is cheap, and subsidizing it may thus appear superior to closing it down and subsidizing unemployment. Nevertheless, subsidies should still go to persons, rather then to the firm, but must be formed in such a way that they do not discourage low-paid employment. This allows such a firm to survive by attracting labour even at low wages, but only as long as better paid jobs do not appear. To subsidize the firm would result in wasting the labour by locking it into such poor uses, and thus preventing the creation of superior alternatives.

Let me now return to the first step of S-privatization, for which price liberalization and phasing out of industrial subsidies were shown to be prerequisites. Another prerequisite is establishment of a government agency

---

[18] Some Western theoretical economists contribute to supporting these objections by their simplified theocies, apparently without seeing these interests.
[19] A variant of this principle was successfully applied in the former Czechoslovakia for taking away subsidies for food without making life too hard for local consumers.

which assumes the role of the formal owner of the commercialized firms. What is not always seen, but the competence argument makes clear, is that because of its origins in politico-administrative rather than market selection, this agency is unlikely to be a highly competent owner. It should indeed be emphasized that democracy is no panacea: the change of the political system from one-party dictatorship to democracy – however valuable this change might otherwise be – does not increase in any substantial way the expected economic competence of politically selected agents. In consequence, this agency should do not much more than be the formal counterpart to the new owners – when these are found – in the transactions of the ownership titles over the privatized firms.

In particular, it would be unwise to entrust it with the highly difficult task of industrial restructuring – with the exception of cutting the oversized government firms into smaller units, for which interested new owners would be easier to find. It should definitely avoid all sophisticated, competence-demanding restructuring and all selective industrial policy which tries to recognize, select, and support future winners. As noted, because of the insufficiency of relevant competence and integrity among public policy-makers, such a policy caused enormous social losses in the developed West, and must therefore be expected to cause even higher losses in a post-socialist economy, where this competence and integrity are likely to be even lower.

The competence and integrity constraints on public policy-making constitute a powerful reason why the bulk of industrial restructuring should be left to the new owners. In other words – and this is the main implication of the competence argument for the sequencing problem – privatization should precede restructuring.

Note that this fully accords with views held by the opponents to privatization that the proper objective is efficient industrial restructuring, which would replace backward industries full of mismanaged firms by modern industries populated by elite firms, and not privatization as such. It is only shown that privatization is a necessary instrument for such restructuring.

At this point it is useful to recall an important lesson of evolutionary economics – which both Western economic experts, fluent in static analysis of already developed market economies, and Eastern planners, used to thinking that all economic changes must be ordered from above, often fail to see. The starting point is the finding that – because of imperfect information and scarce competence – no efficient industrial restructuring can do without experimental trial-and-error processes, which Schumpeter (1942) so beautifully called 'creative destruction' (see also Pelikan, 1987, Eliasson, 1988). In other words, the restructuring cannot manage without closing down many existing plants and entire firms and making room for tentative entries by new firms, not all of which can be expected to succeed. The lesson can be summarized as follows. Only a miracle could keep the 'destruction' in a perfect balance with the 'creation': this would indeed require that all the employees of the old closing firms would immediately be re-employed in some 'just-in-time' newly opened firms of precisely the same total size. In the real world, where miracles do not happen, the destruction can and must go ahead of the creation. Although this results in unpleasant 'destruction–creation gaps' with a temporary growth of unemployment, any policy trying to avoid such gaps by hindering the destruction is unwise. Namely, any slowing down of the destruction by subsidizing the declining firms binds scarce resources to inefficient uses, and thus inevitably also slows down the creation. This delays the structural recovery, destroys macroeconomic stability and currency, and substantially increases the cumulative social costs of the entire transformation.[20] The above-mentioned subsidizing of unemployed persons, but not declining firms, is the only efficient policy by which the negative social effects of the destruction–creation gaps can be alleviated. Creating a favourable environment for entrepreneurship, that is, clearly defining hospitable institutional rules, preventing predatory behaviour by incumbent state-owned enterprises, opening access to international markets, and providing for organization of capital markets is the only efficient policy by which public policy-makers can help to narrow the gaps.

The second step of S-privatization is more difficult and time-consuming than the first one. It consists of finding new owners for each of the privatized firms and transferring to them the effective control over these firms. What makes this step so difficult and time-consuming is usually a combination of several unfavourable factors – in particular the great number of firms to be privatized, the poor shape of most of them, the lack of capital and competence for improving this shape and, in some of the post-socialist economies, the lack of interest among the population for assuming the risks and the responsibilities connected with the ownership role.

None of these difficulties, however, is a good reason for purposefully slowing down, or renouncing, the privatization of state-owned enterprises. Given the competence and integrity constraints on government administration, which are typically much more severe in a post-socialist economy than in a developed Western economy, to retain these enterprises in state ownership is not a reasonable option – contrary to what some Western economists believe (see, for example, Ferguson, 1992). What the above argument emphasizes is that privatization is not merely a political objective, that can be diluted or traded off for other political objectives but a strict

---

[20]   Ukraine can again be referred to as a particularly frightening example.

economic necessity, without which industry cannot be efficiently restructured, capital markets cannot develop, and the entire transformation process must fail (see also Grosfeld, 1992 and Pelikan, 1992).

It may be useful to repeat that China, whose main problem is development and where state-owned enterprises are far from controlling all available resources, is not a relevant example for the highly but wrongly developed post-socialist economies in Europe, whose main problem is restructuring and where the private sector cannot properly grow without first dismantling the state sector (cf. note 2). This argument is strengthened by the (in the West) rarely noted fact that the state-owned firms in these economies, besides locking most of the available resources into inefficient uses, have moreover often engaged in predatory behaviour vis-à-vis the emerging private sector – for example, by refusing to supply inputs, or to pay for outputs.

Given the high priority of post-socialist privatization – at least in the more developed post-socialist economies in Europe – the only hopeful strategy for coping with its extraordinary difficulties is to choose an extraordinary privatization method which could cope with them at lower social costs than the high costs of retaining firms in state ownership.

6.6   THE CHOICE OF THE PRIVATIZATION METHOD

It is above all for S-privatization – the actual finding of new owners and transferring to them the effective control over the privatized firms – that the choice of method poses a problem. Different methods differ in their maximum speed and in their impact on efficiency and equity, especially in the short run. In the long run, of course, if the relevant institutional rules are suitably designed and the capital markets are allowed to do their job, the most serious inefficiencies in the initial distribution of control over firms will be corrected. But this does not mean that short-run effects should be underestimated. They may have important political consequences on which the entire transformation process may substantially depend. Hence not all privatization methods are equally suitable. For example, a particularly unsuitable method, widespread in certain post-socialist economies, is the theft of state-owned firms by incumbent managers (sometimes euphemistically called 'spontaneous privatization'), for both its economic and political consequences are strongly negative. The question is therefore, which methods are more suitable than others?

Ideally, the new owners should meet two conditions: (1) they should have enough financial capital available, both to pay a high price for the firm in order to make a large contribution to the strained state budget, and to invest in the firm itself in order to modernize its obsolete equipment; (2) they should have a high level of relevant competence, in order to provide – directly, or by means of competently appointed and monitored intermediaries – for efficient reorganization and high quality management. The problem is, what is to be done in a post-socialist economy, where candidates meeting both these conditions are in an extremely short supply, even when potential foreign investors are included, given the very large number of the firms to be privatized.

This problem is rarely seen in its full extent. In standard analysis, as noted earlier, the scarcity of economic competence is assumed away, which means that only the first condition is considered. For many Western economists, the privatization problem is indeed reduced to the problem of financing. In consequence, their policy advice is to insist that only those candidates who can fully meet the first condition be eligible. It is now clearly documented by the experience of Hungary and the former East Germany, that this is not very good advice. Hungary, which was first to begin post-socialist privatization, is now lagging in the proportion of privatized firms far behind the Czech Republic and Russia, which started to privatize much later. In the former East Germany, privatization could proceed only thanks to the large number of West German investors, with social and political consequences reminiscent of colonization: very few East Germans could enter into competition for the control of firms which formally belonged to them.

Without underestimating the problem of financing, the present argument is that it is the need to find high relevant competence that is primary. The problem of financing is seen as secondary simply because with low competence, all financial resources are mostly wasted, whereas with high competence new financial resources are likely to be discovered and attracted.

Candidates who meet both the above conditions should certainly not be neglected. But when they are in short supply, compared to the large number of firms to be privatized, the main role of privatization should be seen as a search for new owners of high relevant competence, able to improve upon the inefficient organization and poor management of most of the state-owned firms, with only limited attention paid to their initial capital strength.

This search must inevitably be a process which cannot avoid trials and errors. Indeed, after several decades of non-market selection for top economic jobs, the relevant high competence (or the scarce talents for learning it) may now be dispersed over the most unexpected places on which prior information is nearly impossible to obtain. Moreover, recalling that high levels of economic competence are needed for recognizing high economic competence, no government privatization agency can be expected to have very good criteria for distinguising true relevant competence from mediocrity, often hidden behind impressive formulations. As argued earlier, relatively the best method for conducting such a search is selection by developed capital markets. In any post-socialist economy, however, a well-known difficulty is precisely that such markets are underdeveloped there, if they exist at all.

The present argument shows also that there is an extraordinary privatization method that copes reasonably well with most of the extraordinary difficulties of post-socialist privatization. This is the privatization by (nearly) freely distributed investment vouchers, to be used in auctions of shares in firms. The method is of course not new, for it has already been employed in several post-socialist economies – such as the Czech Republic, Estonia, and Russia – and has been discussed for a long time in Poland. But it has been difficult to show its correctness: it has been rejected by virtually all Western theoretical economists and avoided by many other post-socialist economies – such as Hungary and East Germany. Present argument provides it with a solid theoretical justification and, moreover, specifies some of its more detailed properties.

The justification stems directly from the competence argument. Emphasizing the importance of the search for relevant competence, this argument appreciates voucher privatization above all as a first step towards an efficient EC-allocation. This is indeed the most effective way of starting an open tournament, able to select future champions of industrial organization and management – whom no one can know in advance – from the largest number of initial candidates.

Among the more detailed properties, two turn out to be of particular importance. First, the method must allow for free entry of investment funds, to allow individuals who prefer to be passive owners to choose their delegates and those who on the contrary wish to be active owners to start funds of their own and try to become such delegates. Second, it must allow for immediate secondary trade with the acquired shares. It may appear advantageous to allow for secondary trading at the stage of distribution of the vouchers, as has been possible in Russia but not in the Czech Republic. But, given the above-mentioned importance of economic education, forcing all citizens to be responsible for the use of their vouchers at least until the choice of a suitable investment fund turns out to have a non-negligible pedagogical value. Namely, this forces them to learn about the state and the prospects of different firms and/or investment funds, and the learning may have positive spillover effects on the future working of both market economy and political democracy.

As objections against secondary trade are frequent, even among the advocates of voucher privatization, an additional note may be useful. The usual argument against it is egalitarian, demanding that ownership of capital be and remain equitably distributed. This is to be achieved by preventing less competent owners from selling their vouchers or shares 'too cheaply' to the more competent ones. Clearly, this is the very opposite of what the competence argument shows should happen. To be sure, broad continuing involvement of small shareholders has many positive social, educational and political effects. However, the main purpose of the entire voucher privatization is precisely to find as rapidly as possible a few strong competent owners, able to lead the necessary industrial restructuring, for which neither government officials nor the incumbent managers can be expected to have sufficient competence (some of them may well have this competence, but it is initially not known which ones!). While policies limiting economic inequalities need not be entirely abandoned – as is mentioned below and shown in Pelikan (1993), the competence argument is more hospitable to them than the traditional incentive argument – their impact must be limited to final consumption, without disturbing the allocation of economic competence in the organization and management of production.

Two objections against the very principle of investment vouchers are also instructive to consider. One is due to Kornai (1990), who is preoccupied with the financing problem and objects to the free distribution of state property on moral grounds. For the state firms that cannot be sold at a market price he prefers continued state ownership, which he justifies by the optimistic belief that the state administration is in good health and can guarantee efficient management. This objection can be refuted on at least two points. First, the state property is formally the property of all citizens. Investment vouchers thus give nothing away for free, but only partition an already existing ownership relationship into small tradeable pieces, with which the market search for competent owners can begin. If moral grounds are to enter the argument, I believe them on the contrary to be weaker in the case of a state bureaucracy selling off the state-owned firms, while often cashing in personal rents, behind the back of the population at large. Second – as follows from discussion above – Kornai's belief in state administration as a guarantor of efficient management of firms is grossly over-optimistic.

The second objection is due to Corbett and Mayer (1992), who claim that industrial restructuring in a post-socialist economy should rely on large investment banks and not on competitive capital markets, quoting Japan and Germany as the models to imitate. What this claim forgets is that competent investment banks are also rare creatures that are not easy to obtain, and especially not in a newly liberalized post-socialist economy. Of course, that such banks would be of much help cannot be denied. What the present argument points out is that without competitive capital markets, competent banks are unlikely to emerge and remain competent.

It should also be noted that the present support for voucher privatization does not include all of its methods. For example, what is not included is the method that was about to be adopted in Poland, which allows only a restricted number of government-appointed investment funds to bid for shares of firms, whereas individuals are given vouchers only for shares in these funds. This strongly restricts the competition for the ownership roles; moreover, the fact that the allowed competitors are selected by government administration is a further handicap, likely to favour mediocrity and exclude many true but yet unknown talents. In the short run, to be sure, this method may be more successful than the one which allows for free entry of investment funds – such as in the Czech Republic. The reason is that it guarantees a certain minimum professional standard right from the beginning, whereas the Czechs are likely to commit more errors, including bankruptcies by many of the spontaneously emerged investment funds. In the long run, however, the Czech method is predicted to select more true industrial champions, and thus result in a more advanced industrial structure.

6.7   CONCLUDING COMMENTS

In a post-socialist economy, after several decades of inefficient economic practice and confusing socialist indoctrination, economic competence is an extremely scarce and grossly misallocated resource. As pointed out, the problem of its scarcity and efficient allocation is substantially more serious there than in a developed capitalist economy, where market selection – although often unnoticed by economic theory – has been at work for a long time. Even if this selection has sometimes failed to promote the most competent agents, it has done an invaluable job in demoting the inadequately competent ones.

The main strategy of this paper has been to make the competence problem the central point in the study of post-socialist privatization. The result is a stronger support for such privatization than the one provided by the usual incentive argument. The incentive argument is indeed weakened by all findings that suggest that human beings may be more altruistic creatures than economists usually assume. Moreover, it is also weakened by the fact – demonstrated by both economic theory and managerial practice – that reasonably efficient incentives can often be designed even for non-owners. None of this, in contrast, weakens the present argument based on scarce economic competence. If economic agents are unequally imperfect optimizers and no one initially knows how imperfect different agents, oneself included, are, then even an ideal team in the sense of Marschak and Radner (1972) – whose members need no individual incentives to pursue its objectives – must solve the intricate problem of how to allocate the most important decision tasks to the a priori unknown least imperfect optimizers. It is as a means of solving this problem that private and tradeable ownership of capital and competitive capital markets turn out to be irreplaceable, even within such a perfectly altruistic team. There, of course, capital holdings only determine the decision authority of their owners in organizing production, as opposed to a real economy, where they moreover determine the opportunities for personal consumption. However, regardless of the redistributive policies that might be considered for final consumption, the decisive point is that more competent industrial leaders are likely be appointed by means of private and tradeable ownership of capital than by ministerial decrees or one-person-one-vote elections.

A qualification, however, should be added. If capital markets are to realize their potential in selecting for high relevant competence, they need to be protected by both written and unwritten institutional rules against distortion by other selection criteria – such as ruthlessness or dishonesty. The ways of becoming rich are thus exposed as a matter of public concern, for which social efficiency requires maximum transparency, similar to what is required for those who wish to hold public office. If the nirvana fallacy is to be avoided, however, this qualification in turn needs to be qualified. Failures in the protection of capital markets must not be judged absolutely, but only in comparison with what protection against ruthlessness and dishonesty can be provided in the selection of politicians and government officials. Casual observations suggest that where it is difficult to secure honesty in business, it is usually not less difficult to secure honesty in politics and government administration. In such cases, government ownership may still not be the socially superior alternative, however distorted the selection by capital markets might be.

In addition to providing strong support for post-socialist privatization as such, the competence argument also make it possible to throw new light on several controversial questions about the speed, the sequencing and the method of such privatization. In particular, it is shown that privatization should proceed as rapidly as possible; that it requires liberalization of prices, convertibility of currency, opening of access to foreign markets for both imports and exports, and readiness to admit bankruptcies; and that it is itself a prerequisite for efficient industrial restructuring. The competence argument moreover supports methods of privatization which use (nearly) freely distributed investment vouchers in public auctions, provided that free entry of investment funds and immediate secondary trade are admitted. As the main purpose of privatization is found to be the search for and selection of scarce competent owners, the crucial advantage of these voucher methods is that they allow for open competition in which such owners can be selected from the largest number of initial candidates.

Finally, let me briefly mention why the competence argument is more hospitable to egalitarian values than the traditional incentive argument. The main reason is that scarce competence, or exceptional talents for learning it, may also appear where money is not: some highly talented agents may simply be so poor and mistrusted that they cannot mobilize the minimum starting capital to enter the competition for ownership of firms, which causes their scarce talents to be socially wasted. In an extreme case, this competition may even become limited to a small closed group where the best talents can no longer be found, while self-perpetuating poverty would exclude the rest of the population. Hence mild redistribution that maintains access for scarce competence and talents to entrepreneurial capital (including human capital by means of education) may more than countervail its negative effects on incentives. A warning, however, should be added. The negative effects on incentives, including the very incentives for acquiring competence, should not be forgotten. It is these effects that would prevail if redistribution became too ambitious. Efficient egalitarian policy must therefore be limited to mild redistribution, where the positive effects on broadening the field of competition for ownership still prevail over the negative effects on incentives.

6.8   REFERENCES

Alchian, A.A. (1950), Uncertainty, Evolution, and Economic Theory, *Journal of Political Economy,* vol. 58, pp. 211–22.

Bardham, P. and J.P. Roemer (1992), Market socialism: A Case for Rejuvenation, *Journal of Economic Perspectives,* vol. 6, pp. 101–16.

Buchanan, J.M., R. Tollison, and G. Tullock, eds (1980), *Toward the Theory of the Rent-Seeking Society*, Texas A & M University Press, College Station.

Corbett, J. and C. Mayer (1991), Financial Reform in Eastern Europe: Progress with the Wrong Model, *Oxford Review of Economic Policy,* vol. 7, no. 4, 57–75.

Eliasson, G. (1988), Schumpeterian Innovation, Market Structure, and the Stability of Industrial Development, in H. Hanush, ed., *Evolutionary Economics: Applications of Schumpeter's Ideas*, Cambridge University Press, Cambridge.

Fama, E. (1980), Agency Problem and the Theory of the Firm, *Journal of Political Economy,* vol. 88, pp. 288–307.

Ferguson, P.R. (1992), Privatization Options for Eastern Europe: The Irrelevance of Western Experience, *The World Economy,* vol. 15, pp. 487–504.

Friedman, M. (1953), *Essays in Postitive Economics*, University of Chicago Press, Chicago.

Grosfeld, I. (1992), *The paradox of Transformation: An Evolutionary Case for a Breakthrough in Privatization*, Document 92–94, DELTA, Paris.

Heiner, R.A. (1983), The Origin of Predictable Behavior, *American Economic Review* vol. 83, pp. 560–95.

Jensen, M. and W. Meckling (1976), Theory of the Firm: Managerial Behavior, Agency Costs, and Capital Structure, *Journal of Financial Economics,* vol. 3, pp. 305–60.

Katz, B.G. and J. Owen (1993), Privatization: Choosing the Optimum Time Path, *Journal of Comparative Economics,* vol. 17, pp. 715–36.

Kornai, J. (1990), *The Road to a Free Economy, Shifting from a Socialist System: The Example of Hungary*, Norton, New York.

Lucas Jr, R.E. (1978), On the Size Distribution of Business Firms, *Bell Journal of Economics,* vol. 9, pp. 508–23.

Manne, H. G. (1965), Mergers and the Market for Corporate Control, *Journal of Political Economy,* vol. 73, pp. 110–20.

Marschak, J. and R. Radner (1972), *Economic Theory of Teams*, Yale University Press, New Haven.

Nolan, P. (1993), China's Post-Mao Political Economy: A Puzzle, in J. Eatwell, M. Milgate and G. de Vivo, eds, *Contributions to Political Economy,* vol. 12, pp. 71–87, Academic Press, London and New York.

North, D.C. (1990), *Institutions, Institutional Change and Economic Performance*, Cambridge University Press, Cambridge and New York.

Pelikan, P. (1985), *Private Enterprise vs. Government Control: An Organizationally Dynamic Comparison*, Working Paper 138, The Industrial Institute for Economic and Social Research, Stockholm.

Pelikan, P. (1987), The Formation of Incentive Mechanisms in Different Economic Systems, in S. Hedlund, ed., *Incentives and Economic System*, Croom Helm, London and Sydney.

Pelikan, P. (1988), Can the Imperfect Innovation System of Capitalism be Outperformed? in G. Dosi et al., eds, *Technical Change and Economic Theory*, Pinter Publishers, London.

Pelikan, P. (1989), Evolution, Economic Competence, and the Market for Corporate Control, *Journal of Economic Behavior and Organization,* vol. 12, pp. 279–303.

Pelikan, P. (1992), The Dynamics of Economic Systems, or How to Transform a Failed Socialist Economy, *Journal of Evolutionary*

Economics, vol. 2, pp. 39–63. Reprinted in H.J. Wagener, ed., *On the Theory and Policy of Systemic Change,* Springer Verlag, Heidelberg.

Pelikan, P. (1993), Ownership of Firms and Efficiency: The Competence Argument, *Constitutional Political Economy,* vol. 4, no. 3 (fall).

Sah, R.K., and J.E. Stiglitz (1985), *Selection, Self-Reproduction, and Evolution of Organizations: The Selection and Performance of Managers,* Paper prepared for the World Congress of the Econometric Society, Cambridge.

Schumpeter, J.A. (1942), *Capitalism, Socialism, and Democracy,* Harper & Row, New York.

Simon, H. (1978), Rationality as Process and as Product of Thought, *American Economic Review,* vol. 68, pp. 1-16.

Vining, A.R. and A.E. Boardman (1992), Ownership versus Competition: Efficiency in Public Enterprise, *Public Choice,* vol. 73, pp. 205–39.

Winiecki, J. (1991), *Resistance to Change in the Soviet Economic System: A Property Rights Approach,* Routledge, London.

Winter, S.G. (1971), Satisficing, Selection, and the Innovative Remnant, *Quarterly Journal of Economics,* vol. 85, pp. 237–61.

Wintrobe, R. (1985), *The Efficiency of Public vs. Private Organizations,* Paper presented at the Canadian Economic Association Meeting, Montreal.

7. Investment Incentives in the Formerly Planned Economies

Gunnar Eliasson·

7.1 INTRODUCTION

The institutions of markets supporting property rights are defined and linked via incentives for investment leading to economic growth. The political and business risks affecting investment in formerly planned economies are defined and compared with returns to investment by domestic and foreign investors. Deficient institutional structures in formerly planned economies often make political risks prohibitive. Various ways of reducing the risks to Western levels, or offloading them from investors on to supporting Western governments are discussed. It is found that many problems of opportunistic political behaviour are common to Western and formerly planned economies, the difference being a matter of degree. One conclusion is that while Western economies may be burdened by excessive law and regulation the formerly planned economies lack most of the institutions needed to support a viable market economy. Only a small core of legal codes may be needed to establish critical market functions and precedent. Here, it is essential that the new legal code overrules all other remaining legislation from the communist past.

When the former Soviet empire collapsed, it was believed, quite plausibly, that enormous investment resources would be needed to restore run-down communist economies to industrial nations. This massive investment boom would be privately and socially profitable and would drive up real interest rates in the West, halting expansion there, notably in the not so competitive mature industrial nations. The West would have to live with that situation for years. Even though private savers would be happy, unemployment and low

· Prepared for the Nordic Economic Research Council's (NEF's) conference 'The Baltic States in Transition', 4–5 November 1993 in Riga. Revised April 1994 and September 1995.

real income growth would follow after an initial boom in investment goods industries.

This scenario has failed to materialize, at least so far. What is the reason? Cases from the Baltic region provide an illustration.

7.2   WHY NOT GROWTH?

There are two ways of approaching the investment growth problem in the formerly planned economies. The first, standard approach used by economists is to look at the various national accounts figures involved and observe, as was done above, that neither investment nor growth was showing up, conclude that more investment is needed and suggest that more Western financial support should be administered. This is the *welfare* approach.

The alternative approach is entirely different: it shuns statistics and mechanical analysis, and looks at *the institutions that define the incentives to invest.* Proponents of that policy alternative ask the question: are incentives properly directed and sufficient? Perhaps, one should *not* expect to see the desired investment boom. This is the *institutional incentive* approach.

In this paper I will discuss both the welfare and the institutional incentive proposals. The reason is that without properly structured incentives there will be neither a desired indigenous investment boom, nor a desired growth development based on foreign investment. The institutions, so to speak, define the investment climate of the economy. If incentives are properly directed, the desired welfare targets will eventually be achieved. It all depends on how institutions are designed to support incentives, and how long the people and their political representatives are prepared to wait. On the other hand, if incentives are right, and large-scale investment and rapid growth follow, significant and very unevenly distributed social adjustment will be the consequence. To cope with that a well-designed social insurance system (call it a welfare system) will be needed to gain political acceptance for economic success.

My analysis is organized around the definition of property rights in *Table 7.1,* namely the right to *manage* the property, to *access* and use the profits, and to *trade* in the property rights. Institutions supporting these rights are found in *Table 7.1.* On the one hand, I relate the property rights (through the financial system and financial incentives) to the four investment growth mechanisms in *Table 7.2.* On the other hand, I relate the credibility of the three components of property rights to a hierarchy of risks associated with the various contractual arrangements that support the property rights. These risks also depend on the institutions supporting the property rights and the corresponding investment incentives that generate economic growth through

Table 7.1: Institutions supporting property rights

1.	*Right to manage*	–	New establishment
		–	Corporate governance
		–	Company law
		–	Operations control
		–	Competition
		–	Monitoring and control
2.	*Right to access*	–	Tax law
		–	Exchange controls
		–	Bankruptcy law
3.	*Right to trade*	–	Constitutional property rights
		–	Registration
		–	Rules for identifying property rights with persons
		–	Court recognition of voluntary contracts (enforcement, resolution of conflict, procedure)

the four investment mechanisms in *Table 7.2*. This is all summarized in *Figure 7.1*. We shall find that opportunistic political behaviour constitutes the core growth problem of the formerly planned economies and that the solution lies in the ability of the economic political system to spontaneously create, through deliberate policy, a market for such risks.

Any country, any economy is governed by institutions (legal code, conventions, ethical norms) designed by decree or through evolution and popular acceptance to guarantee certain minimal rights to its citizens and its firms. The most important such institution for the economy is the *property rights* institution (North and Thomas, 1973, North, 1990, Pelikan, 1987). Property rights define ownership and are, consequently, necessary for trade in markets. As repeatedly pointed out by Douglass North over the years, without property rights there is no market economy. You have to own what you sell, and you have to know that you own what you buy. The most sophisticated property rights for an advanced market economy, however (Eliasson, 1993a), is *the right to future profits from investment commitments today*. This property right is the foundation of the standard ownership contract called the stock certificate, and hence also of the stock market. It requires a complex legal and institutional structure to be defined and enforced, and accordingly took a long time to develop. Until recently many advanced industrial countries relied on crude financial substitutes to a full-

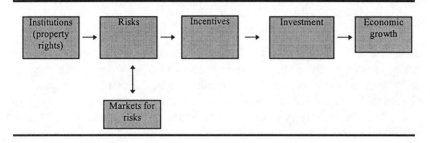

Figure 7.1: The links between property rights, investment incentives and economic growth

fledged financial system. The entitlements to future profits from investments today define the *incentives* for the actors of the economy to engage in growth-promoting long-term investments, and, thereby, the efficiency of the economy. These institutions have to be sufficiently stable to ensure predictability in their application. But there also have to be institutions that allow the incentive system to evolve, to accommodate new technologies and forms of economic organization: in short, to make improvement possible. It is very difficult, probably impossible, to write law that facilitates the realization of all desired improvements. Hence, the procedure should be the opposite. Law should be formulated explicitly to prevent restrictions and hindrances to improvement, and to facilitate improvement through interpretation of law and the building of precedent. I shall call such law *enabling law* in what follows (see further Eliasson et al., 1994).

There is, in fact, when discussing the transition of formerly planned economies to market economies only one reason for going beyond the 'incentives' issue and the supporting institutions, namely *the time dimension,* and the *risks* investors are carrying between their investment and the time (if they succeed) needed to recapture the principal and the rents. If speed is required to prevent a political collapse of the transition process, empirical analysis is needed to assess the quantitative and dynamic time relations involved, and the financial support from the West required.

For instance, there seems to be no feasible way of generating a sufficiently rapid growth path in any of the formerly planned economies, based on domestic savings alone, however appropriate the incentives, to forestall the social and political unrest that will follow if a Western-type market economy does not deliver in pace with boosted expectations.

7.3 THE FOUR ELEMENTS OF ECONOMIC GROWTH – DYNAMICS

To assess the dynamics involved let us assume, for simplicity, that growth in output is the only desired outcome and proceed to break the growth process down into its components. Growth occurs through four basic mechanisms (Eliasson, 1992, 1993b): *entry, reorganization, rationalization* and *exit* (see *Table 7.2*). Each category represents a particular investment activity, the last a disinvestment to make room for new investment and help adjust factor prices.

Table 7.2: The four mechanisms of economic growth

1.	Entry
2.	Reorganization
3.	Rationalization
4.	Exit (shut-down)

Sources: Eliasson (1992, 1993a).

The so-called Salter curves in *Figure 7.2* (see p. 204) illustrate the principles involved. It ranks labour productivities in an economy by firms or establishments, one column representing one firm, and the width of the column the size of the firm as a percentage of the value added of all firms. The lower curve is the matching wage cost level per effective employee, and the difference gross operating profits per employee. In practice, labour market arbitrage makes the wage cost level much more even than the distribution of productivities. The firms at the upper left should apparently be able to pay high wages without suffering in profitability.[1] The dark columns at the far right represent two East European firms[2]. The problem with an East European economy is that its firms would all cluster at the far right, very low end if the productivity distributions of a Western European and an Eastern European economy were to be merged. If a Western European wage level were established in the merged economy, the consequences would be disastrous for the Eastern European firms. The upgrading of the Eastern European industry structure is the vehicle to achieve economic growth. This occurs through the four mechanisms of growth in *Table 7.2*. Reorganization and rationalization raise the columns of existing firms. Exit removes low

---

[1] Note that large capital output ratios will require high profit margins to achieve the same rate of return as a company with a low capital output ratio.

[2] See Eliasson (1993c).

performers at the far right. Entry adds new columns from the left. In practice (see Eliasson, 1991b) entry comes in a very diverse lot, illustrating the fact that the ex ante expected performance characteristics of new, entering firms is often far above ex post realized performance.

Entry, on the one hand, and investment in reorganization and rationalization in existing firms on the other, also operate on *very different time scales.* Rationalization investments combined with exit give immediate and productivity effects, but not sustained economic growth. Long-run growth has to build on new investment in new technologies.

Economic growth is, however, not a matter of independently taken investment decisions in firms. Considerable *clustering of activities* occurs and forms the basis for long-lasting synergies. This was called *development bloc* formation by Dahmén (1950) and has more recently been 'independently' reformulated by Lucas (1988) and Romer (1986) in a thin macroeconomic version, called the 'new growth theory'. The formation of development blocs is a necessary part of the transformation of formerly planned economies. The critical part for the nation is for its industries to find, through experimentation, a viable industrial technology around which to specialize and build new industries. Deciding for this development bloc formation, however, is the establishment of the non-economic institutions, that constitute the backbone of the incentives to invest. To this I turn next. However, the investment elements of the growth process of *Table 7.2* have first to be clarified in terms of the synergies created and the dynamics involved. The kind of growth witnessed among the industrialized nations since the industrial revolution, and desired in the formerly planned economies, cannot take place without

(1)   significant *clustering* of investment, creating large economies of scale (development blocs);

(2)   the transformation of those investments into an *expanded capacity* to produce for international markets and;

(3)   *patience* among investors, during the *time lag* between the enhanced capacity to produce and actual production growth and profits (*dynamics*).

When all four investment activities in *Table 7.1* become viable and active, the growth process will move of itself and nobody has to worry about statistics. This is not the case with the formerly planned economies and therefore it becomes important to ask why. I will do that by linking the future investment and growth mechanisms to incentives, notably to the *risks* associated with property rights (Eliasson, 1993a). A particular issue is the different rules that accompany new entry in the small business sector and the privatization and/or possible exit of the old, mammoth (in employment terms) Soviet production organizations.

I shall then discuss how property rights can be designed to establish incentives that stimulate investments, rather than how to arrange finance for investments. As it turns out such finance will, anyhow, have to come from the West. It is therefore doubly important for investment and growth to make the formerly planned economies attractive economies for direct foreign investment and/or for the financing of domestic investment.

7.4   THE CRITICAL PROPERTY RIGHTS INSTITUTION

In their book from 1973 Douglass North and Robert Thomas concluded that by the early 19th century most of the institutions required to support the functions of a viable market economy were in place in Western Europe, notably the legal functions supporting the property rights system. Property rights can be defined as consisting of three different, supporting elements (see *Table 7.1*): the right to *manage* one's assets, the right to *access* the profits and the right to *trade* in the assets (usus, usus fructus, abusus in Latin). These property rights in turn have to be supported by explicit and implicit *contracts* and institutions designed to *enforce contractual agreements*. This definition of property rights is quite clear when it comes to physical assets like land. *The most important property right for a market economy, however, relates to intangibles, namely the entitlement to future rents from investment resources committed today* (Eliasson, 1993a). This is the property right upon which financial markets are based, notably the stock market. It strongly influences the incentives to engage in long-term investment commitments, namely the present value of the profits generated, discounted by an appropriate interest rate, including all the *business risks* and all the *political risks* associated with the credibility of the property rights institution. Without legal protection and enforcement of financial contracts long-term commitments of investment funds will not take place, because investors cannot feel confident that the rents, even from a successful business, can be recaptured by the owners. And entitlements to future profits cannot be defended by brute force, as was the case earlier with land. The bridging function between today and the future is vested in the institutions that protect the ownership right to financial contracts, underwritten by parties unrelated to the authorities that are responsible for the same institutions.

It is unfortunate that so much of the privatization discussion in the East has focused on physical property. Profitable production does not require that the producer owns the land on which, and the machines with which, production is organized. They can both be leased. But it is essential that *the investor owns the profits that he generates* (has a title to the profits he creates). If investors have no confidence in the institutions that protect such long-term benefits, risks will be considered too high. There will be no long-term financial commitments and economic activity will contract into short-term trading. The ability to induce long-term financial commitments through a reduction in the entire spectrum of risks that are not directly related to the true economic–technical business decision is the basic institutional foundation of an advanced industrial market economy. It is apparent even from recent government practice among socialistically inclined Western economies how difficult it is to understand this simple institutional function of economics. In fact almost the entire economics profession has had great difficulty in reaching this understanding. As a result the few early writers on such matters, such as Douglass North, have for decades languished disregarded in academic backwaters.

7.5   POLITICAL RISKS ARE SHORTENING THE TIME HORIZONS OF INVESTORS

Risks that undermine the property rights institution in financial markets operate in several dimensions (*Table 7.3*). They consist of two principally different types: *political* and *business*. Political risks relate directly to the institutions protecting the property rights. Business risks relate to the competence of the investor to take the right technological and economic decisions. Since some of the economic factors that have to be incorporated in business decisions are indirectly influenced by the institutions of the economy (like inflation), the two types of risks are not entirely independent.

Most Western capitalist nations have managed more or less to organize themselves in such a manner that the property rights system is reasonably well enforced and predictable. There have been great difficulties in getting it properly organized in order that it may function well in the intangible, financial dimension. In fact, it was only in the 1980s that sophisticated financial markets began to function outside the United States. Furthermore, as the ownership of capital and wealth was the focus of dispute between the socialist left and the capitalist right, Western nations with a socialist leaning used the legal system during the 1960s and the 1970s to restrict the ownership of wealth, thereby destroying important resource allocation mechanisms. Here the situation has rather been the deliberate and unwise creation of redundant, unnecessary or hindering institutions.

The normal characteristic of formerly planned economies, on the other hand, is that few or no institutions (whether formal or by convention) exist to

Table 7.3: The risk hierarchy

Political risks
1.　*Force Majeure* – referring to non-economic events (military intervention and so on)
2.　Macroeconomic – refering to uncontrollable macro development (run-away inflation, collapse of monetary system and so on)
3.　Opportunistic political behaviour

Business risks
4.　Opportunistic behaviour of competitors
5.　Pure business risks

---

support private property rights. This is particularly the case with the property rights that support the management and trading of financial wealth. There is a *lack* of the proper institutional functions to support private incentives.

Thus, even in the absence of other political or macroeconomic risks (in *Table 7.3*), the incentives to commit funds long term on private account are virtually absent in most of the formerly planned economies, apart from the hope that the appropriate institutions will soon be introduced. In some economies, notably Poland and the Czeck Republic, the necessary minimal institutions are beginning to be created, and economic growth is slowly beginning to appear.

In addition, political and macroeconomic risks loom to a varying degree over most formerly planned economies. This means, for instance, that investments in local currencies may be suddenly confiscated and/or rendered without value. Hence, it is perhaps not so surprising that we do not see an investment boom in the formerly planned economies, except in places (like Eastern Germany) where a Western government has underwritten the risks. Future expected profits are simply discounted so heavily (because of risks) that only extreme investments become profitable. Rather, the fact that so many private firms, both large and small, have nevertheless committed investment funds in those countries can only be interpreted as reflecting faith in the spirit and political power of the authorities in those countries that the necessary institutions will eventually be introduced. A realistic assessment of the investment and growth prospects of the formerly planned economies must therefore include an assessment of the probability that these nations, or some of them, will successfully build such institutions and/or that Western nations will cover the political, non-business risks. This is synonymous with the assumption that the necessary institutions for a market in such risks will be created.

7.5.1   Case 1: Grand Hotel Europe, St Petersburg[3]

In 1988 a group headed by Reso International Hotels and SIAB teamed up to restore the old hotel Europeijskaja in St Petersburg to a luxury hotel of international standards; 600 million SEK were invested and the hotel began to operate in December 1991. This was about the time that the Soviet Union collapsed as a centralized political system. The first year was a success, with 92 per cent capacity utilization, which was very high by any standard.

During the first year, the hotel had a problem with managing its cash flow. There were no banking services in St Petersburg and the hotel was granted informal permission from Moscow to run its accounts through Nordbanken in Stockholm. In March 1993 banking services had been established in St. Petersburg and the hotel moved its banking services back to St Petersburg. The same year (1993) in June, however, the new tax police in Russia was created. It claimed that it had been illegal to use a foreign bank and ordered the hotel to pay $24 million on the transactions accumulated through the Stockholm account. This case is still pending. If the hotel is ordered by the court to pay, it will go bankrupt and investors will lose their money on account of an arbitrary (opportunistic) reinterpretation of the rules. Since the case has not been cleared, the value and ownership of assets cannot be determined. Thus the Swedish investors have had difficulties in selling their assets and recapturing their investment.[4] The expectation that such legal trouble may arise is synonymous with the elimination of private incentives to invest.

Problems like those of Grand Hotel Europe were compounded by the almost daily changes in the laws of the former Soviet Union, the uninhibited use of retroactive taxation, unclear rules regarding who should pay and which institution should receive payment, and the infighting between local and federal tax authorities on who should receive the tax payments. One example[5] is a tax law that allows tax inspectors to levy a tax of up to 23 per cent on foreign loans to enterprises in Russia. Under such risky circumstances, any

---

[3]   Sources are *Dagens Industri* (15 September, 1993, p. 17, 17 August, 1994, p. 12), and interviews.

[4]   After a drawn-out period of negotiations the 30 per cent share in the hotel held by Reso and SIAB was acquired in September 1995 by Dresdner Bank and the Kempinski Hotel chain. The price for the 30 per cent share was SEK 26 million (*Dagens Industri*, 18 September, 1995, p. 12).

[5]   For details, see *The Wall Street Journal* (20 April, 1994, p. A16).

investment evaluation will heavily discount future profits, rendering most long-term investments unprofitable.

7.5.2   How to Reduce the Risks that Shorten Investment Horizons in the Formerly Planned Economies – The Incentive Issue

The conclusion of the previous section was that it was the lack of credible institutions that protect the ownership right to financial contracts that radically reduces the incentives to take on long-term investment commitments in formerly planned economies, rather than the lack of investment funds. The question then becomes, *first* to identify these institutions in sufficient detail to assess feasibility and *second* to detail the critical time dimension.

In discussing this problem two distinctions have to be made. *First,* we have to distinguish between the rules that regulate entry and small business, notably in the service sector, and the existing big production establishments. This takes us right into the privatization debate. *Second,* we have to distinguish between *domestic* indigenous *investments* and *foreign direct investment.* Free competitive entry is one form of privatization. Turning sluggish Soviet production organizations into privately operated competitive firms is an entirely different form of privatization.

The domestic investor has to raise finance and for that he needs credible collateral, such as a mortgageable house, land and so on. For the foreign investor, with ample finances, this is not the problem. He needs a credible contract to get his money and his profits back. There are two different property rights to consider.

Huge and run-down Soviet production facilities overstaffed with low quality labour with job guarantees are probably not worth having. Why all the fuss about privatizing them, when they may be completely worthless? The ownership of physical assets is not the important property problem, it is the entitlement to future entrepreneurial and competence rents that is the major concern. It may also be the case that the appropriate investment mechanism in *Table 7.2* to apply to most existing physical capital is to achieve a speedy and low cost divestment (exit item 4). Then attention can be focused on the creation of new businesses that efficiently exploit the comparative advantages of formerly planned economies: cheap and fairly well-educated labour. The exit or bankruptcy process is legally complex. There may be something of value even in a bankrupt company. For an investor to be willing to take on a potentially profitable part of a bankrupt company, he has, however, to be able to get rid of all the obligations, such as the debt and employment responsibilities associated with the defunct company. If that cleansing is not well defined in bankruptcy law it has the same negative consequences as the absence of property rights and valuable assets will remain idle. In countries with very few assets of any economic value, this is of course particularly serious.

On the whole, privatization of small businesses is proceeding rapidly in the formerly planned economies, notably in direct household service production. When it comes to new entry, the earlier absence of such phenomena means that investments by means of the new entry of firms is not even covered by statistics. On the other hand, collapsing large firms are well covered statistically. Hence, development of total manufacturing output is probably significantly underestimated.

Turning old production units into private firms is more difficult. While the new firms start from scratch, the old firms employ thousands of people and are in a terrible mess. Only a fraction of the existing workforce can be gainfully employed in production for international markets, and the main management–privatization problem is to get rid of the bulk of the labour force and shut down most of the old capacity. Even after that has been done, the market value of such a firm is often negative, something the Treuhand experience illustrates.

To 'minimize' the social problem privatization authorities often require employment guarantees, notably from foreign investors, which make the investments unattractive. The problem therefore becomes to clarify – given the current state of affairs – what can happen if you engage in long-term investments, and/or what is needed as a minimum requirement in the form of institutions that avoid the risk that such unfavourable things might occur. The problem is how to make a country legally and institutionally attractive for an investor.

7.5.3 How to Make an Economy Institutionally Attractive for Investors

The complex of explicit and implicit code (law and conventions) that coordinates a market economy is immense. Only a fraction of the required rules can be formulated explicitly. The rest has to be developed through precedent 'in the market'. Even if Western law is adopted, the legal expertise to implement it may be lacking. Hence it is impossible for an East European country to institute it all in the short time needed to get the economy moving. In addition old rules, still in force, work against the desired objectives.

All Western legislative practice rests on a vast structure of procedures relating to the implementation, interpretation and enforcement of coded law and precedent. Investors in transition economies face political risks even when written law exists, because interpretation and enforcement practices have not had time to develop. In addition law tends to be changed frequently, sometimes from day to day.

Some formerly planned economies like the Baltic countries, Poland, the Czech Republic, Slovakia and Hungary, and, of course, East Germany, can fall back upon a legal Germanic-French tradition from a not too distant past. This tradition may perhaps be re-established and updated. In Poland, in particular, a functioning market economy based on pre-communist legal traditions has existed parallel to the Soviet rule (Eliasson et al., 1994).

An important *first* source of political uncertainty refers to unclear definitions regarding what is and what is not allowed. The legal system of Western market economies is normally negative. What is not explicitly forbidden in law is permitted. In the socialist economies, prohibitions were instead often of a general nature. Under these rules, economic actions not explicitly listed in law should be thought of as forbidden. Under the new regime, the situation has been turned upside down. 'Anything is allowed', which creates a different type of uncertainty. Another source of business uncertainty in the formerly planned economies is that the socialist legal system has not been generally abolished. Old laws are often allowed to remain in effect until new laws have been explicitly introduced. Similarly, administrative procedures granting licences have remained. Thus, vested interests have been able to prevent new ventures by means of, for example, permit requirements. New and old law may also be in conflict.

As I mentioned earlier, the first important thing that a Western observer learns when looking into the Eastern European economic problem concerns the institutional design of his own so-called market economy, above all the tangle of rules, regulations and legal code that are not needed and the fact that much of the redundant code may hinder economic growth and should be removed.

That insight makes you very cautious when attempting to design the necessary market institutions for the formerly planned economies, especially about the danger of overly detailed specifications, increasing the probability of faulty specification and rigidity of the institutional structures in the necessary adaptation of the legal code to new circumstances through interpretation and evolution.

These considerations lead to the following conclusions.

7.5.4   Enabling Law

With the exception of a full-scale implementation of an already existing institutional system, including all legal code, regulations and interpretations and enforcement practices (as in Eastern Germany), a complete institutional system on the model of a Western industrial economy is not possible within the time frame allowed. Some new intermediate institutional device will be needed.

One should rather opt for what can be called *enabling law* (Eliasson et al., 1994), designed to achieve the more rapid evolution of an informal and formal *common law*.

Enabling laws are a provisional set of explicit and implicit codes which make the market economy workable until the necessary institutional framework has been instituted. If it works well, very few explicit codes may be required. One aspect is to create a list of rights[6] that free a business activity from restrictions and give enabling law superior status. *All other law, especially pre-existing law that contradicts new enabling law, excluding specially listed exceptions, is considered inapplicable.* Exceptions should also be limited by dominant principles. For example, doing harm to a third party should be limited in certain well-defined ways, *although these limitations have to exclude economic damage* to third parties, that is limitations on desired competition. Competition (by definition) means causing economic damage to competitors.

Enabling law has the advantage of speeding up the legal process and preventing bureaucratic use of old law to slow down the process. If old law that contradicts the new enabling laws represents socially important regulations, interest groups that want to see them remain in force have to argue their case explicitly to secure exemptions. This means that only restrictive rules explicitly passed by the political process will be valid. One further advantage is that enabling law can be made effective prior to the exceptions.

Another advantage of enabling rules is that they allow shareholders in corporations to develop arrangements as circumstances change. Mandatory rules, on the other hand, imply one 'standard form contract' as mandatory. All rules may be classified on a scale between the extremes, since even highly flexible enabling rules must have a mandatory component.

Enabling law should, consequently, be seen as a set of guidelines designed to facilitate the interpretation of remaining old law[7] and new minimal code in the interest of economic growth. Such enabling law will automatically

---

[6] An example would be the unlimited right to start a company, provided it is registrered, excepting a *small* number of explicitly listed activities where particular licences are required, for example, in surgery.

[7] A similar suggestion was made for Sweden in *Den långa vägen* (*The Long Road*), IUI, Stockholm 1993, arguing that it would be politically impossible to remove the tangle of legal structure that hinders innovative competitive entry and small business. A general instruction about how existing legal structures should be interpreted and not interpreted would be a more rapid solution.

(through its guided interpretation) make existing law that is detrimental to economic growth invalid (inapplicable). Enabling law should be explicitly written to achieve that result.

This particular design may sound outrageous to the traditional legal expert of the West. To me, however, it represents the only convenient, speedy and democratic way to achieve the desired results sufficiently rapidly. In addition this opportunity not only avoids the risk of writing (however carefully done and however long it takes) redundant and inflexible code that will soon retard growth. It also creates the opportunity for the East to significantly improve upon the West in institutional design.

7.5.5   Case 2: Interviews of Swedish Multinationals and Baltic Firms

A few interviews with Swedish multinational companies operating in the formerly planned economies have been carried out. There are two different motives for being interested in these countries. For the very large companies, it is important to establish a presence in a market that *may* become large and important in the future. For companies of all sizes, where production uses skilled labour intensively, subcontracting of simple component-type production can be profitably located in the East. Many companies are therefore looking for subcontracting arrangements and/or acquisitions of existing firms or building new plants. On the basis of the small number of interviews carried out so far the following picture emerges.

The establishment of subcontracting arrangements and/or production facilities in a formerly planned economy takes time. Management and workers are not used to the discipline, the precision and the technologies required in the West. Existing production plants often (but not always) have to be entirely rebuilt or replaced and the local producer has no financial resources for that. But as long as we are talking about subcontracting arrangements with limited contributions of finance from the Western purchaser things will happen, albeit slowly.

The extreme lack of product development and marketing know-how in the companies of formerly planned economies in a sense makes them attractive acquisition targets, since Western product technology and marketing know-how can be rapidly introduced, without appreciably increasing the wage level in local production plants. This is attractive provided the Western company can prevent the know-how transferred from being used against it later by a potential competitor, and provided it can capture the rents from the same technology transfer (the property rights problem).

When major acquisitions and establishments are concerned the picture is different. Takeovers of existing production facilities are often effectively killed by local employment requirements. The normal situation is that after reorganization of production and modernizing of the plant only a small fraction of earlier employment is needed. If redundant labour cannot be laid off, the business proposition is no longer profitable. Hence frequently nothing happens.

On the commitment of significant funds the investing company always points to the arbitrary rules and regulations, rather than the ownership of facilities, that restrict access to profits, and the possible difficulties of recouping the investment if the company wants to change or sell out. Again we are not necessarily talking about large investments in physical capital but of transfers of know-how. There are few credible rules that protect the investor from arbitrary opportunistic political behaviour and frequent cases of such behaviour have been reported. This uncertainty is often enough to significantly slow down foreign investment.

All firms interviewed emphasized the need to take management control of the operation and impose market discipline on the staff. This was necessary if large financial commitments had to be made. Under current institutional circumstances, arms length management practices were considered impossible.

More important than financial commitments, however, are transfers of potentially learnable Western technology and/or production know-how. Such transfers were not even considered if full management control could not be achieved. If there was no credible guarantee that the know-how would stay under exclusive control of the foreign investor, including the rents created, the investment was not even considered. The latter is a far-reaching requirement that has very little to do with the ownership of physical assets. If the foreign investor cannot count on a long-term presence in the formerly planned economy under Western legal conditions, he won't engage in large-scale, long-term commitments of Western technology. Such technology, if committed, will soon be learned by the local staff and remain as potential competition if he has to pull out for one reason or another. Hence, *credible* commitments among the political authorities in the formerly planned economies to the property rights institutions are essential for major commitments of finance and (in particular) technical know-how by Western firms.

7.5.6   Case 3: Talleks, Estonia[8]

In December 1991 the president of the Supreme Court in Estonia allowed the Government to privatize seven industrial enterprises. *Talleks,* a producer of

---

[8]   See Kukk (1993).

small trucks and earth-moving equipment was one of them. Two joint-stock companies made bids for Talleks, both representing employees of Talleks. The group presenting the most modern business plan won the bid, and began negotiating with the State Property Department (SPD) about how to implement the privatization. The other group, however, led by the former managing director filed a protest with the prime minister. It did so despite the fact that it had only offered one-tenth of the winning bid for Talleks, and had tried all kinds of backstage political manoeuvring to win the case. The prime minister decided the decision of the SPD had been correct. The new owner group began to invest in the firm.

The earlier managing director, however, sued both the SPD and the Ministry of Industry, arguing that both the procedure and the implementation of the principles of the Property Reform Act had been violated. A new government was now in charge. The parliament had amended the contested paragraph of the Implementation Act. It was also revealed that the former director of Talleks was backed by influential circles of Estonian society who were unwilling to lose their status as a result of privatization.

Government, however, explained to the court that the privatization of Talleks was according to the law.

The Tallin City Court nevertheless (in September 1992) declared the purchase invalid. The new owner then appealed to the Supreme Court, which supported the Tallinn City Court. This whole outcome rested on inconsistencies in the new law, even if the practice was in accordance with government intentions. Seven other privatization cases were therefore also at stake, and several companies had made significant investments on the basis of the authorized privatization. Important principles were at stake. The vice-chairman of the Supreme Court then demanded that the president of the Supreme Court consider the case again. In January 1993 the president declared that the privatization had been legally correct.

The former director now turned to the chairman of the New Constitutional Highest Court, the National Court and protested against the privatization deal, citing formal procedural inaccuracies which contradicted the civil code. The privatization of Talleks was once again declared illegal on 12 May 1993, on this occasion by the National Court. However, two days later, the prime minister acted, accusing the former nomenclature of hindering privatization efforts, and proceeded to initiate a special law to privatize Talleks along the already agreed lines. Parliament approved the law on 16 June 1993, and decided that in determining the final price for acquiring Talleks the costs and losses associated with the long lawsuit would be taken into account.

7.6   THE SYNTHESIS: HOW TO CREATE A MARKET FOR RISKS

There are now three ways of dealing politically with the investment issue in a formerly planned economy. The *first,* welfare approach, tried extensively for years in the underdeveloped economies, can be ruled out as non-workable and destructive. Supplying more money will not solve the investment incentive problem, only worsen the economic problems of the formerly planned economies.

The *second* and *third* approaches are related, and probably have to be mixed. The second approach, attempting to build the appropriate *minimum institutional* structure, will have to be the main policy course but will take too long. Therefore it has to be provisionally complemented by an *insurance arrangement* for foreign direct investment, Western countries carrying the political investment risks of their firms.

We are now close to the *first* task of specifying the minimal set of institutions required to support the three elements of the property rights of *Table 7.1* such that non-business risks are sufficiently reduced in *Table 7.3* to make investments viable.

Second, we relate the elements of the property rights definition to the four fundamental mechanisms of economic growth (see *Table 7.2*). These mechanisms can be interpreted as four *investment* mechanisms, the last being a case of disinvestment. In doing this we have established the necessary and sufficient institutional conditions for investments needed to ensure sustained economic growth. The final step (not taken in this paper) will be to discuss the elements in *Table 7.2* that are the most important.

As can be seen from *Table 7.1*, large complexes of law and the associated interpretative and enforcement mechanisms have to be created to achieve the minimal institutions necessary to reduce the risk of opportunistic political behaviour associated with the property rights institutions, notably the ownership of corporate equity. This is only (see further Eliasson et al., 1994) the surface of the complex rule system needed. Most of this rule system does not exist in the formerly planned economies, and the complementary political mentality necessary for the smooth operation of a market economy is lacking.

As long as this situation prevails, business and political risks will mix uneasily. Both indigenous and foreign investments will be discouraged.

Since indigenous investment will not, in the foreseeable future, be sufficient to achieve a reasonable growth rate in formerly planned economies, the focus should be directed towards the conditions needed to stimulate foreign direct investments (see further Eliasson et al., 1994). Again relying on the indigenous development of the necessary legal system, the only way to move will be by way of Western financial support, in principle in the same way as Western Germany is salvaging the former Eastern Germany.

7.6.1   The Insurance Solution

Since it will not be possible in general to implant an entirely new legal system to protect property rights, the solution will have to be to combine (1) a Western financial insurance coverage for political risks *(opportunistic political behaviour)* taken on by firms with (2) strong incentives, directly linked to this support to allow the necessary legal framework to develop. I have referred to *enabling law* as the vehicle to achieve this goal. Only in this way will it be possible to reduce the investment risks in the formerly planned economies such that firms only have to cover their normal business risks. Using an insurance arrangement (as suggested in Eliasson, 1993d) Western government aid to the formerly planned economies could be in the form of a guaranteed insurance against their own opportunistic political behaviour, covering the investing Western companies. There will then be a strong incentive to move rapidly in creating an efficient property rights system.

The problem will be to define operationally the dividing line between business risks in *Table 7.3* to be covered by the firm and the political risks for which Western governments extend aid to the formerly planned economies. To solve this problem in advance of the development of rules and conventions through enabling law, an extensive and imaginative interview study of the experiences of firms in similar circumstances would have to be carried out. It is then not necessary to restrict oneself to recent experience in formerly planned economies. A large reservoir of similar experience exists in the developing countries and in most of the heavily regulated parts of Western industrial nations. Such an inquiry would, in fact, also be very valuable to the Western industrial world.

Let us outline some particular problem areas. One consideration to be borne in mind is that the different legal structures in *Table 7.1* affect different parts of the growth mechanisms in *Table 7.3*.

7.6.2   Bankruptcy Law

Thus for instance, to take a concrete example first, if there is no *bankruptcy law* (see item 2 in *Table 7.1*) there will be difficulties terminating unprofitable operations efficiently (the exit, item 4 in *Table 7.2*), especially when it comes to clearing up financial obligations. Similarly, if there is no enforceable *company law* the founders of a firm would have to formulate their own contract regulating their internal relationships and the external relationships of the firm, for instance to outside lenders. Delegation of operations control would be unclear as would the *right to* manage (item 1 in *Table 7.1*), restricting the possibilities of organizing production efficiently and reducing redundant staff. The absence of standard contracts and enforceable company and bankruptcy law will not prevent firms from being established, but risks and transactions costs will be higher.

7.6.3 The Big Firms

In many formerly planned economies, it is not permitted to fire people. This restriction hinders the *exit* process and the efficient *reorganization* and *rationalization* of big firms. The existing, big Soviet firms pose a particular problem. For one thing, they employ a large part of the existing labour force. While many of these people will not be an asset in the new firms, several will be needed, and part of the transition problem is to induce redundant people to move to new and more uncertain jobs. This means that efficient reorganization and rationalization will be a formidable task under current legal regimes. There are large risks associated with securing new capital to modernize, and then a tremendous risk associated with closing down redundant physical and human capacity. If the large firm does not embody certain unique competence or assets it may be most rational to close down the entire operation, or at least not to pin any hopes on obtaining a contribution to growth. Consequently, the difficulties associated with the exit process will be a real obstacle to the transition process in the sense that it locks up resources and makes available resources more expensive. Hence, *in the long run* newly established firms will represent the main growth factor, and so it appears, this may also have to be the case in the short run.

7.6.4 New Entry

Policy that aims to enhance the transition process should focus on creating incentives that

a) improve conditions for the new establishment and the expansion of small firms; and

b) (if there is a potential) induce foreign firms to invest to upgrade existing plants.

In both cases, however, it will be necessary to establish tradeable property rights in the entitlements to future profits from these business ventures, such that

(1) profits can be freely disposed of, and/or returned to some other country

(2) the entitlement to the business can be transferred to some other party, without any restrictions imposed by political authorities.

These rules have also to be credible in the sense of being enforceable by courts, or by some other means.

Improving such institutional conditions, furthermore, will be a slow process, requiring extreme patience on the part of politicians.

The spontaneous creation of markets for financial risks facing businesses to facilitate the funding of profitable long-term growth investments in formerly planned economies will thus have to await the reduction of the political risks in *Table 7.3*. Here a few conclusions may be drawn.

First, the existence of strong expectations of type one and two 'major' political risks will effectively reduce all major investments in the formerly planned economy. Large foreign firms may gamble on the possibility that such events will not occur and establish a presence in those markets. But this is a far cry from investments involving expansion on a large scale. Small foreign firms in low technology production might engage in subcontracting arrangements of a short-term nature, with limited commitments of funds and technology. Again, if such political risks are expected to be large, they will always maintain supplementary supply relationships in Western economies, a negative circumstance for the East European producer. The strong growth injection will not occur.

Second, this permits the following conclusion to be drawn. Among the couple of dozen or so formerly planned economies those considered most stable in terms of first and second order political risks will receive most long-term investments. There is a case for competition among the nations to establish an orderly and predictable judicial system.

Even if first and second order political risks have been reduced to reasonable levels (remember that significant macro instabilities occur also in Western countries) the third political risk category, *opportunistic political behaviour*, imposes a basic restriction on growth. This is the risk category we have paid most attention to in this paper. We have now reached the detail of *Table 7.1* and we have already concluded that to do it on their own, the formerly planned economies have to face a long time horizon, far longer than most of these nations can handle politically and socially. There is probably only one way to overcome the waiting period, or the time needed to allow the natural evolution of a viable Western legal system, namely to look for Western support. This should not be in the form of financial aid, but in the form of private direct investment and insurance for the foreign investors against political third order risks. There should be plenty of possible arrangements to secure risk reduction under category three with a minimum of moral hazard on the part of receiving countries and investing firms, along the lines developed in Eliasson (1993d). This provision of risk coverage should be the main task of the European Bank for Reconstruction, rather than disbursing finance to firms and formerly planned economies.

The reduction of political risks of all three kinds in *Table* 7.3 is furthermore necessary to enable an orderly development of the institutions of the financial system.

7.6.5   The Investment Calculation

A careful analysis of most firms from any formerly planned economy would reveal the following three facts. The firm *(first)* lacks the management and technical competence and the equipment to develop, to produce and to market products in Western international markets such that costs are covered. *Second,* the country lacks the competence to develop, within a reasonable time, the same competence and the necessary equipment and, hence, is critically dependent on foreign investment in such competence to support an investment and growth rate that matches expectations in the formerly planned economies. *Third,* the economic value of the required competence and capital investment in each firm is enormous compared to the value of existing competence and equipment. Taken together, for all firms and formerly planned economies, the total investment requirement is gigantic. If it had occured during a short period, the consequences would probably have been as was foreseen and indicated in the introductory words of this paper. But the incentives have been lacking because of the high political risks. Investment is not only a question of financing. Valuable competence plays an important role, and the cost to Western firms in terms of increased competition from parting with their technology under uncontrolled circumstances is potentially very high. Hence there will not be an investment boom in the formerly planned economies until the political risks have been eliminated through institutional reform and/or taken on by some other party, say a benevolent and wealthy Western nation (the insurance problem). Suppose, however, that the political risks have been eliminated, how do the profitability prospects then look?

Some firms like the two firms in Eliasson (1993c) can sell their obsolete, but still useful products in Western markets through Western intermediaries, the latter capturing (in the two cases) some two-thirds of value added in the process. Even though the value added created domestically (excluding the part created by the foreign intermediary) is only sufficient to create a labour productivity far below the worst Swedish producer (*Figure 7.2*), very low

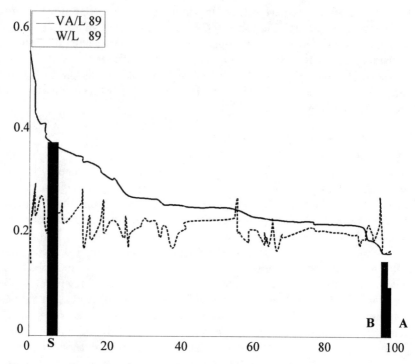

Note: Two East European firms (A and B) and one 'comparable' Swedish
           machine tool manufacturer (S) are indicated. V A/L = Value
           added/employee, W/L = Wage cost/employee. See, further, the text.
Source: Eliasson (1993c).

Figure 7.2: Labour productivity distributions in small Swedish manufactur-
ing firms and subcontractors, 1989

wages (valued in Western prices and currencies) still make the firms
profitable by Western standards (*Figure 7.3*), in fact more profitable than the
'corresponding' Swedish competitor. To raise the performance of the two
East European firms to Western standards, it is not sufficient just to invest in
new equipment and new competence in the form of a marketing and product
development organization. Competent labour and technicians have also to be
trained or hired at significantly higher compensation than the current salary
levels. It is perfectly possible to compare the costs of that transition, using
stylized data and the information in the Eliasson (1993c) study. The political
risks discussed in the main part of the paper can be included in this
calculation. These political risks will apply to domestic and foreign investors

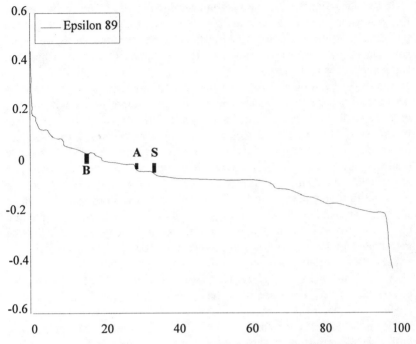

Note: Two East European firms (A and B) and one 'comparable' Swedish machine tool manufacturer (S) are indicated. See, further, the text.

Source: Eliasson (1993c).

Figure 7.3: Rates of return over the interest rate in 1989 in small Swedish manufacturing firms and subcontractors

alike. But the foreign investor will be able to compare his returns net of these political risks with what he can earn from investments in Western markets.

Using the data on two firms from Eliasson (1993c) we find that total capital intensity has to be increased at least three times. First hardware production capital has to be at least doubled by modernizing the equipment. In addition hardware capital has to be added and at least as much for inventories and other current capital. Furthermore, hardware capital amounts, on average in these types of firms, to some 60 per cent of total capital, including also accumulated stocks of product and market knowledge and investments in training the staff. This is a cautious estimate, noting also that these were the best firms in their respective countries (see Appendix). This investment alone will not, however, bring the East European firms on a par with the Swedish firm.

In the long run the investments indicated will have to be made for the firms to become competitive on their own in international markets. There are two critical issues. *First,* to carry out the needed investments, the requisite competence of the receiver has also to be upgraded. *Second,* what will happen to wages in the process?

We have already concluded that the profitability calculation collapses if the necessary business and technical competence cannot be brought in. The only way will probably be to use foreign expertise through foreign direct investments. The foreign investor will then be compensated through a high return on his investments. This can only be brought about at reasonable returns to investment if the property rights are in order, and if wage and salary levels remain much lower than in the West for a considerable time.

In the East German case it has not been possible to keep wages down. It will not be possible in other formerly planned economies under a programme of massive investment and upgrading of existing facilities, requiring the recruitment of labour with a competence that does not exist in sufficient volume. Wage inflation will then follow.

A few firms doing this rapidly and alone with Western inputs of competence would, however, profit handsomely. This is essentially the case for foreign direct investment.

Using the rate of return formula in the Appendix, we can see that the most profitable Western strategy is to acquire an East European firm and use it as a subcontractor only, upgrading the factories with Western technology. This arrangement will considerably improve profitability compared to production in a corresponding Swedish facility. Technically the foreign firm could team up with a domestic subcontractor. It would, however, not be willing to share its own technology with the subcontractor if it could not control its use through an ownership contract. This contract would thus have to be legally supported in the country in question.

Such an arrangement (as the Appendix shows) could support a significantly higher wage cost level. But it would not necessarily be in the interest of the foreign investor to introduce its product design and marketing know-how into the East European subsidiary. It is more profitable (as the calculations show) to keep it as a producer of rents and components. For such know-how to be developed by the domestic producers on their own would require considerable investment that would not be as profitable as a subcontracting arrangement.

7.6.6   Appendix

The *real rate of return* of a company is defined as:

$$R = \frac{PQ - WL - rK}{K}$$

where:

Q = output volume

P = output price deflator

W = wage cost per unit of labour import

L = unit of labour input, say man years

K = capital, replacement value

ρ = depreciation factor

It follows immediately:

$$R = \left(1 - \frac{W}{PQ/L}\right)\frac{PQ}{K} - r$$

or

$$R = M - \frac{PQ}{K} - \rho$$

where M is the gross profit margin as a percentage of value added and $M = (1 - \text{unit labour cost})$.

From Eliasson (1993c) we have data expressed in international currencies on Firm B in *Figures 7.2* and *7.3*. Firm B is the best machine tool manufacturer in one East European country. Firm S is the best machine tool manufacturing company in Sweden. The two firms happened to be of roughly comparable size in terms of value added. This means that we have adjusted the Swedish data so that the two firms produced (in 1989) exactly the same output in SEK. The data are explained in detail in Eliasson (1993c). The comparison is shown in the table below.

If production facilities are modernized to Swedish standards, assuming blue collar labour is capable of producing as efficiently as Swedish labour, but earning the same wage as before, the profitability calculation improves considerably to $R = 19$ per cent. It is, however, important to observe that wages mean something, but not very much. This is the most optimistic case a

Table 7.4: Performance rates of the Swedish and East European firm

	Swedish Firm	East European Firm
Value added (=pq)	220 million SEK	220 million SEK
Employment (=L)	600	1 500
Labour productivity (= PQ/L)	367 000	147 000
Wage costs (=w)	250 000/employee	30 000/employee
Machines and buildings	350 million	350 million
Total visible capital in balance sheet (Replacement values)	700	700
R (per cent)	0	15

foreign investor will meet, using the East European firm only as a subcontractor. If wages escalate to half the Swedish level, the rate of return will decrease to 11 per cent. This is still the case of an East European firm being used as a subcontractor by its Swedish parent. If the East European firm tries to go it alone acquiring the needed marketing and product know-how at Western costs, the rate of return collapses (assuming half the Swedish wage) to R = 5 per cent. This is higher than for the Swedish firm, but below the common level and with no margin for political risk coverage.

7.7   REFERENCES

Carlsson, B. and R. Henriksson (1991), *Development Blocs and Industrial Transformation, The Dahménian Approach to Economic Development*, IUI, Stockholm.

Dahmén, E. (1950), *Svensk industriell Företagarverksamhet. Kausal analys av den industriella utvecklingen 1919–1939*, IUI, Stockholm.

Eliasson, G. (1987), *Technological Competition and Trade in the Experimentally Organized Economy*, IUI Research Report no. 32, Stockholm.

Eliasson, G. (1990), The Firm as a Competent Team, *Journal of Economic Behavior and Organization*, vol. 13, no. 3 (June), pp. 275–98.

Eliasson, G. (1991a), Modeling the Experimentally Organized Economy: Complex Dynamics in an Empirical Micro-Macro Model of Endogenous

Economic Growth, *Journal of Economic Behavior and Organization*, vol. 16, no. 1–2 (July), pp. 153–82.

Eliasson, G. (1991b), Deregulation, Innovative Entry and Structural Diversity as a Source of Stable and Rapid Economic Growth, *Journal of Evolutionary Economics*, no. 1, pp. 49–63.

Eliasson, G. (1992), *The Economics of Technical Change*, IUI Working Paper no. 349b, published 1995 in Revue d'Économie Industrielle, Numero Exceptionnel.

Eliasson, G. (1993a), A Note: On Privatization, Contract Technology and Economic Growth; in R.H. Day, G. Eliasson, C. Wihlborg eds, *The Markets for Innovation, Ownership and Control*, IUI, Stockholm and North-Holland, Amsterdam.

Eliasson, G. (1993b), Företagens, institutionernas och marknadernas roll i Sveriges ekonomiska kris (The Role of Firms, Institutions and Markets in the Crisis Management of the Swedish Economy); in *Nya villkor för ekonomi och politik*, SOU 1993:16, bilaga 6.

Eliasson, G. (1993c), The Micro Frustrations of Privatizing Eastern Europe, in H. Genberg, ed., *Privatization in Economies in Transition*, ICMB pp. 45–89, Geneva.

Eliasson, G. (1993d), *Reducing Political Risks and Moral Hazard in East West Financial Relations*, IUI Working Paper no. 388, Stockholm.

Eliasson, G. (1994), The Theory of the Firm and the Theory of Economic Growth – An Essay on the Economics of Institutions, Competition and the Capacity of the Political System to Cope with Unexpected Change; in Magnusson, L., ed., *Evolutionary and Neo-Schumpeterian Approaches to Economics*, Kluwer Academic Publishers, Boston/Dordrecht/London.

Eliasson, G., T. Rybczynski and C. Wihlborg (1994), *The Necessary Institutional Framework to Transform Formerly Planned Economies – With Special Emphasis on the Institutions Needed to Stimulate Foreign Investment in the Formerly Planned Economies*, IUI, Stockholm.

Kukk, M. (1993), Privatization in Estonia, IUI Mimeo, Stockholm.

Lucas, R.E. (1988), On the Mechanics of Economic Development, *Journal of Monetary Economics*, vol. 22, pp. 3–42.

North, D.C. (1990), *Institutions, Institutional Change and Economic Performance*, Cambridge University Press.

North, D.C. and R.P. Thomas (1973), *The Rise of the Western World: A New Economic History*, Cambridge University Press.

Pelikan, P. (1987), The Formation of Incentive Mechanisms in Different Economic Systems, in S. Hedlund, ed., *Incentives and Economic System*, Croom Helm, London and Sydney.

Pelikan, P. (1992), The Dynamics of Economic Systems, or How to Transform a Failed Socialistic Economy, *Journal of Evolutionary Economics*, vol. 2, no. 1.

Romer, P. (1986), Increasing Returns and Economic growth, *American Economic Review*, vol. 94, pp. 1002–37.

8. Structural Adjustment, Efficiency and Economic Growth

Thorvaldur Gylfason

8.1 INTRODUCTION

This paper is intended to show that the potential static and dynamic output gains from economic reforms are substantial under conditions that are relevant for the Baltic countries and for other previously planned economies.

The purpose of the paper is:

(a) to demonstrate that national output may be increased by reducing or eliminating relative price distortions through price reform and free trade and thereby increasing macroeconomic efficiency at full employment;

(b) to present an explicit formula in which the potential static output gain from structural adjustment through economic liberalization is approximately proportional to the square of the original distortion;

(c) to provide a rudimentary quantitative assessment of the potential output gains from adjustment by numerical examples; and

(d) to suggest how more efficient use of productive resources will lead not only to a higher level of output per capita, but also, probably, to a higher rate of economic growth in the long run.

To set the stage, consider an economy characterized initially by full employment of all available resources and excess aggregate demand, repressed inflation, and a general shortage of goods and services. The planned economies of East and Central Europe before the collapse of communism are cases in point. The supply of all factors of production is held fixed by assumption.

When prices are set free, the general price level rises in response to market forces. This general price increase is accompanied by a change in relative prices because prices tend to increase mostly in those sectors where the initial excess demand was largest. At first, output contracts and unemployment spreads as inefficient firms go bankrupt in those parts of the economy where

211

relative prices have fallen. The resulting contraction of aggregate supply increases the pressure on the price level. The slump in aggregate demand may also reduce output and employment temporarily in those markets where relative prices have risen, owing to the spillover effects of bankruptcies across sectors.

This process continues until the new profit opportunities and incentives arising in markets where relative prices have increased begin to be exploited by innovative entrepreneurs. When this occurs, resources are drawn into more productive employment than before and the decline of aggregate output is gradually reversed. Output continues to rise until all profit opportunities have been exploited in full and full employment has been restored at a higher level of output than initially. Even though the initial output loss is temporary and the ultimate output gain is permanent, the structural adjustment may or may not increase the present discounted value of output, because the output loss is suffered before the gain materializes. The cure may conceivably be worse than the disease, but this seems a remote possibility.

8.2   STATIC OUTPUT GAIN: A SIMPLE FORMULA

What is the relationship between the ultimate increase in output and the extent of the initial disequilibrium?

Imagine two sectors, agriculture and industry, where productive resources are fully, but inefficiently, employed initially and the relative price of industrial goods in terms of agricultural goods is lower at home than in world markets. This means that more resources are devoted to agricultural production at prevailing domestic prices than would be the case under free trade at world market prices.

In *Figure 8.1*, the initial full-employment equilibrium position is described by point E where the domestic relative price line with slope $-\pi$ is tangential to the production possibility frontier. At point E, domestic production equals domestic consumption and no trade takes place. The steeper line with slope $-\pi^* < -\pi$ describes the ratio of the prices of the two goods in world markets. The intersection of this line through point E and the horizontal axis gives total output Y (i.e., Gross National Product) measured in terms of industrial goods:

(1) $$Y = I + \left(\frac{1}{\pi^*}\right) A \,.$$

Suppose now that the economy is liberalized by lifting restrictions on foreign trade and by reforming the structure of domestic prices. Trade begins at world market prices. Agricultural output falls. The economy moves downwards from point E in *Figure 8.1* to a point such as J inside the production possibility frontier. Unemployment emerges. If the contraction of agricultural production spreads to industry, that is, if the decline in purchasing power in agriculture reduces the demand for industrial goods as well, industrial production first falls and then rises again on the way from E to J. Aggregate output is lower at J than at E by equation (1).

Sooner or later, however, the business opportunities created by the increase in the relative price of industrial goods will begin to be exploited by profit-seeking entrepreneurs. As resources are transferred from agriculture and idleness to industry, the economy begins to move to the right from the interior point J towards point F on the production possibility frontier.

One possible adjustment path is described by the locus $EJHF$. Along the segment EJ, output is lower than initially in both agriculture and industry. At J, industrial output is restored to its original level, but national output is still lower than initially. At H, national output has returned to its initial level, but full employment is not restored until the new equilibrium point F is reached. Gradual adjustment trajectories of this type involving unemployment of labour and other factors of production can be derived from optimal producer behaviour if the adjustment itself is costly (see Mussa, 1982).

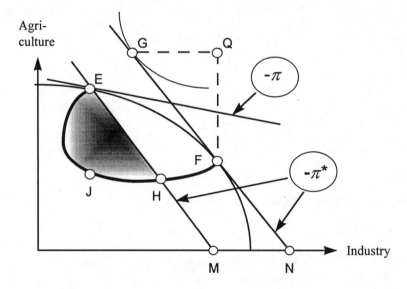

Figure 8.1: Output gain from agricultural trade liberalization

When point F on the production possibility frontier is reached, aggregate output has increased by an amount indicated by the thick segment MN of the horizontal axis in *Figure 8.1*. Domestic production of agricultural and industrial goods in the new equilibrium is described by point F in the figure, and domestic consumption by point G. Industrial goods are now exported in exchange for agricultural imports. As exports GQ are equal to imports FQ at world market prices by construction of the trade triangle GQF, the current account is in equilibrium.

The welfare cost of the status quo is, however, different. This cost is measured by the external transfer of resources that would be required at domestic prices without trade to lift the economy to the same level of social welfare as could be achieved by structural adjustment through free trade. In *Figure 8.1*, the welfare cost in terms of industrial production is indicated by the horizontal distance between the domestic relative price line tangential to the production possibility frontier at point E and the parallel price line (not shown) tangential to the upper social indifference curve that goes through point G. Generally, this hypothetical welfare cost of the status quo is different from the output gain from structural adjustment denoted by the thick segment of the horizontal axis, and will not concern us further here.

The output gain from moving from E to F in *Figure 8.1* depends on the magnitude of the initial distortion and the curvature of the production possibility frontier (see Gylfason, 1993). Suppose that the relationship between domestic and world market prices is given by

(2)		$\pi = (1-c)\pi *$

where c is a constant that reflects the extent of the initial distortion $(0 < c < 1)$. The distortion parameter c reflects the angle between the two relative price lines where they cross at point E in the figure.

Moreover, suppose that the production possibility frontier is described by the function

(3)		$A = F(I)$

where $F' < 0$ and $F'' < 0$. It then follows that

(4)		$F'(I) = -\pi *$

at point F in the figure and, correspondingly, $F'(I) = -\pi$ at point E.

The increase in industrial production from E to F is therefore approximately

(5)		$\Delta I = -F''^{-1}(I)(\pi * - \pi) = -F''^{-1}(I)c\pi *.$

The approximate reduction in agricultural production is obtained by evaluating a second-order Taylor expansion of equation (3) around point E in the figure:

$$(6) \qquad \Delta A = F'(I)\Delta I - \left(\frac{1}{2}\right)F''(I)(\Delta I)^2 .$$

The approximate increase in total output from E to F is found by substituting from equations (5) and (6) into equation (1) after taking first differences on both sides at given world market prices. This gives

$$(7) \qquad \Delta Y = mc^2$$

where m denotes the multiple $\frac{1}{2}(F'/F'')$.

In words, the expansion of output is approximately proportional to the square of the initial distortion. The factor of proportionality, $m = \frac{1}{2}(F'/F'')$, depends solely on the shape of the production possibility frontier. Alternatively, this multiplicator may be expressed as $m = \frac{1}{2}Ie$ where $e = F'/(F''I)$ is the elasticity of industrial production with respect to relative prices.

The simple formula developed above is a variation on a well-known theme in welfare economics. The welfare gain from removing a single distortion (a tax or a tariff, for instance) is approximately proportional to the square of the initial distortion (see Harberger, 1964). The square of the distortion enters the formula because the welfare gain is approximated by an area enclosed by a right-angled triangle whose short sides are both proportional to the tax rate. However, in the reviews of the theory of optimal taxation provided by Atkinson and Stiglitz (1980) and Dixit (1985), the aggregate output gains from improved allocation of resources are not linked to the theory and measurement of deadweight welfare loss from inefficient taxation.

8.3   AN ANALYTICAL EXAMPLE

To make the simple formula in (7) operational as a rough guide to the potential magnitude of the responsiveness of output to structural adjustment, it is necessary to assume the production possibility equation (3) to take a particular functional form.

Consider, for example, the following quadratic function:

$$(8) \qquad A = a - \left(\frac{1}{2b}\right)I^2$$

where a and b are positive constants. The slope of the production possibility frontier at point F is

$$(9) \qquad \frac{\partial A}{\partial I} = F'(I) = -\left(\frac{1}{b}\right)I = -\pi^*,$$

so that

$$(10) \qquad I = b\pi^*.$$

The change in industrial production can now be written as

$$(11) \qquad \Delta I = b(\pi^* - \pi) = bc\pi^* = cI.$$

Similarly, the change in agricultural production can now be written as

$$(12) \qquad \Delta A = -\left(\frac{1}{b}\right)I\Delta I + \left(\frac{1}{2b}\right)(\Delta I)^2 = -\left(\frac{1}{b}\right)cI^2 + \left(\frac{1}{2b}\right)c^2 I^2.$$

The change in total output is found by substituting from equations (11) and (12) into equation (1) as before. This gives

$$(13) \qquad \frac{g}{1+g} = \left(\frac{1}{2}\right)\left(\frac{I}{Y}\right)c^2$$

where $g = \Delta Y/Y$ is the proportional increase in output from E to F in *Figure 8.1* (with initial output as a base) and I/Y is the share of industry (that is, manufacturing, construction, trade and services) in total output after the structural adjustment has been completed. The elasticity of industrial production with respect to relative prices, $e = F'/(F''I)$, equals 1 in this case, see equation (10).

This simple formula (13) makes it possible to map the proportional static output gain g as a function of the initial price distortion c and of the ultimate share of industry in output I/Y. The more severe the initial distortion c, the larger is the correction that is needed and, hence, the greater will be the gain in output. The more ambitious the structural adjustment that is undertaken, the larger is the share of the industrial (or 'modern') sector I/Y at the end of the day and, hence, again, the greater will be the gain in output.

8.4   NUMERICAL EXAMPLES

To appreciate the possible macroeconomic and empirical significance of increased efficiency in the allocation of resources, let us now proceed to plug plausible parameter values into our formula in an attempt to get a feel for the possible magnitudes involved. This is inevitably a highly speculative exercise in consideration of the simplicity of the formula and the unavailability of reliable evidence about the explanatory parameters.

Let us assume domestic relative prices to be out of line with world market prices initially by a factor of 2, 3, 4 or 5, so that c takes the values 0.5, 0.67, 0.75 and 0.8. This seems reasonable as the prices of many commodities have risen manyfold following selective price liberalization in Poland at the beginning of 1990 and in Russia two years later, for example.

Moreover, let us assume the share of the industrial sector in aggregate output following structural adjustment to range from 0.5 to 0.9. The latter number corresponds roughly to the current situation in Western Europe where agriculture and other related activity that is similarly sheltered from foreign competition to a large extent accounts for about 10 per cent of GNP.

The proportional output gains that follow from these assumptions are shown in *Table 8.1*.

Table 8.1: Static output gain as a function of the initial distortion and the ultimate share of industry in output

$e = 1.0$	$I/Y = 0.5$	$I/Y = 0.7$	$i/Y = 0.9$
$c = 0.5$	$g = 0.07$	$g = 0.10$	$g = 0.13$
$c = 0.67$	$g = 0.13$	$g = 0.19$	$g = 0.25$
$c = 0.75$	$g = 0.16$	$g = 0.25$	$g = 0.34$
$c = 0.8$	$g = 0.19$	$g = 0.29$	$g = 0.40$

These numbers indicate that the proportional static output gains from structural adjustment can range from 7 per cent to 40 per cent once and for all. These gains are permanent, other things being equal.

We have assumed that the relative price elasticity of industrial production is equal to one. A higher price elasticity would entail even greater gains.

Given a discount rate of 5 per cent per year, the present value of these gains amounts to 1.4 to 8 times annual national output once and for all. For comparison, the lowest figure in the table ($g = 0.07$) exceeds the rough estimates of the permanent static output gains expected to emerge gradually from the market unification of Europe in 1992 according to Cecchini (1988).

If these numbers are indicative of the results that would emerge from detailed empirical case studies, it seems reasonable to conclude that abstaining from structural adjustment may be expensive indeed, provided that the initial slump in output is not too deep and enduring.

8.5   DYNAMIC OUTPUT GAINS: ENDOGENOUS GROWTH

The path of output following economic liberalization of the kind discussed above is shown in *Figure 8.2*. Consider an economy that is stagnant up to time t_1 when an economic reform programme is launched. Output at first declines and then rises along the trajectory *EJHF*, as in *Figure 8.2*. The shaded area enclosed by *E, J* and *H* corresponds to its namesake in *Figure 8.1*. At time t_2, output exceeds its initial level by $\Delta Y = mc^2$ by equation (7). This is the static output gain from economic liberalization.

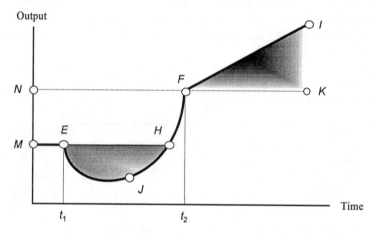

Figure 8.2: The path of output following structural adjustment

But where does the economy go from here? If output is produced by labour L and capital K according to a simple Cobb–Douglas production function, $Y = AL^\alpha K^{1-\alpha}$, and if the accumulated technological know-how represented by A is tied to capital by $A = EK^\alpha$ where E reflects efficiency (as in Romer, 1989), then we have simply

(14) $Y = EK$,

assuming that the labour force is constant at $L = 1$. Then output per capita Y depends solely on the capital stock K in a broad sense and the efficiency E with which it is used in the production process. In other words, output depends on the quantity and quality of capital.

Moreover, if saving S is proportional to output and equals gross investment, that is, $I = \Delta K + dK$, where d is the depreciation rate, then we have $S = sY = I = \Delta K + dK = \Delta Y/E + dY/E$ for given E, so that

(15) $g = sE - d$

where $g = \Delta Y/Y$ as before. The rate of economic growth, in words, equals the multiple of the saving rate s and the efficiency of capital use E less the depreciation rate d.

Generally, E reflects the efficiency of resource allocation in the economy. By implication, all improvements in efficiency, including price reform and trade liberalization as shown in *Figure 8.1*, and also privatization, education, and even macroeconomic stabilization, result not only in a higher level of output by equation (7), but also a higher rate of growth of output by equation (15). Therefore, the economy follows the sickle-shaped path *EJHFI* rather than *EJHFK* in *Figure 8.2*. The shaded area *FIK* represents the dynamic output gain from economic reform.

How large is this potential growth bonus? Consider, for example, an economy where saving is 30 per cent of output ($s = 0.3$), depreciation is 10 per cent of the capital stock ($d = 0.1$), and the efficiency parameter E is 0.33 initially. Then, by equation (15), the growth rate g is zero as shown in *Table 8.2*. Assume now that the efficiency of capital use increases by 50 per cent in the sense that output rises by that much for a given capital stock, broadly defined (compare *Table 8.1*). This means that the rate of economic growth rises from zero to 5 per cent per year. This increase in growth is permanent by the construction of the production function (14).

Table 8.2: Economic growth as a function of the saving rate and the efficiency of capital

$d = 0.1$	$E = 0.33$	$E = 0.5$	$E = 0.67$
$s = 0.1$	$g = -0.067$	$g = -0.05$	$g = -0.033$
$s = 0.2$	$g = -0.033$	$g = 0.0$	$g = 0.033$
$s = 0.3$	$g = 0.0$	$g = 0.05$	$g = 0.1$

Specifically, the mechanisms that prevented increased efficiency and increased saving from stimulating growth permanently in the models of Harrod and Domar and Solow are absent here because the production function (14) exhibits constant returns to capital. In the neoclassical growth model, by contrast, structural adjustment is equivalent to a technological innovation that increases the rate of growth of output while the economy moves from one steady-state growth path to another, higher path. This adjustment process may take a long time in the Solow model. The medium-term properties of the Solow model may, therefore, be difficult to distinguish empirically from the long-run properties of the Romer version of the endogenous-growth model employed above.

8.6   CONCLUSION

In this paper an attempt has been made to clarify the effects of structural adjustment through economic reform and free trade on national income and its rate of growth in the long run. The static output gain from eliminating a single relative price distortion in a two-sector general-equilibrium model with full employment was captured in a simple formula in which the gain is approximately proportional to the square of the original distortion. This formula is analytically equivalent to Harberger's (1964) triangular measure of the deadweight welfare loss from inefficient taxation. Substitution of plausible parameter values into the simple formula indicates that the aggregate output gain from adjustment may be substantial. Because of the efficiency boost that results from an improved allocation of resources among sectors, economic growth increases permanently according to the new theory of endogenous growth, or at least in the medium term by the neoclassical growth model. The dynamic output gain is also likely to be large.

8.7   REFERENCES

Atkinson, A.B. and J. E. Stiglitz (1980), *Lectures on Public Economics*, McGraw-Hill, London.

Cecchini, P. (1988), *The European Challenge 1992*, Gower, Aldershot.

Dixit, A. (1985), Tax Policy in Open Economies, Chapter 6 in *Handbook of Public Economics* 1, North-Holland, Amsterdam.

Gylfason, T. (1993), Output Gains from Economic Liberalization: A Simple Formula, in Laszlo Somogyi, ed., *The Political Economy of the Transition Process in Eastern Europe,* pp. 67–87, Edward Elgar, Aldershot.

Harberger, A.C. (1964), Taxation, Resource Allocation, and Welfare, in *The Role of Direct and Indirect Taxes in the Federal Revenue System*, The National Bureau of Economic Research and The Brookings Institution, Princeton University Press, Princeton, N.J.

Mussa, M. (1982), Government Policy and the Adjustment Process, in Jagdish N. Bhagwati, ed., *Import Competition and Response*, pp. 73–120,

The University of Chicago Press and The National Bureau of Economic Research, Cambridge, MA.

Romer, P. (1989), Capital Accumulation in the Theory of Long Run Growth, in Robert J. Barro, ed., *Modern Business Cycle Theory*, pp. 51–127, Harvard University Press, Cambridge, MA.

9. The Role of Institutions in the Transition to a Market Economy

Michael D. Intriligator*

9.1 THE TRANSITION FROM A CENTRALLY PLANNED TO A MARKET ECONOMY: SOME FUNDAMENTAL QUESTIONS

The transition from a centrally planned to a market economy, particularly in the case of Russia, Ukraine and the other successor states of the Soviet Union, including the Baltic states, is one of the most important questions facing the world today. How to accomplish this transition is certainly one of the most important challenges to economics since the reconstruction of Europe after World War II.[1] The Soviet economy had until recently been the second largest economy in the world, but its successor states are now in a state of economic collapse. The fundamental problem is that the Soviet successor states have disbanded the institutions of central planning but they have not yet established the institutions of a market economy. In the vacuum that resulted from the absence of those bodies that enable an economy to function, whether it be a centrally planned or a market economy, there have been unprecedented economic declines in the Soviet successor states. These

* This paper builds on Michael D. Intriligator, 'Reform of the Russian Economy: The Role of Institutions,' *Contention*, Winter 1994. The author acknowledges, with appreciation, the research assistance of Kenneth Serwin and the comments and suggestions of Fuad Aleskerov, Michael Barnes, Vladimir Keilis-Borok, Axel Leijonhufvud, George Murphy and Slava Tchoudinov. Support from the UCLA Office of International Relations and Overseas Programs is gratefully acknowledged.

[1] See, among others, Milner and Lvov (1991), Åslund (1991), Marer and Zecchini (1991), Alexeev et al. (1992), Wolfson (1992), Fischer and Frenkel (1992), Sachs, (1992), Abalkin (1992), Fischer (1992), Summers and Nordhaus (1992a), Ellman (1992), Dyker (1992), Clague and Rausser (1992), Eberwein (1992), Leijonhufvud (1993a).

declines include sharp reductions in output, enormous increases in prices, large and growing actual or functional unemployment, increasing numbers of workers who are not being paid, reductions in real wages and living standards, the loss of social services, and capital flight, resulting in potential political and social instability.[2] In addition, some of the Soviet successor states have become riddled with crime, including asset stripping by managers of newly privatized establishments and tremendous increases in the role of the mafias in the economy.[3] Thus, a functioning market economy remains a rather distant prospect.

Overall, the question of the transition of the formerly centrally planned economies to a market economy is one of how to get from 'here' to 'there', where 'here' is an economic vacuum characterized by steep declines in the economy and 'there' is a growing market economy. Should the transition use a gradual evolutionary approach or a sudden revolutionary one?[4] In January 1992, President Boris Yeltsin introduced in Russia the radical reform represented by the 'SLP' approach of stabilization, liberalization and privatization under the name of 'shock therapy.' The other Soviet successor states have also introduced some elements of this SLP approach. The 'stabilization' part of SLP refers to macroeconomic stabilization, with limits on government deficits, on growth in the money supply, on imbalances in the balance of payments and so on, involving macroeconomic, monetary and international stabilization. The 'liberalization' part of SLP refers to price

[2] These declines in the economies of the Soviet successor states, particularly those in Russia and Ukraine, and their consequences for political and social instability represent perhaps the greatest threat to global security today. To appreciate their significance, one must take account of the size and population of Russia and Ukraine, their geostrategic position, their arsenals of nuclear and other weapons, their relations with the near abroad nations that had been part of the Soviet Union, and the possibility of Bosnia-type wars within or between these nations. There is a potential in these countries for the advent of neo-communist, fascist or militaristic governments, with adverse consequences for the world that world leaders have generally ignored. The potential threats to global security stemming from these nations are, for example, of far greater potential consequence than such issues as proliferation, the arms trade, terrorism, local conflicts and so on.

[3] See Intriligator (1994).

[4] See Murrell (1992, pp. 79–95). As to the contribution of economics, while there had been a debate among economists over centrally planned versus market economies in the 1930s, there has been remarkably little discussion of the transition from one system to the other. On the transition and economic theory, see Fischer and Gelb (1991, pp. 91–106), Winiecki (1992, pp. 171–90) and Nove (1993, pp. 20–33). On the lack of applicability of the previous transition literature, which concerns mainly the transition from right-wing authoritarian regimes, to the post-Communist transition, see Meiklejohn Terry (1993).

liberalization, freeing prices and allowing them to move to realistic market prices through the pressure of market forces. The 'privatization' part of SLP refers to privatizing the former state enterprises, turning them into corporations, as in Western market economies. Given the declines experienced following the introduction of this SLP approach, a reasonable question is whether it should continue or whether it should be replaced by some other approach. In particular, what should be the role of supporting domestic economic, legal, political and social institutions? In addition, what should be the role of the rest of the world, especially the United States, Western Europe, Japan, the International Monetary Fund, the World Bank, the European Bank for Reconstruction and Development, the Organization for Economic Cooperation and Development, and other nations and international organizations?

9.2   THE IMPORTANCE OF INSTITUTIONS FOR A MARKET ECONOMY

In response to these fundamental questions, this paper contends that it is necessary to establish the relevant economic, legal, political and social institutions in order to prevent the further collapse of the economies of the Soviet successor states. It further contends that the SLP approach will not spontaneously create these institutions and, thus, the government or perhaps local governments, with help from external public and private sources, should take a major role is establishing these institutions.

These conclusions follow from a consideration of the basic transactions of a market economy and the institutions necessary for such transactions to take place. The most important of the institutions needed for a market economy are a legal system, including both business law and property law; a related system of property rights; a credit system; a system of commercial and investment banks; classified advertising; an accounting system, and other institutions, including a sound currency and a social safety net. In the absence of these institutions, enterprises, whether privatized or not, will not have the proper incentives to produce and to invest. Unfortunately, most of our received economic theory omits the institutions of the economy, taking them for granted or simply assuming that they are present. The experience of the Soviet successor states demonstrates that these institutions are essential for any economy and that they must not be ignored. It is probably neither possible nor desirable to return to a system of central planning in the Soviet successor states, but a relatively greater economic role for the government may be the way – and perhaps the only way – to facilitate the development of those institutions needed for a market economy. There is a strong sentiment against a major role for the government, which is understandable as a result of the long experience of a centrally planned economy. Nevertheless, there must be a recognition of the need for government to take initiatives in the establishment of these institutions, which would take an unacceptably long time, if ever, to form in the absence of such initiatives. The establishment of institutions is itself a political process, and a necessary first step will be the creation of an effective government in these nations that can work with their parliaments in taking the appropriate initiatives. In general, the goal should not be a pure *laissez-faire* market economy, but rather a mixed economy like those of Western industrialized economies. Such economies are not completely decentralized in that they involve the government acting as a regulator, as an initiator and, in other capacities as well, influencing the economy. In particular, the prescription for improved economic performance should come not just as a part of the usual form of the SLP approach. I will argue that institution building is much more important at this point in the transition, specifically the formulation of policies that would foster the establishment of the institutions of a market economy or direct initiatives to establish them.[5]

9.3 THE FOUNDATIONS OF A MARKET ECONOMY

An appreciation of the role of institutions follows from considering the foundations of a market economy. One economist from one of the Soviet successor states has referred to the 'secrets of a market economy', but a market economy involves few if any secrets. The basic transaction of a market economy is extremely simple: one economic actor, whether an individual or an enterprise, has something to sell and another wants to buy it, so they make a mutually profitable transaction. This basic transaction is multiplied an astronomical number of times in a functioning market economy. Now consider what is necessary for this basic microeconomic transaction to happen. First, both the buyer and seller must know what they own and what they can buy, making necessary a system of property rights. Second, each must know about the other, so they have a way of finding each other, leading to advertising, especially classified advertising, trade journals and other information systems. Third, they must have some way of enforcing their agreements to buy and sell and of settling disputes that may arise over the transaction, making necessary contracts, laws, courts, a commercial code and so on. Fourth, they may find it necessary to finance their transaction,

---

[5]   For discussions of the role of institutions in the transition to a market economy, see Oppenheimer (1992, pp. 48–61), Koslowski (1992, pp. 673–705) and Nagy (1992).

making necessary a financial system, including both commercial and investment banks and other financial intermediaries. Fifth, they must be able to insure what they have bought and sold, making necessary an insurance system. Sixth, they must be able to account for what they have bought and sold, making necessary an accounting system. Seventh, to avoid barter, which requires an improbable coincidence of wants, they must have access to money both as a unit of account and as a means of payment.

Starting with a basic market transaction, it is thus possible to identify many of the institutions that are necessary for a functioning market economy. The absence of these institutions in the Soviet successor states has led to a situation in which the managers of the state enterprises have neither the incentives of a market economy nor the regulations of a centrally planned economy. As a result, nothing constrains them from acting in their own personal self-interest, often to the detriment of the state enterprises themselves and of society as a whole.[6] The lack of profit incentives and regulatory constraints has let the managers engage in mismanagement and even outright criminal behaviour, including the diversion of hard currency earnings out of the country, asset stripping of enterprises and significant corruption. Lack of control and corruption have led not just to increased crime but have enabled organized crime networks, the mafias, to control major sectors of the economy. Indeed, the economic reform carried out so far has created a system that is virtually ideal for the transfer of property to either second echelon bureaucrats or organized crime. The situation in these nations is like the 'robber baron' period of unfettered capitalism during the last century, but even more extreme, where the current robber barons are the mafias and corrupt bureaucrats, including enterprise managers.

The building of the economic and other institutions needed for a market economy is totally different from the current privatization campaign that exists in some of the Soviet successor states. Some former Soviet and Western economists have virtually measured the move to a market economy by the degree of privatization, but this campaign, like several of Gorbachev's earlier economic campaigns, either will not accomplish much or will actually make matters worse. Simply changing the labels on existing entities will not change much, particularly if the same managers are running the same institutions, using the same workers and the same (largely obsolete) capital and technology. There is also the problem of asset stripping, where the managers of the enterprises find it much more profitable to sell off raw materials inventories and plant and equipment than to sell finished products,

---

[6]   See Cooter (1992).

lodging the proceeds in their private offshore bank accounts.[7] The issue is not that of changing labels on existing entities, but rather that of creating those new institutions that would make possible private market transactions. These institutions, which lie at the core of a market economy, evolved over centuries in Western economies, but they must develop rapidly in the Soviet successor states to prevent their further economic decline. These states do not have the time needed for such institutions to evolve. That will require an activist government, ideally with help from other nations and international organizations to foster their creation or to create them directly.

It will require more than just the creation of these institutions, however, to solve the economic problems of the Soviet successor states. While these institutions are necessary for a market economy, they may not be sufficient. The former East Germany, for example, was able to have access to all these institutions as a result of unification, but it is still experiencing severe economic difficulties in its transition to a market economy. An activist government is necessary not only to create the market institutions but also to ensure their use. Government policy must focus not only on creating those institutions necessary for a market economy but also on fostering the creation of new economic entities to use them. These new producing and other entities can then bid away the resources of labour and capital from the current ones. Policy initiatives should focus on the creation of new efficient economic entities that can compete effectively in the world economy, such as have been established recently in China and elsewhere. They could, for example, be fostered through industrial development offices organized on both an industry and a regional basis. They could also be organized as state-owned development banks or other establishments by either national or local governments. By contrast, current policy in the Soviet successor states appears to concentrate on sustaining the existing inefficient production units through privatization, direct subsidies and so on, rather than creating efficient new economic entities.

9.4 THE FUTURE OF THE ECONOMIES OF THE SOVIET SUCCESSOR STATES

To understand the future of the economies of the Soviet successor states, one must be aware of their past and present, particularly the history of past economic reforms and the results of the current SLP-type reforms. The

---

[7] An estimated $23 billion left Russia in 1993 alone to go into private offshore accounts in Cyprus, Bermuda, Switzerland and other locations, dwarfing the amounts that the IMF and other nations have delivered to Russia.

system of central planning was abandoned as a result of the dissolution of the Soviet Union in December 1991, but many of the institutions and people from the earlier system were left intact. Central planning lasted in the Soviet Union from 1928 until 1985, with some reforms under Khrushchev in 1962 and additional ones under Brezhnev in 1965. It is currently fashionable for both Westerners and people from the former Soviet Union to criticize central planning, but it did lift what had been a backward and largely agricultural economy to the level of the second largest economy in the world, with the world's largest production of steel, coal, oil, wheat, shoes, and so on. This economy, built under central planning, was also able to fight and to win the biggest war in the history of the world against the Nazis, with relatively little help from its allies in the West. The postwar period under central planning witnessed significantly rising living standards and the modernization of the economy. Thus, one must give at least some credit to central planning, which, despite its well-known deficiencies and excesses, 'worked' in the Soviet context. The Soviet economist Dyachenko argued in the 1930s that the need for central planning is inversely proportional to the level of development of the economy. Just as Dyachenko had suggested, central planning, which had played the major role in the transformation of the backward economy in the earlier period, functioned less and less adequately in the later period, as recognized by all Soviet leaders since Stalin.

Even more relevant is the failure of economic reforms in the Gorbachev era, from March 1985 to the end of 1991, in the last years of the Soviet Union. Gorbachev recognized the need for fundamental reforms in the system, and he introduced various economic 'campaigns' to improve economic performance, or, in his own words, 'to raise productivity to world standards', 'to catch up', 'to accelerate development', 'to shed "sluggishness" and 'inertia,' and 'to leave behind the "era of stagnation"'. One was the anti-alcoholism campaign to reduce drunkenness, particularly in the workplace, by making vodka difficult or expensive to obtain. Instead, it had the effect of stimulating home production of vodka, with the side effect of the disappearance of sugar and a substantial reduction in tax collections. Another was the acceleration campaign to speed up the production of goods, which failed to increase output. A third was the quality improvement campaign to improve the quality of consumer goods, but which instead led to the wholesale rejection of low-quality goods by inspectors whose prior experience had been to ensure quality of military goods. A fourth was the conversion campaign, which attempted unsuccessfully to convert military plants to produce civilian goods. A fifth was the campaign for joint ventures and private initiatives that stimulated some interest but did not lead to much activity once domestic or foreign entrepreneurs assessed the difficulties and risks involved. These various attempts all failed. Each tried to do something that was impossible: to change the Soviet economy without changing the institutions of the economy. By way of contrast, while Gorbachev's economic reforms had little success, his political reforms came much closer to achieving their purpose, resulting, for example, in open elections and a free press. The establishment of political institutions but failure to establish economic institutions may, in part, explain why his political reforms achieved their purpose but his economic reforms did not.

The present situation in the Soviet successor states involves an attempt to establish a market economy through some or all of the elements of the SLP programme of stabilization, liberalization and privatization. It has, however, instead resulted in economic decline, impoverishment of the vast majority of the populations of these states, and social polarization. While more far-reaching and revolutionary than those of the Gorbachev period, the economic reforms in the Soviet successor states have a basic flaw similar to the various Gorbachev reforms to improve economic performance. Like the Gorbachev reforms, they do not take account of the lack of the relevant institutions and have little chance of succeeding without them. Conversely, if these institutions were in place, the current reforms would be much more effective. A major example is privatization as the route to a market economy. This reform is largely superficial in that little or nothing has really changed when an establishment has been privatized. As already noted, the privatized firm has the same capital, labour, management, sources of supply, sales channels and so on., as its predecessor. Thus, privatization is like a new 'Potemkin Village', where appearances only hide the reality. The incentives supposedly created by privatization fail to produce output and investment in the absence of market institutions. Rather, the incentives for managers under current conditions are to take as much as possible out of the privatized enterprises by stripping them of assets and lodging the proceeds in foreign accounts.

Altogether, privatization, whether of small enterprise or of major industry, is absorbing too many resources, including capital, managerial talent and government activity, with too little of these resources devoted to the development of new private firms and the institutions of a market economy. A better approach would have a more activist government involved in establishing such institutions and encouraging the formation of new enterprises. This more activist government might well be the national governments in the Baltic states and the smaller Soviet successor states and the local governments in Russia (the oblasts) and other large Soviet successor states.

9.5   PUBLIC AND QUASI-PUBLIC INSTITUTIONS OF A MARKET ECONOMY

Consideration of both the microeconomic foundations of a market economy and past economic reforms has led to an appreciation of the importance of the institutions of a market economy. The creation of these institutions should be a major part of the economic reform programme, with the government either fostering their creation or, if necessary, creating them directly. Some, such as the legal institutions, are the province of government in any case and are thus public institutions. For others, such as entities in banking and finance, accounting and insurance, it is possible for the government to create them and then spin them off to the private sector. They are the quasi-public institutions.

Three public institutions are of fundamental importance in establishing a market economy and, each being the province of government, their creation requires governmental initiatives, ideally in the first phase of reform. The first is a system of property rights, which would establish the basis for ownership and clarify the issue of who owns the assets in the economy.[8] Legalizing the right to own and to sell property is not enough in a society in which the state had owned many assets. The title for these assets, including much of the productive capital in the economy, land and natural resources, is now clouded in that it is not clear precisely who owns them. In many cases there are competing claimants for this capital, including managers, workers, local councils, regions and others. For the future, ownership of existing property must be determined, and, in general, property rights must be defined and understood, including such basic concepts as exclusivity (that is, the right to exclusive use of the property) and alienability (that is, the right to sell or to transfer the property). Failing this, individuals will not exercise their rights to resources in a manner facilitating production and investment.

Closely related to property rights is the second such fundamental public institution, a legal system, including a civil code and a commercial code. Property rights are part of the legal structure and lead to contracts, which form the basis of a functioning market economy. Without contract rules and mechanisms for their enforcement a market economy cannot function. Business law, including a commercial code and anti-monopoly laws, is also essential for providing a framework for market transactions of all kinds. The legal system requires much more, however, than just legislation of laws. The

---

[8]   For discussions of property rights and economic reform see (Winiecki, 1992) and (Koslowski, 1992).

government must also provide the necessary enforcement mechanisms and develop appropriate forums for the settlement of disputes.

The third such institution is a stable currency. Individual agents in a market economy must have a viable currency both as a means of making transactions as well as a unit of account and a store of value. In the absence of such money, some of the trade among enterprises has been conducted on the basis of barter arrangements, but this is an extremely inefficient way of making economic transactions, making it difficult for producing units either to obtain material inputs or to sell their products. The trade between enterprises that is not arranged on the basis of barter is being carried out in most circumstances under traditional supplier networks, with each enterprise building up debt to the others. This debt, however, must eventually be paid off by the government through increased subsidization, thereby fuelling the inflation. These old-style relationships have led to a huge inter-enterprise arrears crisis of overdue payments for goods and services that is severely undermining stabilization efforts.[9] A stable currency must be the goal of monetary and fiscal policy. This goal would be facilitated by the establishment of an efficient system of tax collection and closer control of government expenditures and the money creation process.

Other public institutions that would facilitate the formation of a market economy include state legal and regulatory agencies to prevent corruption, monopolization and other criminal activities that are not only costly in themselves but that also undermine popular support for a market economy. It is also important to develop a social safety net to replace the social services that had previously been provided by state enterprises. Both of these institutions should be part of a new social contract to replace the earlier one. The earlier social contract called for unqualified support of the party in return for its provision of subsidized housing, food and fuel, and its direct provision of social services such as education, health care and pensions. There is not yet a new social contract, but it might involve the provision of a social safety net and protection from criminal activities in return for support of the current political-economic system. The establishment of a new social contract is important to gain public support for the transition to a market economy.

In addition to these public institutions that are all the exclusive domain of government, there are several other institutions that are also essential to a functioning market economy. They are typically provided through the private

[9] The naive belief that 'hard budget constraints' could simply be applied to the old enterprises is directly responsible for this inter-enterprise arrears crisis. No one now believes that hard budget constraints will work, but the crisis is one of enormous proportions. See Whitlock (1992, pp. 33–8) and Ickes and Ryterman (1992, pp. 331–61).

sector in Western economies, but they could be provided by the government and are thus quasi-public institutions. While the history of Western economies suggests that these institutions could come into being through private initiatives, the fact is that it took centuries for their evolution in the West and the Soviet successor states do not have the time needed for their private formation. It will take governmental initiatives to foster their creation or, even better, to establish them directly, possibly to spin them off eventually to the private sector.

The first is a banking and credit system, which could finance new enterprises. Such a system of financial intermediaries is not provided by the current banks in the Soviet successor states. It may be easier to establish new entities to provide these services, including commercial and investment banks, rather than to try to change the existing ones in view of the traditional ways in which they operate and the problem they have of writing off their bad debts. Second is classified advertising, trade journals and other information systems that enable buyers and sellers to find each other. In their absence, transactions depend on traditional networks among established entities, fledgling commodity markets that help but are inadequate, use of computer networks that are innovative but inadequate to the task, and street bazaars among individuals. The government should help create markets by organizing information exchanges among potential buyers and sellers, such as publications advertising items for sale or purchase, including help wanted and jobs sought. Third is accounting, which plays a very different role in a market economy from the one it plays in a centrally planned economy. As in the case of banking, it may be easier to establish new entities to provide these services than to change the existing ones. Fourth is insurance, another quasi-public institution that plays a key role in a market economy, and the government should establish organizations providing insurance services, including special guarantees for investment. These quasi-public institutions, once established, could eventually be privatized.

9.6   POLICY ALTERNATIVES FOR THE SOVIET SUCCESSOR STATES

The official programmes of the Soviet successor states involve a continuation of some elements of the SLP approach as the strategy for reform and as a way of treating the steep declines in their economies. This approach, which has been endorsed by some Western governments and international organizations, includes further privatization and price liberalization, bankruptcy of non-viable enterprises, and control of government spending.

However, this SLP approach has already had and will continue to have significantly negative results. There was no preparation for the rapid introduction of free markets and a consumer-driven social order in terms of the establishment of the basic institutions of a market economy.[10] Furthermore, while the Communist Party hegemony has collapsed, much of its structure remains, including the social structure and culture of state socialism, the state apparatus, and the Communist Party members themselves. The managers of the state sector are resistant to change, believing that reform would undercut their position.[11] Thus, the SLP attempt at a transition to a market economy both inherited many of the institutions of the prior system and did not create the institutions necessary for a market economy. The result was not transition to a market economy but rather the collapse of the economy and its criminalization.

The International Monetary Fund has proposed its standard solutions of governmental fiscal restraint and restricted growth of the money supply, with attention focused on stopping the ongoing inflation and on balancing the international accounts. These components of the stabilization part of the SLP approach were developed for Latin America, particularly to treat the structural inflation of that region, and they involve a totally different set of problems and a different history. In particular, the Latin American economies have the market institutions that are lacking in the Soviet successor states. The Soviet successor states, in fact, have much to build on to become successful economies in the international community. They have a skilled labour force, access to some advanced technologies, a complete infrastructure and an internal market. The question is how will the necessary investment incentives be created to convert these assets into marketable products and services and to convert decline into growth?

9.7 THE CHINA MODEL

The China example might be a model for creating the necessary investment incentives. While the Soviet successor states have been experiencing declines

---

[10] By contrast, Poland was far more prepared for a policy of shock therapy owing to the prior existence of some market institutions, a strong corporatist relationship between the government and unions, and a healthier overall economic condition at the time of implementation. For discussions of the economic reform in East Europe and in other Soviet successor states see Kornai (1992, pp. 1–21), Koslowski (1992) and Ellman (1992) regarding Poland; Leijonhufvud (1993), Simonetti (1993, pp. 79–102), regarding Hungary, Poland, the Czech and Slovak Federation, and East Germany.

[11] See Winiecki (1992).

in output, employment, investment and so on, China has been growing at one of the fastest rates of any major economy in the world. It experienced a 13 per cent growth rate in both 1992 and 1993 and, while its growth may be declining, it will probably remain at or near the double-digit level for the next few years.[12] It is a mistake to dismiss the China model owing to perceived and valid differences with Europe. The fact is that much can be learned from this example.

China achieved a high growth rate by following several principles. First, it avoided political risk by postponing political reform until after economic reform had taken place. Second, it started its reform in the rural regions, thereby making the peasants rich and creating an internal market that had not existed earlier. Third, it then set up special economic zones in coastal areas, particularly in south China near Hong Kong, and in east China across from Taiwan. These zones have attracted export-oriented industry and have helped make China a leading exporter, thereby earning needed foreign exchange. The rest of the world assisted China through granting it Most-Favoured-Nation (MFN) status, helping it to create a huge export sector. Fourth, and often overlooked, China focused on the creation of new enterprises, particularly those oriented to exports, rather than on privatizing existing old enterprises. Instead of wasting scarce resources on privatizing the old economy, it concentrated on building a new economy of mainly state-owned enterprises, many of which were established by the local governments (provinces) and townships or villages. China was much more pragmatic and flexible than the other economies undergoing the transition, not insisting on changing ownership or on private enterprise, but instead requiring that the new firms be modern and export-oriented, using current technology, having good managers and workers and so on. The result has been stunning, with not only very high growth rates but also tremendous flows of capital into China

---

[12] The contrast between the steep output declines in the Soviet successor states and the huge output increases in China is a stark one. If economists had been predicting the effects of the attempted transitions to a market economy in the Soviet Union and in China as of the late 1980s, they could well have concluded that the attempt would succeed in Russia but would fail in China, given the contrast between their levels of output, particularly on a per-capita basis; given the presence of a huge internal market in the Soviet Union but its absence in China; given the presence of communications, transportation and other infrastructure in the Soviet Union but their absence in China; given the presence of a highly trained workforce in the Soviet Union but its absence in China, and so on. In fact, the outcome was just the opposite, with great increases in China and great decreases in the Soviet Union. The major explanation for the differences between the outcomes in these formerly centrally planned economies must be the differences in their approaches to economic reform.

from all over the world. China's competence in managing the transition has had an enormous pay-off. This is a model that could be followed in other nations, including the Soviet successor states, that have focused on the 'old economy', keeping old establishments going through privatization.

9.8 AN ALTERNATIVE TO PRIVATIZATION AS THE ROUTE TO A MARKET ECONOMY

There is an alternative to privatization as the route to a market economy. This alternative is to focus the programme on the 'new' economy rather than the 'old' economy, establishing new enterprises, as in the case of China, rather than concentrating on privatizing old enterprises. The contrast between these two routes to a market economy is a stark one. Consider the various aspects of enterprise involved in privatization versus the creation of new enterprise. As to managers, privatization retains the old incompetent or corrupt managers, while the creation of new enterprises leads to a search for competent and honest managers. As to workers, privatization retains the old poorly motivated, low productivity workers, while the creation of new enterprises leads to a search for the best workers. Similarly for capital, technology, distribution channels and so on.

The first step in the transition to a market economy should be the creation of the institutions on which such an economy is based, as without them a market economy cannot exist. The second step should then primarily be that of the creation of new enterprises and secondarily the reorganization of old enterprises into viable and profitable firms, which have competent managers, productive workers, modern capital and technology, secure sources of inputs and markets and so on. These firms can be state-owned or private. The third step is then that of privatization of those firms that are state owned by spinning them off to the private sector. By delaying privatization to this point, the enterprises, including newly created state owned enterprise, will be viable and valuable, making use of both the financial and other institutions of the market economy that can facilitate such a transition.

The system of privatization adopted by the Soviet successor states represents an attempt to salvage existing enterprises, which are uneconomic and thus amounts to a waste of resources, throwing 'good money' after 'bad'. By contrast, the alternative approach, based on the Chinese model, is that of focusing resources on building a 'new' economy through the creation of new enterprises, many of which are state-owned enterprises. It is at best wishful thinking to believe that these enterprises could be created from the old state enterprises, given the incompetent managers, obsolete capital, use of outmoded technologies, inappropriate scale, and so on in such enterprises.

Equally, it is wishful thinking to believe that they would be created spontaneously as new firms, given the lack of management skills, the scarcity of capital, the huge risks involved, and the policy of the state to tax profits in every way possible.

It is more realistic to base the creation of these enterprises on the actions of interested parties, including the same parties that might play a role in the development of the institutions of the economy. The state itself or local governments could play the role of a catalyst. Another possibility is investment banks, one of the financial institutions that should be created for this very purpose. External bodies might also help in the creation of the new enterprises, including foreign multinational firms; Western governments and consortia of governments such as the G7 and the Organisation for Security and Cooperation in Europe; and international organizations, including the International Monetary Fund, the World Bank, the European Bank for Reconstruction and Development, and the Organization for Economic Cooperation and Development. They could provide the Soviet successor states with the technical assistance needed to establish and to develop the basic institutions of functioning markets. A sister nation approach might also be valuable, pairing nations or groups of them with Western nations that would assist their formerly centrally planned partners in creating the modern enterprises that would form the production base for a market economy.

9.9   CONCLUSIONS AND IMPLICATIONS FOR A NEW TYPE OF POLICY

By contrast to past and current governmental and international organization policies, which involve some or all of the elements of the SLP approach, the analysis presented here implies that there may be a better route to a market economy. This alternative would entail a radically different type of policy that reconstructs the very structure of the economies of the Soviet successor states. This approach requires more activist governments than those found in the Soviet successor states after the dissolution of the Soviet Union, governments that would take major initiatives and not rely entirely on delegating economic matters to the private sector. These governments must play a major role in the transition between the centrally planned economy, which now no longer exists, and a market economy, which still does not yet exist. Activist governments should be establishing those institutions of a market economy that could not be provided by the private sector, including a system of property rights, a legal system and a sound currency. They should also be establishing and enforcing a legal code and establishing regulatory bodies to prevent asset stripping, monopolization of markets, extortion and corruption. The governments should also be establishing those quasi-public institutions that could be provided by the private sector but would take too long to develop, including entities providing accounting, advertising, banking, insurance and other services. The governments should also help in the establishment of new producing and other entities that would make use of such institutions. Finally, they should be establishing social safety nets as part of a new social contract.

As to the rest of the world, the issue is not simply that of providing foreign aid. The amounts that have been proposed are much too small to be meaningful and the Soviet successor states could well be sieves for these funds, which end up in private offshore bank accounts. It must be recognized that there are limits on what the West can do, but that the West can definitely help. It can provide technical assistance to help establish those institutions needed for a market economy to function. National governments, international organizations and consortia of governments should provide the Soviet successor states with the technical assistance needed to develop functioning markets. Such governmental or intergovernmental technical assistance should ideally be augmented by assistance from the private sector. For example, professional associations of lawyers, bankers, accountants, advertising executives and so on in the West might furnish groups of volunteers, such as recently retired professionals, to provide advice and assistance at nominal cost. Such public and private assistance should be channelled through new activist governmental programmes and new non-governmental organizations in the Soviet successor states.[13] Equally important, Western nations should open their markets to goods from the Soviet successor states, facilitating increased international trade with these states. They should also provide information and insurance and other forms of protection to encourage foreign direct and portfolio investment in these states and joint-ventures. They should also encourage visits by managers and students to Western institutions so they can appreciate what is meant by a 'market economy', which remains a mystery to many in the former Soviet Union. Access to foreign markets; to what can be provided by foreign firms in terms of capital, management, marketing skills and so on; and to learning how markets function are all of basic importance to the rebuilding of the economies of the Soviet successor states and their transition to a market economy.

---

[13] For a discussion of how aid distributed to the government should be conditioned on the implementation of institutional reforms and how aid should be directed towards the firms and individuals actually making the transition, see (Leitzel 1992, pp. 357–74).

Private capital markets would be prepared to provide financing, provided there is a reasonable prospect of profit at an acceptable level of risk. An example is China, where huge sums are flowing in from throughout the world, demonstrating that there is a global capital market. Indeed, a market test of reform is precisely whether such capital is forthcoming, whether from internal or external sources. Assuming there is market access, the forward and backward linkages from international trade could assist in establishing institutions and markets, particularly those involved in exports and imports of the Soviet successor states. Another market test of reform is whether the economies of the Soviet successor states are able to capitalize on those products that have potential markets in the West. These include not only the traditional natural resource exports, especially oil and gas, but also the products of advanced technologies that have been developed for military or space use but that have commercial potential in Western markets. Ideally, high technology products would be produced by new firms established in the Soviet successor states for export to distributors in the West, who would market them throughout Western markets. This approach would combine the high technology products and production facilities in the Soviet successor states with the marketing capabilities of firms in the West.

9.10   REFERENCES

Abalkin, L. (1992), The Current Crisis and Prospects for the Development of the Soviet Economy, *Problems of Economic Transition*, vol. 35 (June), pp. 6–13.

Alexeev, M., C. Gadd and J. Leitzel (1992), Economics in the Former Soviet Union, *Journal of Economic Perspectives*, vol. 6 (spring), pp. 137–48.

Åslund, A. (1991), Prospects for Economic Reform in the USSR, *World Bank Economic Review*, pp. 43–66.

Clague, C. and G.C. Rausser, eds (1992), *The Emergence of Market Economies in Eastern Europe*, Blackwell, Cambridge, MA.

Cooter, R.D. (1992), Organization as Property: Economic Analysis of Property Law Applied to Privatization, in C. Clague and G.C. Rausser, eds, *The Emergence of Market Economies in Eastern Europe*, Blackwell, Cambridge, MA.

Dyker , D.A. (1992), *Restructuring the Soviet Economy*, Routledge, London and New York.

Eberwein, W.-Dr.   (1992), Transformation Process in Eastern Europe: *Perpectives from the Modelling Laboratory*, Peter Lang, Frankfurt am Main.

Ellman, M. (1992), Shock Therapy in Russia: Failure or Partial Success?, *RFE/RL Research Report*, vol. 1 (28 August), pp. 112–61.

Fischer, S. (1992), Stabilization and Economic Reform in Russia, *Brookings Papers on Economic Activity*, pp. 77–111.

Fischer, S. and J. Frenkel (1992), Macroeconomic Issues of Soviet Reform, *American Economic Review*, vol. 82 (May), pp. 37–42.

Fischer, S. and A. Gelb (1991), The Process of Socialist Economic Transformation, *Journal of Economic Perspectives*, vol. 5 (fall), pp. 91–106.

Ickes, B.W. and R. Ryterman (1992), The Interenterprise Arrears Crisis in Russia, *Post-Soviet Affairs*, vol. 8, pp. 331–61.

Intriligator, M.D. (1994), Privatization in Russia Has Led to Criminalization, *Australian Economic Review*, no. 2, August.

Kornai, J. (1992), The Post-Socialist Transition and the State: Reflections in the Light of Hungarian Fiscal Problems, *American Economic Review*, vol. 82 (May), pp. 1–21.

Koslowski, R. (1992), Market Institutions, East European Reform, and Economic Theory, *Journal of Economic Issues*, vol. 26 (September), pp. 673–705.

Leijonhufvud, A. (1993a), The Nature of the Depression in the Former Soviet Union, *New Left Review*, vol. 199 (May–June), pp. 120–26.

Leijonhufvud, A. (1993b), Problems of Socialist Transformation: Kazakhstan 1991, in Lazlo Somogyi, ed., *The Political Economy of the Transformation Process in Eastern Europe*, Edward Elgar, Aldershot.

Leitzel, J. (1992), Western Aid and Economic Reform in the Former Soviet Union, *World Economy*, vol. 15, pp. 357–74.

Marer, P. and S. Zecchini, eds (1991), *The Transition to a Market Economy*. OECD, Paris.

Meiklejohn Terry, S. (1993), Thinking about Post-Communist Transitions: How Different Are They? *Slavic Review*, vol. 52, pp. 330–37.

Milner, B.Z. and D.S. Lvov, eds (1991), *Soviet Market Economy: Challenges and Reality*, North-Holland, Amsterdam.

Murrell, P. (1992), Evolutionary and Radical Approaches to Economic Reform, *Economics of Planning*, vol. 25, pp. 79–95.

Nagy, A. (1992), Institutions and the Transition to a Market Economy, in C. Clague and G.C Rausser, eds, *The Emergence of Market Economies in Eastern Europe*, Blackwell, Cambridge, MA.

Nove, A. (1993), Transition to the Market and Economic Theory, *Problems of Economic Transition*, vol. 35, pp. 20–33.

Oppenheimer, P.M. (1992), Economic Reform in Russia, *National Institute Economic Review*, vol. 82 (August), pp. 48–61.

Sachs, J.D. (1992), Privatization in Russia: Some Lessons from Eastern Europe, *American Economic Review*, vol. 82 (May), pp. 43–8.

Simonetti , M. (1993), A Comparative Review of Privatisation Strategies in Four Former Socialist Countries, *Europe–Asia Studies*, vol. 45, pp. 79–102.

Summers, L. and W. Nordhaus (1992), Stabilization and Economic Reform in Russia, *Brookings Papers on Economic Activity*, pp. 112–26.

Whitlock, E. (1992), A Borrower and a Lender Be: Interenterprise Debt in Russia, *RFE/RL Research Report*, vol. 1 (October), pp. 33–8.

Winiecki, J. (1992), The Transition of Post-Soviet-Type Economies: Expected and Unexpected Developments, *Banca Nazionale del Lavoro Quarterly Review*, vol. 181, pp. 171–90.

Wolfson, M. (1992), Transitions from a Command Economy: Rational Expectations and Cold Turkey, *Contemporary Policy Issues*, vol. 10 (April), pp. 35–43.

10. Introducing New Currencies in the Baltic Countries: A Comment

T.M. Rybczynski

My task is to comment on the analysis and evaluation of the process of introducing new currencies and policy implications discussed in the chapter by Sutela and Lainela.

The chapter covers four topics. They are, why a new currency was introduced; how the new currency was introduced and to what extent this process differed in three countries; to what degree and in what way results and consequence differed in the three countries; and the problems facing these countries at present.

Before taking up these issues, there are two problems which deserve a brief comment: the first is that the introduction of new currencies in the three countries was not unprecedented. They had to tackle similar tasks and somewhat similar problems had to be resolved by the three Baltic countries and Finland after World War I when, together with Central European countries, they became independent. All of them had to set up a central bank, or similar authority, endow it with statutes governing its working and decide on the nature of its link with the international monetary system. In those cases where the problem was entirely new, the solution was more difficult to find and took much longer. However, to the extent that the model then developed and accepted in the West was virtually the same as reflected in the 'conventional wisdom' embodied in the recommendation of the Genoa Conference favouring the adoption of a gold exchange standard, the choice was limited. However, it was not until 1927 when Estonia formally adopted the gold exchange standard that the process of building the new institution and accepting new constraints was completed. This contrasts with the period of only four years that it has now taken to cover a similar path. The shorter time taken on this occasion is a reflection of what is described as a 'collective learning' experience accumulated and embodied in the general cultural wealth and used to assist the process of rebuilding the institutional framework previously created.

The second general issue that deserves comment is the significantly greater complexity of the task facing the authorities in these countries. This was owing to the need to fundamentally re-orient their monetary, financial as well as productive and trade structure from being a fully integral part of the economy of the former USSR and to link it with world prices, commerce and production, thereby breaking their almost complete insulation and isolation from activities outside Iron Curtain countries.

The re-establishment of the new institutional framework governing economic and political fields required the introduction of formal and informal rules as well as an enforcement mechanism for their observance. While formal rules (laws, constitution and so on) are and have been built on the basis of those created in the inter-war period, informal rules (conventions, self-imposed codes, norms of behaviour), along with their enforcement mechanism require a long period to be fully understood and accepted. Furthermore, at a micro-level, an entirely new complex of skills has come into existence in the West, as with for example rules relating to accounting auditing, banking, risk evaluation and assessment, investment ranking, quality standards, patents and so on, which had to be learned virtually from the beginning.

At a macro-level, new rules have to be introduced relating to the proper operation of markets, for example, competition, freedom of entry based on and revolving around the three central pillars of a democratically based market economy, property rights, an independent judiciary and a multi-party political structure.

The introduction of these new modes of behaviour and rules was bound to be more difficult, especially in the initial stage after World War II because prior to the 1917 Revolution, the Baltic states were reasonably well integrated into the world economy having in essence institutions based on similar principles, that is, reasonably free and unrestricted trade, currency convertibility (the rouble was on the gold standard) and the benefits of unhindered and free capital movement. To tackle, rebuild and re-orient profoundly distorted social, institutional and economic structures, including monetary architecture, posed an especially formidable problem.

The fact that the phase of building and rebuilding the basic institutional framework for a market economy took only four years testifies to the strength of political determination and the importance of 'path dependence' in the evolution of countries and nations.

Let us now examine the first of the four topics, discussed in the chapter, that is, the reasons for introducing a new currency. There is of course wholehearted agreement with the view put forward by the authors that a new currency is of crucial importance and significance as a sign of sovereignty and independence especially for countries which had been subject to a prolonged period of foreign rule. The psychological impact of the introduction of a country's own currency is undoubtedly particularly significant and has had and continues to have far-reaching political consequence.

Alongside the psychological benefits, there are also fairly mundane but not entirely unimportant gains of seigniorage whose contribution to the public sector's receipts cannot be disregarded.

The second reason for introducing a new currency adduced by the authors is that it enables the authorities to pursue an independent monetary policy. This, however, must be qualified. It must be emphasized, that the introduction of a new currency does not necessarily have to be associated with the pursuit of independent monetary policy. Independent monetary policy gives the authorities the power to regulate the money supply (and short-term interest rates but not long-term interest rates) in any way that they deem desirable. A rapid increase in the money supply – to finance a public sector deficit or to stimulate activity and employment – may, however, result in strong inflationary pressures, a deterioration on current account and ultimately a depreciation of the currency, if a floating exchange regime is adopted, or a forced devaluation if a fixed exchange rate regime is in existence.

The choice of pursuing an independent monetary policy and all that this implies need not be taken because the authorities may prefer to link the new currency to a non-inflationary currency by adopting a currency board arrangement. Under this arrangement, all domestic money supply must be 100 per cent covered by foreign currency reserves and money supply will be determined by the behaviour of the balance of payments: expanding when there is a surplus or contracting when there is a deficit. The main arguments used in favour of currency board arrangements are that they prevent inflationary financing of a public sector deficit and create an anchor of stability.

In a wider context, the question of the degree of independence of monetary policy must be linked with the degree of convertibility and restrictions on current and capital account. Full convertibility on current account and a fairly liberal approach to capital inflow in a world characterized by free capital movements amounting at present to over $1 trillion a day (in Anglo-Saxon terminology) means that the net inflow of capital over and above the current account deficit will also lead to an increase in the money supply. This capital inflow gives rise to inflationary pressures unless it is sterilized and in the medium and long run offset by a tighter fiscal policy.

For countries where the financial system is in a relatively early phase of development, that is, where capital and credit markets are shallow and banks are the main savings-collecting and saving-allocating institutions, sterilization may be impossible.

Looked at from this point of view the question of independence of monetary policy is linked to the type of exchange regime. Here there are a number of possibilities starting from a fixed but adjustable exchange rate, which accidentally includes currency board arrangements, to a fully floating regime.

One additional reason, that supports the case for new currency and foreign independence with the central bank pursuing the objective of price stability, is that this will be conducive to the development of financial institutions and markets on the 'bottom up' basis. This, in turn, might reinforce the process of economic growth by stimulating financial innovation on the one side and necessitating the creation of an appropriate supervisory framework on the other. Such a framework is indispensable in order to provide security for savers and investors and to avoid financial instability.

The decision to introduce a new currency must take into account these various elements and the benefits and costs that they will bring to existing conditions. There are some benefits such as confidence in a currency whose benefits in the short term are very large indeed; there are medium-term costs and benefits such as those associated with the choice of exchange rate regime and convertibility which change over time and which are not possible to quantify. All of these must be judged by reference to the ability of the authorities to pursue the aim of price stability while smoothing adjustment to shocks arising outside and within a country.

The second issue raised by the authors is 'how to introduce a new currency'. The main questions here are the timing of the introduction, the degree of cohabitation with the old and other currencies, the conversion coefficient employed and, in the case of the Baltic countries, the use of the rouble in the hands of the authorities.

These questions are partly questions of logistics, that is, the arrangements for printing distribution and storage, the period allowed for conversion and announcement, the coefficients applied to various types of deposit and the treatment of non-resident assets and liabilities. All these aspects involve costs and benefits. Questions of policy are also involved in relation to conversion term and treatment of non-resident claims and assets.

The different approaches adopted by the three Baltic countries, the reasons behind them and the somewhat different problems they face are analysed in a perceptive way by the authors providing a clear picture of what has happened.

The three Baltic countries selected different combinations of these three elements. While there has been a significant degree of convergence since the original decision, the present mix adopted by each of the three countries differs from each other. Estonia opted for a 'shock treatment'. Its mix comprised an immediate exchange of roubles into new currency (the kroon) in June 1992, a simultaneous banning of the use of other currencies and the pegging of exchange rates to the deutschmark by means of a currency board. There were also minor restrictions on current and capital account convertibility which were, however, largely phased out first in 1993 and then removed completely in March 1994.

Latvia adopted a gradualist approach. She introduced the Latvian rouble in May 1992 and its own currency, the Lat, in June 1993. Although prices had to be expressed in Lats, the use of foreign currencies was allowed. The gradualist approach to the introduction of a new currency was combined with the adoption of a flexible exchange rate regime until February 1994 when the Lat was pegged to the SDR.

This flexible exchange regime was of the dirty float variety with the central bank intervening directly to maintain the exchange rate at a desirable and fairly stable level. The floating regime in place until February 1994 and the subsequent pegged regime has been accompanied by full convertibility on current and capital account for residents and non-residents alike.

Lithuania also adopted a gradual but also prolonged approach. A temporary new currency, tallons, was introduced in May 1992 circulating alongside the rouble. In September 1992, the tallons became the sole legal tender and the rouble was withdrawn. However, foreign currencies could be used with special permission. The tallon was replaced by a new currency, the litas, in June 1993 and the use of foreign currencies was banned. Until the autumn of 1993, there were dual exchange rates: the free market rate and the official rate. From the autumn of 1993 until April 1994, the exchange rate regime was a floating rate with the authorities intervening directly to preserve stability in terms of the US dollar at around 3.9 litas. However, since April 1994, the litas has been pegged to the US dollar by means of a currency board arrangement. The litas has been convertible on current account since the introduction of national currency. Capital account convertibility is controlled but the approach is liberal.

The present position is that all three countries have a national currency. All three countries peg their exchange rate. However, Estonia pegs to the deutschmark, Latvia to SDRs and Lithuania to the US dollar. Estonia and Lithuania have currency board arrangements and cannot pursue an independent monetary policy. Latvia's link with the international monetary system is through the Latvian central bank intervening to maintain stability of the exchange rate. All three countries have full convertibility on current account but Lithuania has some modest restrictions on capital account.

The next topic discussed in the chapter by Sutela and Lainela is the results achieved by introducing new currencies and the factors underlying the introduction. One outstanding result that all three countries have achieved is a reduction of inflation on a monthly basis to a single digit figure by early 1994 accompanied by the prospect of a further slow-down. This result cannot be only attributed to a tight monetary policy associated with the exchange rate regime but also to a highly supportive fiscal policy stance, involving a balanced budget, accompanied by price liberalization, privatization and above all the initial adoption of a low external value of currency. The adoption of a low external value resulting in a large gap between the real values of their currencies and the currencies to which they are pegged (and those linked to them) has enabled them to absorb strong inflationary impulses emanating from cost pressures, the deterioration in the terms of trade and the overall balance of payments surplus linked to inflow of capital.

The three lessons that the experience of the Baltic countries provides are that stable exchange rates require the support of a responsible fiscal policy, as pursued consistently by all of them; that stability of external values can be helped by the adoption of a peg; and that the adoption of an undervalued exchange rate provides a cushion and room for manoeuvre for the absorption of external and domestic shocks. However, the time purchased is not unlimited and must be used for creating arrangements conducive to stable and non-inflationary growth.

The last topic relates to the problems presently confronting these three economies, especially in relation to monetary aspects. The inflationary pressures, although declining, are appreciably higher than in the countries to which their currencies are pegged. Thus, the question is how and when existing arrangements relating to exchange rates (that is, currency boards or formal peg) are changed and in what way. Apart from the fact that the present rate will have to be lowered sooner or later, there is no doubt that the process of changes in relative (domestic) prices has still some way to go, and further inflationary impulses (domestic and external) are bound to occur.

The pressure for changing the originally accepted exchange rate arrangements have been reinforced recently by a large net inflow of capital. In addition to direct investment, this inflow has also comprised financial investments to benefit from high interest rates and convertibility. To deal with their problems, a simple change in 'parity' in the case of currency board arrangements may still be conducive to stabilization policy as would be also a shift to an adjustable peg (of a Latvian variety). The former has some attraction because currency boards cannot change the peg more than once or twice, following which its credibility disappears. At the same time, an adjustable peg arrangement appears to be conducive to the development of an independent financial structure (institutions and markets) which may not only assist the implementation of monetary policy but may also be conducive to economic growth. Another approach is to adopt a reasonably wide range of fluctuations around parity, that is, an adjustable peg with a wide band.

Ultimately the choice between these basic approaches – and I exclude flexible rates and 'tablita' since they lack domestic and foreign credibility – will depend on the importance attached to the credibility of monetary policy as such and the importance attached to the need to build a viable and expanding financial structure. In the longer perspective, this choice was not available after World War I when a fixed exchange rate and membership of the gold exchange standard was the only option. Viewed in this light, the choice of future path and the character and role of monetary policy in the overall economic policy mix will be more difficult and will be determined mainly by the trade-off between inflation and employment in the context of political pressures and friction. To that extent, this problem is not dissimilar to that experienced by both developing and developed market economies. The latter are now characterized by the emergence of three currency blocs and the marked volatility of their currencies in terms of each other, affecting the external values of currencies linked to them and posing the question of the nature of the external link they adopt. To that extent their current problems are more formidable than they were after World War I and require different approaches.

What is the net balance of costs and benefits from the introduction of new currencies in the Baltic states? To answer this question we compare two alternatives. The first is that the Baltic countries had remained in the 'Rouble Area', and the second consists of adopting a somewhat different approach as regards 'technical' aspects such as timing, announcement, cohabitation with the rouble and other currencies, conversion terms and so on.

Using the basic test of being able to improve price performance there is no doubt that the Baltic countries have been quite successful. It must likewise be said that they have accepted that the main aim of monetary policy must be the achievement of price stability with regard to the shocks and pressures emanating from abroad. A particular source of external shocks has been the rouble area in relation to the import prices of energy, raw materials and other products.

The Baltic countries have succeeded in re-establishing appropriate institutions and clearing mechanisms to run monetary policy and conduct all types of international transactions. They have created different types of links with the international monetary systems in relation to the direction and composition of trade and capital movements. They have created and established appropriate supervisory frameworks designed to help the development of financial institutions.

Furthermore, they have opted for different mixes of monetary and foreign exchange policies but all of them have emphasized the need for prudent fiscal policy. In retrospect it now seems that the differences in timing and the methods adopted can be attributed predominantly to 'technical' factors and the need to arrive at an intelligible and politically acceptable approach. This holds true particularly in relation to the phasing-out of the rouble, the conversion coefficients for the rouble balances, the management of these balances vis-à-vis the former USSR and the convertibility on current and capital account. In introducing the new arrangements, the three countries were able to rely on gold and foreign exchange reserves returned to them by the Western countries where they were deposited before World War II.

The decisions taken regarding the determination of the currency values in the three countries have had to take account of the need to adopt tight fiscal policies in order to maintain convertibility. The implementation of such policies has necessitated the disciplining of financial institutions, particularly banks, with the result that some 'bailing out' operations have been needed and may still be needed in the future. This has also been true of other post-Communist (as well as Western) countries and must be regarded as a part of the 'learning process' in establishing a new financial system and an entirely new currency.

Sutela and Lainela's chapter is bound to help our understanding of the basic factors at work when introducing a new currency and the special conditions which have operated in the case of the Baltic countries.

11. Eastern Europe in Transition

Oldrich Kyn

11.1 INTRODUCTION

It has been said many times that the fall of communism in 1989 came to many as a big surprise. It was a surprise even to most experts on Soviet and East European politics and economics. What was really surprising – at least to me – was not just the fall of communism but the relatively peaceful way that the communists gave up power in most of the Soviet Union and Eastern Europe. Of course, Bosnia and Chechnya keep us aware that there were exceptions to this dictum.

It was not long after 1989 that the international community was exposed to additional surprises. First, we learned that the transition from a totalitarian system to political democracy and from central planning to the free market economy is much more difficult than anyone could have believed. It has taken longer than expected and all the countries in transition suffered unparalleled economic setbacks. Second, once we were finally convinced that the East European peoples had departed once and for all from that period of their history, they started to re-elect the former communists to power. Finally, at the same time as the arguments about the merits and weaknesses of shock therapy and privatization reached a climax, almost all the East European countries resumed economic growth irrespective of the strategy that they actually adopted.

All these surprises suggest that we may have misunderstood or misinterpreted the historical circumstances and conditions and that some reconsideration of conventional wisdom may be due. I shall start by formulating alternative hypotheses and then reflect on the evidence from the Baltic and other East European countries as presented in the papers and discussions of this conference and in various other publications.

11.2 WHY COLLAPSE?

The first question which comes to my mind is 'Why did communism collapse?' This question was rarely asked, perhaps because the collapse and its abrupt arrival appeared ex post inevitable. The answer to this question may hold important clues for the understanding of the bewildering developments in today's Eastern Europe. Let me state three – not necessarily exclusive – hypotheses about the possible reasons for collapse.

A1:   The unsoundness of central planning hypothesis: administrative central planning was unable to reach a sufficient level of economic coordination so that the economic collapse as well as the ensuing political collapse were inevitable.

A2:   The insufficient dynamism hypothesis: although central planning may have been able to achieve a certain basic level of economic coordination it had not been able to generate such vigorous technical change and innovations as the free market economy. As a result the centrally planned economies lagged behind the West in the rate of economic growth. Communism collapsed because the population was not willing to tolerate the increasing gap in the standard of living any further.

A3:   Bad implementation hypothesis: there is nothing wrong with the idea of socialism and central planning, it was just badly implemented.

The next set of hypotheses relates to the difficulties of economic transformation.

B1:   The improved allocative efficiency hypothesis: the transition to a market economy will improve incentives and lead to a more efficient allocation of resources.

B2:   The misdiagnosis hypothesis: official statistics misrepresent reality. In particular, they fail to sufficiently capture spontaneously growing private economic activity and also overstate the decline in real consumption.

B3:   The vacuum or discoordination hypothesis: according to this hypothesis, market economy and command economy are two distinct coordinative mechanisms that work on completely different principles. During transition one has to be dismantled before the other can be created, leading to a temporary discoordination.

B4:   Cost of transition hypothesis: transition to a market economy requires reallocation of resources, retraining people and creating new institutions. All that is costly and time consuming.

B5:   Fragmentation hypothesis: the end of communism resulted in the breakup of COMECON and the dissolution of multinational states.

Fragmentation cut the supply links and reduced the internal markets for domestic products.

B6: Demand 'pull-down' hypothesis: uncertainty in relation to the transition caused a radical decline in investment which together with the already mentioned decline of foreign demand and real consumption led to diminished aggregate demand.

B7: Wrong transition strategy hypothesis: politicians who obtained power were either incompetent or wrongly advised and chose incorrect transition strategies.

Several if not all of the B hypotheses may actually be valid at the same time. The point is not to accept or reject any of them but rather to show how much and in what time frame each of them contributed to the perils of transition. This knowledge is relevant especially for judging the appropriateness of various transformation strategies. The problem is, of course, that it might be impossible to separate the effect of the factors mentioned from the effect of the strategy itself. The hypothesis B7 states that wrongly chosen strategies may have been a significant cause of the economic decline during transition. This could also explain why different countries did not suffer equally. It is quite obvious that no country escaped a significant decline in GDP and industrial production, increase of unemployment and at least a temporary surge of inflation. It is, however, equally clear that the extent of these setbacks was quite different in different countries. For example the estimated fall in GDP amounted only to 20–25 per cent in Visegrad countries (Poland, the Czech Republic, Slovakia, Hungary) and Slovenia, while it reached 40–60 per cent in other East European countries and the successor states of the former Soviet Union. Even larger differences have been observed in rates of inflation and unemployment. Are these disparities owing primarily to different strategies used or do they have some other causes? Three additional hypotheses can be formulated to explain the differences mentioned.

C1: Geographic location hypothesis: East European countries located in close proximity to Western Europe suffered less.

C2: Level of economic development hypothesis: more developed countries could make the transition to market economy with lower costs.

C3: Historical and cultural traditions hypothesis: historical experiences, customs, beliefs and attitudes made some nations better inclined to part with communism and accept a market system.

Let us now look more closely at the individual hypotheses. The first hypothesis A1 corresponds to the old views of von Mises and Hayek. It had little support after World War II but became quite popular again after 1989. It is probably true, although I am not sure whether it can ever be proved independently of hypothesis A2. Maybe the centrally planned command economy could actually work if completely isolated from capitalism on some remote planet preferably outside the Solar system. It seems clear, however, that it has not been able to keep up in competition with the vigorous dynamics of capitalist economies as postulated by hypothesis A2. Of course, this is my personal view which is perhaps shared by some of my colleagues but other people may have different belief about the validity of these hypotheses.

For example Michael Ellman clearly rejected A1 when he wrote: 'it seems to me wrong to place the blame for the collapse on the system exclusively. In an earlier period, the system was quite compatible with rapid economic progress. I see the collapse of the Soviet economic system at the end of the 1980s as a contingent phenomenon, resulting from the interaction of the system, the economic policies pursued, and the domestic and international environment in which it found itself' (Ellman, 1993, p. 2). He then vehemently supports hypothesis A2: 'The former Soviet system collapsed, in my opinion, because of its inability to compete successfully with the OECD countries and because of the response of its leadership to this failure. The crucial spheres of this competition concerned personal consumption and technical progress' (Ellman, 1993, p. 3).

Grzegorz Kolodko also rejected A1: 'one should not oversimplify the conclusion drawn from the historical experience of the CPEs. It is not true, as recently and quite often suggested, that under a centrally planned economy allocation of resources was always inefficient and investment was largely wasted . . . One cannot negate the fact, that in several cases . . . the CPEs exercised firm economic growth' (Kolodko, 1993, pp. 44–5). He then seems to suggest that what appeared to be the economic collapse of communism, may have been – at least partly – explainable by cyclical fluctuations in rates of economic growth and by external shocks: 'During 40 years of their history there were some sort of growth cycles . . . For a more recent period, however, . . . the picture is less bright. The condition has clearly deteriorated in almost all CPEs . . . due mainly to the CPEs' lack of proper adjustment to the supply shocks of the 1970s' (Kolodko, 1993, p. 45). If I read it correctly Kolodko implies that the system might have not collapsed if it could only have been isolated from external shocks.

11.3   SYSTEM DESIGN

The relative inefficiency of the Soviet-type system has been documented many times. One of the striking pieces of evidence – quoted in Niels Mygind's chapter – is the finding (Dellebrant, 1992) that Estonia and Finland were at about the same level in 1940 and that in 1990 Estonia had only around 40 per cent of Finland's GDP.

The question about the causes of the collapse of communism is closely related to another question, namely why the capitalist market economy proved to be more efficient and dynamic than the centrally planned command economy. There are several and again not necessarily mutually exclusive answers:

1) Traditionally the most common answer has been that the neoclassical view of allocative efficiency and the Pareto optimality of the market economy has been superior to the distortions and misallocations of the command economy.

2) A second explanation is based on the informational efficiency of decentralized markets and the costs of overcentralization in a command economy.

3) Third, the better incentives in privately owned firms lead to more rational management decisions, more intensive innovations and more rapid technical change.

4) In several recent papers, Pavel Pelikan has promoted an innovative view of the importance of private ownership for the efficient allocation of 'economic competence'.

5) Finally, one can see also a substantial difference in the way the two systems change their organizational structure. The centralized reorganizations in a command economy are acts of social engineering which can have disastrous effects because they have not been subjected to the 'survival' tests before being implemented. On the other hand the market economy is a self-organizing system in which spontaneously appearing mutations survive only if they prove to be viable. Its evolution resembles Darwinian natural selection. The crucial difference is in the opportunity to try diverse structures. Private ownership of capital guarantees that a multitude of new ideas is tried, even if some of them may appear absurd on the first glance. In a command economy with public ownership only what seems to be most rational to the members of the 'committee' will be tried.

Depending on their perceptions of these causes, different people may regard different target systems and different transitional strategies as desirable.

The important questions to decide are:

a)   How essential is the rapid liberalization of internal and external markets?

b)   How essential is the rebuilding of the institutions of the free market economy and especially how essential is rapid privatization?

c)   What kind of role should government play in the target system and during the transition towards it?

Answers to these questions may be important for understanding the motives of post-communist politicians. Do they aim for the free capitalist market economy based on private property and minimal government intervention, or for some kind of third way 'social market economy' with government 'guiding' the market by enforcing strong social policies and possibly maintaining a large chunk of the economy in state ownership? The reluctance to liberalize markets rapidly and to privatize state-owned firms may be an indication of the latter position.

11.4   THE THIRD WAY

Probably only a minority believes today in hypothesis A3. Hardly anybody would openly ask for the restoration of Soviet-type communism, but some may still believe that market socialism or some kind of the 'third way' rather than the return to capitalism should be the target.

Immediately after the 'Velvet Revolution' in 1989, Ota Sik, the father of the 'Third Way' concept, returned to Prague with the hope of implementing his ideas there. According to his own description (Sik, 1990), the target system was not to be much different from some versions of Western capitalism. Markets for goods, labour and capital were supposed to be almost completely free and government was supposed to avoid discretionary interventions as much as possible. The main role of the government was to set the institutional framework for the economy and to use the tools of economic policy for achieving social goals. Sik did say, though, that he favoured some forms of 'macroeconomic programming'. Some remnants of socialism would be encountered in combining various forms of property rights: private, cooperative, state and employee co-ownership in private firms. Employees would be able to participate in management and profits. Sik claimed that such a system – he was not sure whether to call it socialist or not – would guarantee full employment, economic efficiency and elimination of the conflicts between labour and capital. But even that was too much for the post-communist generation.

They refused to listen to him and set the country on the path leading directly to a highly liberal form of capitalism. Their idea is succinctly summarized in the following recent statement of Vaclav Klaus:

The fashionable ideologies of the fifties and sixties suggesting the crucial role of governments, state ownership, planning, development agencies and development aid are over. The old utopian dreams of social engineering are forgotten and it has been more and more accepted that everything starts with an individual human being, with his or her behavior and activity, with free markets, private property, and private initiative. The collapse of communism gave a final blow to the previous etatist thinking (Klaus, 1995).

Mario Nuti believed that market socialism was feasible and would have been an improvement over the traditional Soviet-type system. He blamed communist politicians for their inability to implement the appropriate reforms:

> speculation about a possible alternative model of "market socialism" - a "Third Way" – is a purely intellectual exercise . . . It cannot possibly involve claims to superiority over the capitalist system but it might well have been an improvement over the half measures taken in the name of reform. However, market socialism today cannot be regarded as a blueprint for action in Central Eastern Europe: obtuse procrastination on the part of past and present socialist leaders . . . has made it impossible for anything but a version of capitalism to be the target model for Central Eastern European countries: when a boat is sinking, it is no time to experiment with the floating properties of alternative rafts (Nuti, 1992, pp. 19–20).

Historical developments also forced John Roemer to revise considerably his idea of market socialism. It now differs from pure capitalism mostly by using 'coupons' to simulate popular ownership of capital.

> My intent is to propose an economic mechanism that differs quite modestly from the successful capitalist market economies: a lesson of the Bolshevik experience is that one is ill-advised to redesign too many moving parts in a complex machine at the same time. . . . The market socialism that I have outlined is a pale shadow of what Marx thought possible, or of the Bolsheviks' utopian dream. It is a society in which many of the conflicts of capitalist society would remain (Roemer, 1993, pp. 105–06).

Niels Mygind pointed to the importance of a 'value system'. He is certainly right about that, but he also seemed to imply that people of Eastern Europe with histories, cultures and value systems different from the West should aim for target systems that are more akin to them, that is for systems that presumably lie somewhere in between the decentralized individualist capitalism of the West and the former centralized collectivist system of the East. I disagree. What is here perceived as the value system of East Europeans may have been just the value system of their rulers. In a totalitarian society it is impossible to determine what people really want, because their will cannot be manifested, and because they are subjected to intense ideological manipulation. But let us admit that people – whether this was their 'natural' preference or not – actually embraced the collectivist values imposed on them by past propaganda. Does it mean that some mix of market and planning will be better suited for them than the pure market economy? I do not think so. I doubt that any combination of (command) planning and market forces is appropriate. Certainly, market systems have had variations relating to diverse cultures and historical traditions; however, not all of these variants were equally efficient. Any large interventions by the government that severely restricted or deformed private property rights, free pricing and competition always resulted in reduced performance by the market system. It is a misconception to believe that owing to different cultures and historical traditions the optimal arrangements of, for example, Asian markets should be substantially different from the optimal arrangements of European or American markets. Similarly, it is bad advice to tell East Europeans that because of their values and traditions they should preserve a higher degree of planning and collectivism in their economic system.

The preference for a 'third way' solution is even more visible in the chapter by Hans Aage. He pleads for a partial retention of state ownership and claims that 'the requirements of restructuring are so overwhelming that they can hardly be fulfilled by the invisible hand of the market, unless it receives some badly needed assistance from a firm and visible government policy'. How does Aage support this position? First, he says that 'a well functioning market economy . . . is not an original, natural state of economic life' and that 'it requires a complex system of legal, political and social structures that took five centuries to establish in Western Europe, and a further 200 years to establish a civilized, socially acceptable system'. Second, he says that high taxation restricts private property rights anyway: 'a 50 per cent profits tax that has full loss offset corresponds to a 50 per cent state ownership concerning the right to income. A tax on capital gains is similarly the equivalent of state ownership of part of the right to the capital value.' Third, he brings forward a frequently repeated example of some Asian growth economies (Japan, South Korea, China) that used 'comprehensive state intervention' to achieve fast growth. Fourth, he mentions the case of some Polish state enterprises that were reported to improve their efficiency during transition. Finally, he suggests that 'there is growing scepticism, for both theoretical and empirical reasons, towards unregulated market forces and trade liberalization.'

I am not impressed. Should we believe with Aage that because the East European countries missed seven centuries of the development of market institutions they would be better off retaining some state ownership? This is ridiculous. Eastern Europe missed at most 50 years of those seven centuries

(70 years in the case of the former Soviet Union), and the economic implications of the difference between private and state ownership goes far beyond the 'taxation equivalence'. The crucial thing is who makes decisions. It is true that 50 per cent taxation restricts private property rights somewhat, but the decisions are still made by owners and managers of private firms. If state ownership were to be retained, decisions would remain in the hands of state bureaucrats who would most likely continue to produce negative value added. It may be true that under the pressure of hard budget constraints some managers of state-owned enterprises began to behave in a more business-like manner, but there is also plenty of evidence to the contrary. In any case managers of state enterprises would probably need strong guarantees that their enterprise would not be privatized in the foreseeable future to prevent the 'pre-privatization malaise'. Pavel Pelikan showed in his chapter quite well why China may not be a good model for Eastern Europe. I want to add just one point here: political freedom and democracy were among the main goals of the recent revolutions of East European people. I do not think they would welcome our suggestion that in a Chinese manner they should postpone the achievement of these two goals until after the economic transition was accomplished in a well-organized way under the firm hand of the government.

Michael Intriligator came out with another version of 'historical tradition' and 'third way' solution. Not unlike Ellman or Kolodko, he believes that Soviet planning played a positive role at low levels of development and became a burden only in recent years. 'Thus, one must give at least some credit to central planning, which, despite its well-known deficiencies and excesses, "worked" in the Soviet context.' He also makes a reference to the controversial view of Dyachenko that 'the need for central planning is inversely proportional to the level of development'. Intriligator believes that sudden liberalization and privatization is a bad policy. At least for the foreseeable future, the goal should have been not a *laissez-faire* system, but a mixed economy with strong activist government that would concentrate on institution building and reorganization of the economy. The inefficient state-owned gigantic firms should not have been privatized but rather either left to wither away or to be privatized at some future date, when their efficiency improved. The new efficient enterprises should be created by state, local administrations, investment banks, foreign firms and international organizations.

Now I move to the B hypotheses. Again, I want to draw attention to the difference between what has actually been happening and what may have been perceived by people or politicians. At the very beginning, that is in 1989 and 1990, people mostly expected a relatively short period of economic adjustment, a quick increase of efficiency and resumption of economic growth.   This was partly based on casual observations and partly on neoclassical economics.

11.5   THE ROAD TO ECONOMIC GROWTH

When the Iron Curtain was raised, and people were allowed to travel more freely, they immediately noticed the significantly higher standards of material consumption in Western Europe. Naturally they attributed the discrepancy to the higher efficiency of the market system and believed that the transition to a market economy would allow them to attain Western consumption standards. As Niels Mygind puts it: 'some people in the euphoria of freedom had expected that their country would take a jump into the Western market economy and the Western standard of living'.

In terms of economic theory, this is a question of an efficiency or welfare gain owing to improved allocation of resources. It was presumed that owing to distorted prices and faulty incentives, central planners and firm managers misallocate resources and therefore Pareto optimality could not be reached under a command economy. Transition to the market would remove price distortions and lead to a more efficient allocation of resources. A welfare gain would be noticeable almost immediately.

The variation of the above neoclassical view is represented in the chapter 'Structural Adjustment, Efficiency, and Economic Growth' by Torvaldur Gylfason. Although he analyses the efficiency gains from the liberalization of international trade rather than from the liberalization of the domestic market, the basic logic of the argument is the same. According to his estimates based on 'plausible parameter values', the liberalization of international trade can increase efficiency by 7– 40 per cent. Using the same resources every year, the country's output may be increased by that proportion now and every year thereafter. Gylfason concludes that the present value – at a 5 per cent discount rate – of the infinite stream of increased production amounts to 1.4– 8 times the GDP of the country. And this is only the external trade liberalization effect. The effect would be much greater when domestic market liberalization is taken into consideration. But even this is not all. A more efficient market economy would lead a more rapid rate of economic growth increasing even further the present value of future economic gains.

Gylfason's figures of 1.4–8 times GDP look really very impressive. But what does a present value of the future stream of GDP mean? Drawing the parallel with a single firm, it ought to be the market value of its assets. At a 5 per cent discount rate, the present value of the constant annual GDP of size 1 would give us a market value of assets equal to 20. The annual size 1.07 would give 21.4 and the annual size 1.4 would give the asset value 28. We are back to more realistic figures of 7–40 per cent increase of national wealth. This looks more moderate but it is still not what happened in Eastern Europe. GDP has been declining for at least three to four years and the market value of economic assets decreased if anything. This example epitomizes the problems with allocative efficiency hypothesis B1. Neoclassical economics need not be wrong about the allocative efficiency of markets, but Gylfason's type of analysis disregards the cost and the time needed for transformation. Here hypothesis B4 becomes relevant. It is naive to think that the new system can use the same resources and just allocate them more efficiently. Some of the old equipment is so obsolete that it has to be discarded. The restructuring of the economy is costly. People need to be retrained and need time for adjustment. Certainly Gylfason does talk about temporary disequilibriums and a decline of output before 'resources are drawn into more productive employment than before and the decline of aggregate output is gradually reversed'. But he does seems to imply that eventually all the resources will be reallocated into more productive uses. 'Output continues to rise until all profit opportunities have been exploited in full and full employment has been restored at a higher level of output than initially'. He must also be thinking about relatively rapid adjustments, because in his present value calculations, everything happens within the first year.

Let me give a counter-example. Assume a middle case in which the efficiency is permanently increased by 20 per cent. I will use, however, a 10 per cent discount rate to reflect a higher level of risk. (Note that the average stock market risk premium in the USA has been around 9 per cent.) Using Gylfason's approach with an immediate increase of efficiency, we obtain a 20 per cent increase in present value. If we assume more realistically that output will first decline and only later increase, we will achieve a very different picture. For example the time path of output may look as follows: 90 per cent, 70 per cent, 60 per cent, 70 per cent, 80 per cent, 90 per cent, 100 per cent, 110 per cent, 120 per cent, 120 per cent . . . This pattern of transition will give us a decline of present value by 5 per cent. Note that from year nine onwards output is always 20 per cent above the initial state, although the temporary decline in the first three years combined with a high risk premium still results in a 5 per cent decline of the market value of economic assets. Even less favourable results would be obtained if we acknowledged that some of the resources would be lost or expended in transition so that the final increase of output would be less than 20 per cent. Strangely enough this indicates that the transition from command to market economy might never have been accomplished as a private investment venture since it is too costly and too risky. This may explain why the promises of massive financial aid by Western governments never really materialized. As Gunnar Eliasson puts it: 'When the former Soviet empire collapsed, it was believed, quite plausibly that enormous investment resources would be needed to restore run-down communist economies to industrial nations. This massive investment boom would be privately and socially profitable. . . . This scenario has failed to materialize, at least so far.'

The misdiagnosis hypothesis B2 surfaced soon after the data began to show that the popular expectations of quick efficiency gains were not materializing. Probably the most outspoken proponent of this hypothesis was Jeffrey Sachs who in numerous lectures, discussions and publications claimed that the observed fall of output and real consumption in Poland immediately after the Big Bang in January 1990 was mostly imaginary.

> The usual listing of the costs is well known, because it is almost a mantra repeated by reporters and political opponents of the reforms: living standards down by a third, unemployment soaring, and real output down by 30 percent. All of that sounds rather dreadful, but fortunately it reflects an exaggeration of the costs of transformation, rather than real disaster. There has been no significant fall in living standards. Real incomes did not plummet. Unemployment, while high, is not soaring to the levels that were feared. And the lost production reflects the cutbacks in production of enterprises that lack customers, mainly the cutback of Poland's excessively large heavy industrial sector (Sachs, 1993, p. 67).

Sachs cited the inability of official statistical methodology – which was developed for the purposes of central planning – to capture vigorous growth of the small-scale private sector. He also argued that the reported decline of real wages resulted from overestimation of real wage growth in the year preceding Big Bang. 'This alleged drop in living standards was largely illusory, since back in November 1989, Poles faced crippling shortages at the official prices, so that living standards on the eve of reform were much lower than the official statistics had suggested' (Sachs, 1993, p. 62).

Niels Mygind also provides at least partial support for hypothesis B2:

> In all Eastern countries in transition, production has fallen sharply in the first years after the start of the transition. This has also been the case for the three Baltic countries. In 1990–92 GDP fell nearly by 40 per cent in all three countries. Part of this fall can be explained by lack of registration of the new growing private activities and under reporting of the results in state-owned firms. The new private firms and some state-owned firms may have an incentive to underreport to avoid taxes. For firms facing privatization the managers might want to give a bad picture of the results, if they have an interest in a low price for the enterprise.

My position is that although the official statistics may have overestimated the extent of decline in output it would be very difficult to argue today that all that decline was in fact compensated by the unrecorded growth of the private sector. It is also indisputable that there was a significant actual and not just imaginary decline in the standard of living of the population in all the countries in transition. The misdiagnosis hypothesis cannot be the main explanation for the observed setbacks.

The vacuum or discoordination hypothesis B3 was probably first formulated by Hayek in *The Road to Serfdom*:

> most people still believe that it must be possible to find some middle way between 'atomistic' competition and central direction. Nothing, indeed, seems at first more plausible, or is more likely to appeal to reasonable people, than the idea that our goal must be neither the extreme decentralization of free competition nor the complete centralization of a single plan but some judicious mixture of the two methods. Yet mere common sense proves a treacherous guide in this field.
>
> Although competition can bear some admixture of regulation, it cannot be combined with planning to any extent we like without ceasing to operate as an effective guide to production. Nor is 'planning' a medicine which, taken in small doses, can produce the effects for which one might hope from its thoroughgoing application. Both competition and central direction become poor and inefficient tools if they are incomplete; they are alternative principles used to solve the same problem, and a mixture of the two means that neither will really work and that the result will be worse than if either system had been consistently relied upon (Hayek, 1944, p. 42).

For about two decades after the end of the World War II, a fairly different concept of optimal mixture of market and planning prevailed, at least in the West. Many economists believed that the decentralized market system and centralized command economy are only idealized limiting cases with a continuous spectrum of real 'mixed systems' in between. An optimal combination of market and central planning was supposed to eliminate the deficiencies of both pure systems and significantly improve economic coordination and efficiency.

The idea of incompatibility was resurrected during the economic reforms of the 1960s especially in Czechoslovakia.

> The Czechoslovak economists believed that the market and command principles are two radically different forms of economic organization which do not easily mix together. Their view of this dichotomy was derived partly from their own historical experience and partly from Wlodzimierz Brus's (1961) influential book which contained an excellent analysis of the differences between centralized (i.e. command) and decentralized (i.e. market) models of socialism (Kyn, 1975, p. 141).

Ota Turek (1967) analysed an 'intermediate model' based on a mixture of command planning and elements of the market economy. He concluded that such a model is organizationally unstable and sooner or later would degenerate back to a directive system.

This opinion was also shared by other economists who believed that both a command economy and a market economy were, in a certain sense, 'stable' organizations, while the intermediate forms containing mixtures of command and market elements were unstable, and would tend to move either toward a command system or toward a complete market system. To use an analogy from physics, it looked as if the command and market systems each had its own 'gravitational pull' which could cause a return to the original system when only a small deviation from it was made. Once, however, steps in the direction of the other system reach a certain border line, the gravitational pull of the other system prevails and the transformation could be accomplished (Kyn, 1975, p. 142).

Similar views reappeared in the 1980s during 'perestroika' in the Soviet Union and other East European countries. They were expressed in slogans of the type: 'You cannot jump over the abyss in two steps'. On the other hand some Soviet economists, for example Shatalin, Zaslavskaya and Gaidar, dismissed the model of centralized hierarchical coordination in favour of a 'bargaining model' (Sutela, 1991, pp. 139–47). The 'bargaining model' is based more on decentralized decisions and lateral communication channels and, therefore, may not appear to be as incompatible with the market mechanism as the centralized command model. After the collapse of communism the vacuum hypothesis reappeared again. For example Kolodko wrote: 'the planned mechanism of allocation has been dismantled, but the market one is not yet in place, so one has to see a sort of systemic vacuum' (Kolodko, 1993, p. 58). Vacuum hypothesis is in the core of Dornbusch's argument against gradualism: 'If reform proceeds hesitantly, economic collapse is certain and the market economy experiment becomes discredited before it even had a chance to be born' (Dornbusch, 1991, p. 181)

11.6   THE ROLE OF INSTITUTIONS

In his chapter Michael Intriligator formulates a version of the vacuum hypothesis:

> The fundamental problem is that the Soviet successor states have disbanded the institutions of central planning but they have not yet established the institutions of a market economy. In the vacuum that resulted from the absence of those bodies that enable an economy to function, whether it be a centrally planned or a market economy, there have been unprecedented economic declines in the Soviet successor states. . . . a functioning market economy remains a rather distant prospect.

Intriligator's interpretation differs from the previous interpretations of the vacuum by identifying it as the lack of institutions. This is very much in line with the recently growing recognition of the importance of property rights and other economic and legal institutions for the efficient operation of a market economy. Certainly, the full significance of private property had not yet been recognized by the Czech reformers in the mid-1960s. Their idea was that Western-style economic efficiency could be attained by moving from a command to a socialist market economy while still preserving some form of public – although not necessarily state – ownership.

A similar delusion also existed among Western neoclassical economists. This is confirmed by the following quotations from the recently published book by Joseph Stiglitz:

> The idea of market socialism was a powerful one. It suggested that it was possible to have all the advantages of market economies without the disadvantages attendant to private property and the frequently associated large concentrations of wealth. Market socialism, it was thought, could at the same time avoid the major pitfalls facing Soviet-type socialism (Stiglitz, 1994, p. 9).

> The neoclassical paradigm, through its incorrect characterization of the market economies and the central problems of resource allocation, provides a false sense of belief in the ability of market socialism to solve those resource allocation problems. To put it another way, if the neoclassical paradigm had provided a good description of the resource allocation problem and the market mechanism, then market socialism might well have been a success. The very criticisms of market socialism are themselves, to a large extent, criticisms of the neoclassical paradigm (Stiglitz, 1994, p. 13).

Although I think that such a stark denouncement of the neoclassical paradigm is exaggerated I do agree with most of the contemporary economic community that the market economy cannot operate efficiently without clearly determined rules of the game, that is, without well-established property rights and other institutions. I do, therefore, wholeheartedly agree with the main proposition of Michael Intriligator's chapter, namely that the successful transition to the market economy requires fast creation of the relevant economic, legal, political and social institutions. The importance of speedy change in property rights with related legal norms, civil and business laws, codes, contracts, and regulations cannot be overestimated. What I do not understand, however, is that from this premise Intriligator arrives at bitter criticism of the existing strategies of transition. He blames Western advisers, IMF and the World Bank, for not recognizing that East European countries are different from other nations and for imposing a faulty strategy of stabilization, liberalization and privatization (SLP) on them. He regards this strategy and particularly its radical version nicknamed 'shock therapy' the main contributor to all the transition troubles (hypothesis B7). He claims that because central planning was abandoned while the institutions of a market economy had not yet been created no one except for criminal elements was in charge. He concludes that such a transition is not a transition to market economy as known in the West but, rather, to an economy riddled with crime and corruption with economic disarray and collapse.

It appears that there is some misunderstanding in the use of the term 'institutions'. While this term now usually means formal 'rules of the game' that impose constraints on economic decision-making – such as laws, customs and so on – Intriligator uses this term in a much broader sense which also includes actual organizations and even some other economic phenomena. His list of institutions of a market economy includes not only property rights, civil and commercial laws and so on, but also banks, insurance companies and other organizations of the financial markets. This has very important implications. Many of us would agree that the major role of the government in the transition process is the creation of institutions in the narrower sense of the rules of the game. Michael Intriligator wants, however, much more; he wants the government to take full responsibility for the actual creation of banks, insurance companies, advertising companies and even the new 'more efficient' industrial firms. He has not given up the idea of social engineering.

Almost everybody has now abandoned the idea that the economy can be efficiently coordinated through the centralized hierarchical organization of the decision-making process. The superiority of the market economy lies not just in its decentralized organizational structure, but also in the fact that decisions about changes in the organizational structure are themselves decentralized. Market is a self-organizing mechanism in which spontaneously created new structures only survive if they are economically viable. Private ownership is an essential precondition of the self-organizing function of the market. This is because correct decisions lead to the growth of capital and consequently of the decision-making power of the owner. Intriligator seems to believe that government bureaucrats can design and implement the optimal reorganization of the economic system from the top. I believe that the successful transition strategy requires to start up the self-organizing function of the market as early as possible. This also implies that private owners rather than government bureaucrats should select managers of firms as Pavel Pelikan shows convincingly in his contribution on allocation of competence.

The point I tried to make above can be documented by comparing Polish and Czechoslovak privatization schemes. Mutual funds played an important role in both designs. The Polish proposal assumed that government would create and run a small number of large mutual funds through which all the citizens would acquire diversified ownership in the formerly state-run firms. This was a social engineering scheme to be implemented by government bureaucrats from the top. No room was given to the preferences of people and to the initiative of private entrepreneurs. Although originally already developed in 1989 it has not yet been implemented. The Czechoslovak design did not originally involve mutual funds. The *laissez-faire* rules of the game allowed a rapid spontaneous increase in hundreds of mutual funds, which contributed immensely to the success of the privatization process.

It is not that I disagree with the vacuum hypothesis, but I think that Intriligator is drawing the wrong conclusions from it. My conclusions would still be similar to the conclusion of the Czech economists in the mid-1960s, namely that the existence of the vacuum calls for rapid, comprehensive change rather than the piecemeal gradualist approach. My disagreement with Intriligator's interpretation is also based on the belief that the vacuum is not just in institutions. A market economy needs substantially different skills and decision-making behaviour. These cannot be decreed by government or imported from abroad. When I returned in 1990 to Czechoslovakia after 23 years' absence, I came to the conclusion that the greatest damage that the communist system did was to human capital. In the 1960s, there were still many who were trained before the communist takeover. In 1990 there were only a few. An entirely new generation with distorted work attitudes dominated. Newly emerging private firms commonly tend to avoid people with experience in the field because of their acquired bad work habits. Institutions are enormously important but the smooth operation of the market requires that people also learn how to make decisions in new situations. Most of this will be necessarily learning by doing. It is unrealistic to think that people could learn just from textbooks without real life experience. Prices must be liberalized for people to learn how to react to price movements. Property must be privatized for people to learn how to exercise their property rights.

Michael Intriligator's arguments are inconsistent. He criticizes stabilization policies but lists stable currency among the institutions that government should create first. He wants a market economy but attacks domestic price and foreign markets liberalization. He pleads for the preferential establishment of property rights but denounces privatization. Does he really believe that government can create a stable currency by decree without imposing a strict control over the supply of money and budget expenditures? Does he believe that government can create market institutions without letting the market operate? Does he have no doubts about the attempts to establish property rights with virtually no private enterprises?

Michael Intriligator says that the current privatization campaign will not change things significantly because it just changes the labels on existing entities. The same managers are running the same 'institutions' (!) with the same workers he says, implying that the privatized enterprise will continue to be inefficient. My response is that this may be true only when the government continues to pay subsidies to inefficient firms. Private property rights mean responsibility for one's own losses. Without subsidies or unlimited credits guaranteed by government, inefficient firms would go bankrupt. Only those privatized firms would survive whose managers and workers learned and adjusted their behaviour to the new environment. Bankruptcies are crucial. Monetary and fiscal restriction is needed to eliminate subsidies and skyrocketing credits to inefficient firms. Pressure of the market and the threat of bankruptcy or unemployment is the most effective way to change the behaviour of workers and managers. Certainly, it will take some time. Certainly, many old dinosaur enterprises will not survive. Why not close them without privatization? Because no government bureaucrat or even economic adviser can predict with sufficient accuracy which firms will remain inefficient in the future. Only competitive markets can solve this problem. Why not let them wither away without privatization? Because it is much more difficult for government to stop subsidies to state-owned enterprises than to private firms. Certainly new firms and organizations need to be created, but I would not trust government bureaucrats or even foreign economic advisers if they told me that they knew the right products and technologies and that they could improve economic efficiency before the market starts functioning in full.

Michael Intriligator seems to believe in optimal sequencing of reform measures. Vaclav Klaus lost such a belief when he became a politician and discovered that political forces and events are unpredictable and hardly controllable. For what is the optimal design worth if you cannot get crucial bills through the parliament in the desired time? Klaus likened the reform process to the game of chess. You must make your moves conditional on the moves of your opponent. The reality of vicious partisan fights in political democracies should cure us from the naive presumption that it is possible to prepare all the market institutions ahead of time before starting the liberalization and privatization process. Frequently you cannot convince politicians about the urgency of certain legislative action before they actually witness the approaching emergency. In the Czechoslovak parliament, the bill on investment privatization funds was sidestepped for months and quickly rushed through only when it became obvious that the Harvard Fund and a few others might acquire an exceedingly large share of privatization vouchers. The fear of concentration of economic power was what finally worked.

Michael Intriligator's severe criticism of the SLP strategy is based almost solely on the Russian experience. However, in many East European countries, the SLP strategy worked with far fewer negative repercussions than in Russia. Particularly in the Visegrad countries, the decline of output and the accompanying inflation were much milder. The Czech government took all the supposedly wrong steps and completed the transformation process more rapidly than any other country and with the massive support of the population. Poland which initiated the big bang strategy has now quite a vigorously growing economy. Both the Czech Republic and Hungary are attracting billions of dollars of private foreign investment. Although Baltic countries suffered much deeper setbacks than the Visegrad countries, they also seem to be already close to a recovery path. In none of these countries have criminal elements had such an extreme role as in Russia. Intriligator's suggestion that SLP would be likely to cause a complete economic collapse and his slogan 'privatization leads to criminalization' are highly inaccurate and misleading.

Intriligator's claim that the SLP strategy was imposed on East European countries by the IMF, World Bank and foreign advisers is false. There is a good deal of evidence that at least in some countries domestic reformers arrived independently at similar proposals. I am convinced that it is the only workable strategy, although ex post we always find out that many things could have been done differently. Foreign advisers and international organizations were well aware of the importance of education, training and institution building. In democratic countries institutional changes have to be implemented through the internal political process. It helps to have a stable well-functioning government, but it should restrict its activity primarily to the creation of clear and consistent rules of the game and leave most of the rest to private business.

11.7 THE BALTIC TRANSITION

Many Western experts judge the success of East European transformation strategy quite differently from Michael Intriligator. This can be documented by the following excerpts from the recent article in *The Economist*:

> The fastest-reforming economies, by the EBRD's and most other reckonings, are to be found in Central Europe. They include Poland, the Czech Republic, Slovakia, Hungary, Slovenia and the Baltic states of Estonia, Latvia and Lithuania. All have the foundations of a market economy securely in place. Poor as the post-communist countries may be, their economies compare promisingly with those of Western Europe. The Czechs, for example, fulfil the Maastricht-treaty criteria for sound public finances better than most present EU members. Despite the economic upheaval, unemployment rates are generally lower than, say, that of Spain . . . If the success of these efforts is far from assured, they do indicate that a watershed has been passed. Across the whole region, the possibility and desirability of creating capitalism has now been accepted, even by the laggards. . . . countries escaping from communism have shown that they can indeed change the economic

structure of their societies in as little as three years. What is more, they have done so with little outside help. (*The Economist*, 3 December 1994)

This evaluation is well complemented by the following two tables: 1) EBRD ranking of the East European countries' progress on the way towards market economy and 2) the dynamics of real GDP in the transition period. The first six columns of *Table 11.1* give scores – from 1 (little or no progress) to 4 (a lot of progress) – on essential aspects of the systemic change. The last column is my calculation of the unweighted average of these scores.

Table 11.1: Marking to market

	L	S	R	P	F	B	A
Czech Rep.	4	4	3	3	4	3	3.5
Poland	3	4	3	3	4	3	3.33
Hungary	3	4	3	3	4	3	3.33
Slovakia	3	4	3	3	4	3	3.33
Estonia	3	4	3	3	4	3	3.33
Slovenia	2	4	3	3	4	3	3.16
Croatia	3	4	2	3	4	3	3.16
Lithuania	3	4	2	3	4	2	3.0
Latvia	2	3	2	3	4	3	2.83
Macedonia	2	4	2	3	4	2	2.83
Kirgizstan	3	4	2	3	3	2	2.83
Romania	2	3	2	3	4	2	2.83
Russia	3	3	2	3	3	2	2.66
Bulgaria	2	2	2	3	4	2	2.5
Albania	1	3	2	3	4	2	2.5

Note: The meaning of columns: L=Large privatization, S = Small privatization, R = Restructuring of companies, P = Prices, competition, F = Trade – foreign exchange, B = Banks, A = Average. Score: 4 = market economy, 1 = little progress.

Source: European Bank for Reconstruction and Development as published in *The Economist*, 3 December 1994. Ranking of the remaining countries by average score: 2.16 Moldova, 2 Uzbekistan, 1.83 Armenia, 1.66 Belarus, Kazakhstan, and Tajikistan, 1.33 Azerbaijan, Georgia, and Ukraine, 1.16 Turkmenistan.

Table 11.2: Index of real GDP

1988 = 100							
	1989	1990	1991	1992	1993	1994	1995**
Czech Rep.*	101.40	100.99	86.65	80.50	80.50	82.92	87.06
Slovakia *	101.40	100.99	86.65	80.50	77.28	81.14	84.39
Poland	100.20	88.58	82.38	83.20	86.53	90.85	95.40
Hungary	99.80	95.81	84.31	80.43	78.82	80.40	82.81
Slovenia	98.20	93.58	84.88	79.36	80.16	84.17	89.22
Estonia	103.30	99.17	86.28	63.84	61.93	65.03	68.93
Latvia	106.80	109.90	100.78	56.43	49.66	51.15	52.69
Lithuania	101.50	96.43	83.79	54.47	45.75	46.67	48.53
Moldova	108.80	107.17	94.42	74.30	67.62	50.71	50.71
Romania	93.10	86.21	74.40	62.94	63.57	65.48	67.44
Bulgaria	98.10	89.17	78.74	72.68	63.96	49.89	46.39
Albania	109.80	98.82	69.27	63.87	70.90	75.86	79.65
Russia	101.90	98.23	87.43	69.94	61.55	52.32	48.65
Kirgizstan	103.80	107.12	101.77	76.32	64.11	57.70	58.86
Belarus	108.00	104.76	101.51	90.35	79.50	62.01	57.67
Ukraine	104.10	100.56	86.98	74.81	64.33	49.54	50.53
Kazakhstan	98.00	90.16	78.71	66.90	58.87	44.16	38.86
Tajikistan	93.50	92.94	84.85	58.55	42.16	31.62	n.a.
Turkmenistan	93.10	94.50	93.93	89.23	80.31	64.25	61.04
Uzbekistan	103.10	107.53	106.57	91.65	89.81	87.12	83.63
Armenia	114.20	104.49	92.16	87.55	74.42	74.42	74.42
Azerbaijan	99.40	87.97	86.30	60.41	52.56	40.99	36.89

Note: * Czechoslovakia before 1993. ** Forecast.
Sources: EBRD and WIIW.

In his chapter, Niels Mygind produced an enormously rich base of empirical facts. They may be quite useful for getting an insight into both general and specific aspects of the transformation process in the Baltic countries. I would disagree with only a very few statements and conclusions of his chapter. However, this is partly because they mostly conform with conventional wisdom on the transition.

His initial attempt to construct a general model of interactions among various economic, social and political factors in the transformation process is somewhat disappointing. Although I do think that it is impossible to fully understand the complexities of the transformation process without having such an interaction in mind, I could not see from the brief presentation at this conference what kind of conclusions one could draw from it. A quick look into his book *Societies in Transition* (Mygind, 1994) revealed the problem. It appears that Mygind is aiming for some grand synthesis of at least five different paradigms: 1) Marxian 'historical materialism'; 2) the 'decision–information–motivation' (DIM) approach to the theory of comparative economic systems, (Neuberger, 1971); 3) neoclassical economics; 4) new institutionalist economics of Williamson, North and others; and finally 5) 'the cultural approach' of Gollestrup (Mygind, 1994, p. 13). This is not only a very difficult, but also a very dangerous path. I cannot keep myself from making a comparison with the past theories of 'optimal mix' of capitalism and socialism, or at least of some of their ingredients, plan and market, public and private ownership and so on. It seemed to some that if those systems had different drawbacks, some combination of them ought to be better than any of the pure types. But, as discussed above, if the distinct systems are based on incompatible 'rules of the game' or incompatible coordinative mechanisms, their mixing would worsen the performance, not improve it. Similarly historical materialism, neoclassical economics, the DIM approach or new institutional economics have their own drawbacks and limitations, but you do not necessarily get better theory by mixing them together. They are based on distinct paradigms, start from quite different assumptions and often use very different methodological tools.

Mygind's 'model' is flawed because 1) it is not clear what the underlying assumptions are; 2) the individual elements of his 'model' are defined only vaguely; 3) it is hard to see how some of these elements would respond to changing inputs from the rest of the system; 4) the overall interactive structure of the model is not very convincingly specified. Analysis of this kind of model can hardly lead to firm conclusions about the resulting processes. In some cases Mygind formulates 'results' that seem to be verified by what has been actually happening in many transitional economies. The problem is, however, that these 'results' do not clearly and necessarily follow from the behaviour and interactions of elements of the model as he has formulated it. Mygind's language with statements like 'this will result in . . . ' or 'it will have positive (or negative) effect on . . .' is misleading because it presents what has been observed to happen as if it followed necessarily from the assumptions of the model, but it does not.

Let us now inspect Mygind's chapter from the point of view of transition hypotheses. He attributes the major part of the economic setback to economic fragmentation (hypothesis B5) and to the decline of aggregate demand (hypothesis B6). Mygind acknowledges certain aspects of the cost of transition hypothesis B4, but does not seem to give it a prominent place in the explanation of transition difficulties.

Mygind points out that the disintegration of the USSR and COMECON between 1990 to 1992 led to a sharp fall in demand for Baltic products from Russia and the other republics of the former Soviet Union as well as from other countries in COMECON.

The disintegration of the former Soviet Union, and the transition to world market prices have led to a disruption of former trade links and serious problems on the supply and the demand side for the industry. . . . Trade with the former Soviet Union fell by more than 50 per cent in 1991, and this trend continued in 1992.

Furthermore,

The general development in 1990–92 was a sharp fall in the demand from Russia and other republics in the Former Soviet Union and also from other countries in COMECON. Most of the trading partners, especially in the Former Soviet Union could simply not pay for the goods. This resulted in increasing interfirm arrears and a change to barter trade, but first of all it resulted in a sharp fall in trade. All three Baltic countries were seriously hit by this development.

It started with the politically motivated economic blockade of Lithuania in the spring of 1990, spread to all three countries when the blockade began to disintegrate, continued when Baltic currencies were removed from the rouble zone, and reached a peak in 1992 after Russia liberalized its own prices and allowed the prices of exported raw materials to jump to world market levels. This was a severe shock for the Baltic economies which resulted in hyperinflation, and a sharp reduction in the supply of energy and other essential raw materials so that 'many firms had to stop or drastically cut production, and in most houses and official buildings the temperature was much lower than normal'. The desperate attempts to redirect trade away from the countries of the former Soviet bloc did not work sufficiently fast, because Finland the closest and most natural partner of Baltic countries was also affected by the Soviet disintegration. A peculiar brief interlude occurred in 1991 because the Baltic countries started price liberalization before Russia while still being in the rouble zone. Russians, who faced empty shops in their own country, generated an extra demand for Baltic products.

In a more or less standard way, Mygind also attributes the decline in aggregate demand in all three Baltic countries to the very strict stabilization policy. Not only did declining real incomes reduce household demand but also 'the credit squeeze made it difficult for the firms to cover their deficit by bank loans. They had to cut down production that could not be sold at prices covering costs'.

Niels Mygind's chapter also adduces some evidence that suggests that all three hypotheses, C1, C2 and C3 claim to explain the differential success of individual countries in transition may be true. This holds both for the group of all three Baltic countries in comparison with other East European countries and the rest of the former Soviet Union as well as for the differences within the Baltic group itself. The Baltic countries as a whole are clearly more successful than the rest of the former Soviet Union but not as successful as Visegrad countries (Poland, the Czech Republic, Slovakia and Hungary).

Within the Baltic countries, Estonia seems to be ahead of the other two. The comparison of Latvia and Lithuania is much less clear.

This can be explained partly by geographic proximity (hypothesis C1). Baltic countries, and specifically Estonia, are very close to Finland and Sweden but not as close to the rest of Western Europe as Visegrad countries and Slovenia. Geographic proximity has made the reorientation of trade links from East to West much easier and with fewer transaction costs. As long as East European communication (telephone, fax, mail and so on) and banking services (slow transfer of funds) remain backward, the advantage of reaching the country in a few hours by car, train or boat unquestionably helps not only trade but direct foreign investment as well. Geographic proximity also allows much more frequent commuting by East Europeans for shopping or work to West European countries or at least to watch West European television and thus get better information about the workings of the Western free market democracies.

The geographic proximity is closely related to the 'historical and cultural traditions hypothesis' C3. In their histories, the neighbouring countries may have mutually exchanged portions of their populations and almost certainly have had a need for frequent communication. As a result, at least part of the population usually knows the language and idiosyncratic national characteristics of their neighbour. This certainly facilitates the transition both because Westerners can present their business proposals in a more understandable and acceptable form while Easterners may learn faster from the West about how to operate in the market economy.

11.8   CONCLUDING REMARKS

The fact that Poles, Czechs, Slovaks, Hungarians and Slovenes have had for more than a thousand years permanent political, cultural and commercial interactions with German-speaking neighbours certainly made the resumption of commercial ties with Germany and Austria after 1989 much easier. For Baltic countries, however, it works in two ways. On the one hand they had strong historical links to Finns and Germans which greatly facilitates reorientation to the West. On the other hand, the traditional links to Russia and the significant presence of a Russian population somewhat complicated the transition process. The historical and language differences also contributed to the greater success of Estonia as compared to the other two Baltic countries.

The higher degree of market-orientated values in Estonia can also be connected to influences from the surrounding world. The close linguistic relationship with Finland made the Estonians able to follow Finnish television and radio. Many

Estonians lived in exile in Sweden, Finland and North America. This was to a certain extent also the case for Latvians and Lithuanians, but the language barrier implied that the influence of the Western style of living was smaller in these countries. . . . Latvia did not have such close links to the West as the Estonians did in relation to Finland. (Mygind)

The level of development hypothesis C2 seems to have some explanatory power as well. The Visegrad countries, and especially the Czech part of the former Czechoslovakia, were traditionally the most industrially developed part of Eastern Europe. Baltic countries and specifically Estonia and Latvia were not very far behind.

Both Estonia and Latvia were industrialized before the Soviet occupation. Tallinn and especially Riga were already important trade centres at the beginning of the century. Lithuania on the contrary had a large population in agriculture after World War II. Therefore the industry here was mainly built up under Soviet rule (Mygind).

The last observation is particularly important. For the countries that achieved a significant level of industrial development before the communist takeover, the transition process may be easier because it means rebuilding something that had already been there. There are three areas in which the previously achieved level of development may by crucially important.

First, there is a good deal of evidence that the industrial structure can itself be adjusted with more ease in a country where communist industrialization was built upon an industrial base created under capitalism. In such situations at least some of the huge socialist 'dinosaur' enterprises were created as amalgamations of previously existing smaller capitalist firms, whose skeletons and 'DNA' may be at least partially recovered even after half a century. It is much more difficult to restructure 'dinosaurs' that have been entirely newly created by socialist industrialization.

Second, the country that was already industrialized before communism must have had a stock of managers, entrepreneurs and people with skills needed in the capitalist market economy. A lot of that must have been lost as I have already mentioned above. Nevertheless, the recreation of these skills and professions may be easier than creating them anew in a country which has had very little business tradition.

Third and probably most important is the 'institutional memory' of such a country. It is much easier to recover and modernize the old economic and legal institutions in a country that once had a well-developed system of property rights, commercial law and so on than in a country that has little or no tradition in that area.

11.9 REFERENCES

Brus, W. (1961), *Ogolne problemy funkcjonowania gospodarki socjalistycznej*, Warsaw, PWN, translated into English in 1972 as: *The Market in a Socialist Economy*, London and Boston, Routledge & Kegan Paul.

Dellebrant, J.A. (1992), Estonia's Economic Development 1940–1990, in A. Åslund, ed., *Market Socialism or the Restoration of Capitalism*, Cambridge University Press.

Dornbusch, R. (1991), Strategies and Priorities for Reform, in *Transition to a Market Economy*, OECD, Paris.

Economist, (1994), Counter-revolution, *The Economist*, 3 December.

Ellman, M. (1993), General Aspects of Transition, in M. Ellman, Gaidar and G.W. Kolodko, *Economic Transformation in Eastern Europe*, Basil Blackwell.

Hayek, F.A. (1944), *The Road to Serfdom*, The University of Chicago Press,

Klaus, V. (1995), *Speech for the World Summit for Social Development*, Copenhagen, 11 March.

Kolodko, G.W. (1993), Recession and Growth during Transition to a Market Economy, in M. Ellman, Y. Gaidar and G.W Kolodko, *Economic Transformation in Eastern Europe*, Basil Blackwell.

Kyn, O. (1975), Czechoslovakia, in H.-H. Hoehmann, M. Kaser and K.C. Thalheim, *The New Economic Systems of Eastern Europe*, C. Hurst & Company, London.

Mygind, N. (1994), Societies in Transition, Institute of Economics Copenhagen Business School. This is a draft of the English version of the previously published book: *Omvaeltning i Ost*", Samfundsletteratur.

Neuberger, E. (1971), Classifying Economic Systems, in M. Bornstein ed., *Comparative Economic Systems*, Irwin, Boston.

Nuti, D.M. (1992), Market Socialism: The Model that Might have Been – But Never Was, in A. Åslund, ed., *Market Socialism or the Restoration of Capitalism?* Cambridge University Press.

Roemer, J.E. (1993), Can There Be Socialism after Communism?, in P.K. Bardhan and J.E. Roemer, eds, *Market Socialism: The Current Debate*, Oxford University Press, New York.

Sachs, J. (1993), *Poland's Jump to the Market Economy*, The MIT Press.

Sik, O., ed. (1990), *Socialism Today*, Macmillan, London.

Stiglitz, J.E. (1994), *Whither Socialism?*, The MIT Press.

Sutela, P. (1991), *Economic Thought and Economic Reform in the Soviet Union*, Cambridge University Press.

Turek, O. (1967), *O planu, trhu a hospodarske politice*, Svoboda, Prague.

Index

agriculture
  foreign trade, 112; 213; 217; 273
  labour supply, 19
  privatization, 25–29; 35; 43–52
Albania, 268
allocative efficiency, 250; 253; 259
arbitrage, 186
balance of payments, 90; 223; 246
Baldwin R., 119; 128–32
Baltic Free Trade Agreement, 103
Bank of Estonia, 29; 31; 74–83
Bank of Latvia, 33; 46; 84–89
Bank of Lithuania, 38; 90–93
banknotes, 66; 85
bankruptcy, 31–38; 57; 96; 161; 162; 192; 200; 232; 266
barriers to transition, 3; 4
Belarus, 68; 131
big bang, 267
Bolshevik, 255
Bosnia, 249
Brazauskas A., 28
budget
  budget constraint, 31; 55; 57
  budget deficits, 5; 72; 107; 112
  budget discipline, 5
Bulgaria, 268
business risk, 12; 182; 188; 199; 200
capital account, 75; 92; 245
capitalism, 226; 252–55; 267; 270

capitalist system, 8; 11; 255
capitalists, 11; 44; 45
central bank, 8; 9; 28; 30; 38; 70–77; 82–92; 244; 245
central bank of Russia, 77
central planning, 150; 222; 224; 228; 249–62
Central Privatization Commission, 49
Chechnya, 249
China, 101; 151; 162; 227; 233; 234; 257
CIS states, 62; 79; 93
Clinton B., 101
Comecon, 4
command economy, 3; 17; 22; 62; 250–62
commercial code, 225; 230
communism, 250
Communist Party, 17; 23–27; 233
comparative advantage, 120–22; 133
competition, 34–38; 55; 56; 101; 112; 124; 125; 138; 165; 174–79; 197; 202; 203; 217; 252; 256; 261
constitution, 18; 24; 27; 242
convergence, 90
corporate income tax, 79; 103
coupons, 91; 92
creative destruction, 163
credibility, 9; 38; 70–73; 82; 92; 93; 183; 188; 246; 247

credit squeeze, 31; 55; 56; 61; 271

credits, 36; 38; 266

Croatia, 268

currency, 2; 6–9; 29; 33–38; 51–56; 66–93; 99; 112; 224; 226; 231; 241–48; 265
   convertibility, 37;54; 70; 75; 79; 83; 88–93; 169; 178; 242–48
   currency board, 29; 38; 72–92; 112; 243–46
   currency reform, 2; 6–9; 71–90
   currency system, 9

current account, 74; 92; 214; 243; 245

customs, 109; 264

Czechoslovakia, 170; 265; 269

devaluation, 30; 243

development bloc, 187

discretion, 81

Dyachenko Y., 228; 257

East Germany, 40

EBRD, 63; 105; 107; 115; 268; 269

EC, 31; 153–61

economic competence, 11; 152–77

economic growth, 5; 10; 249; 250; 252–58
   currency reform, 72
   financial sector, 244; 247
   foreign trade, 142
   goverment activity, 100; 101; 111; 114
   investment incentives, 13; 182–90; 194–99
   liberalization, 14
   structural adjustment, 211; 219; 220

economies of scale, 120; 187

education, 61; 98; 110; 111; 123; 127; 133; 140

EFTA, 31; 37; 54; 128; 147

Ellman M., 252

emigration, 20; 21

employment, 14; 20; 33; 42; 50; 58–61; 188; 193; 197; 211–13; 220; 243; 247; 259

enabling laws, 13; 195

energy, 19; 20; 24; 30; 35; 57; 129; 136; 142–44; 170; 271

energy options, 142

enterprises, 25; 53; 224; 229; 234; 256–257
   and government, 5; 97–103; 109–11; 114; 226
   balance of payments, 74–78; 84–92
   financial sector, 34; 38; 51; 52; 57; 232
   legislative framework, 191; 197; 265
   restructuring, 3; 10; 11; 18; 19; 29–31; 39–49; 55; 59–62; 150; 172; 173; 231; 235; 236; 260; 266; 273

entry of firms, 165; 175–78; 187; 188; 192–95; 242

environment, 121; 125; 126; 172; 252

Estonian Currency Reform Committee, 68

Estonian Privatization Agency, 42

Estonian Privatization Enterprise, 42

EU, 31; 35; 37; 54; 131–35; 141; 267

evolutionary, 4; 8–11; 159; 171; 223

exchange rates
   fixed exchange rates, 9; 72–74; 243

foreign exchange, 70–77; 86–92; 248

floating exchange rates, 38; 88; 243–245

exit of firms, 154; 165; 166; 186–92; 201

external shocks, 247

financial markets, 11; 15; 151; 162; 188; 189

Finland, 19; 22; 32; 54; 94; 127; 241; 271–73

fiscal policy
  design, 4; 5; 79; 93; 114
  fiscal stance, 246
  fiscal trap, 112
  goverment budget, 5; 29; 35; 102; 104; 112
  implementation, 3; 70
  inflationary pressure, 99; 243
  monetary regime, 53; 79; 93; 233; 248
  targets, 6; 16; 33; 79; 231; 246; 248; 266

flat tax rate, 103

foreign capital, 32; 42; 56; 75

foreign trade, 4; 9; 31; 32; 35; 62; 69; 75; 96

France, 127

free capital movements, 9; 243

Free Trade Unions Confederation of Latvia, 33

Friedman M., 112

fullfledged central bank, 8

Gaidar Y., 274

GATT, 135

Germany, 40; 127; 176; 200; 272

Godmanis I., 25

Gollestrup M., 270

Gorbachev M., 98; 228; 229

Hanson A., 21

hard budget constraints, 100; 231; 257

Hayek F. v., 150; 261

Hungary, 39; 96; 114; 116; 174; 175; 267; 268

hybrid form of currency board, 74

IME, 26; 40; 71

IMF, 7; 26–28; 35; 37; 40; 63; 64; 68–71; 94–96; 227; 263

immigration, 19–21

imperfect information, 171

implementation, 2; 8; 14; 16; 55; 77; 85; 194; 198; 237; 248; 250

implementation of the currency reform, 77; 85

incentives, 12; 13; 39; 55; 57; 110; 152–62; 177–92; 201; 203; 212; 224–33; 250; 253

independence movement, 23; 41

indexation, 24; 36

industrial clusters, 126; 140; 147

industrialization, 22; 273

inflation, 18; 32; 34; 49; 60; 206; 251
  banking, 81; 82
  economic growth, 16; 61; 112; 113; 189; 211; 246; 266
  foreign trade, 29; 31; 76; 99
  hording, 53; 54
  hyper-inflation, 24; 30; 38; 48; 231
  hysteresis, 61; 62
  incomes policy, 30; 37
  inflationary financing, 72; 73; 98; 112; 243
  inflationary push, 30; 31
  monetary policy, 33; 70–77; 81–92; 233; 243; 247
  price reform, 24; 30; 38; 48; 231

informational efficiency, 253

infrastructure, 111; 122; 126; 127; 133; 144; 147; 233; 234

institutional incentives, 183
institutional system, 18; 22
interest rates, 57; 61; 81; 90; 182;
    243; 246
International Monetary Fund, 233
investment
    disinvestment, 186; 199
    foreign investment, 12; 42; 44;
        47; 51; 58; 59; 188; 203; 272
    investment climate, 10; 12; 183
    investment funds, 12; 46; 48;
        160; 177; 178; 188; 190
    investment incentives, 13;
        182–90; 194–99; 233
    investment vouchers, 11; 176;
        178
    risks, 4; 10–13; 63; 90; 172;
        183–93; 199–205; 209; 228;
        238
Iron Curtain, 242; 258
Japan, 125; 126; 176
Kazakhstan, 68; 239
KGB, 46
Kirgizstan, 268
land reform, 47; 51
large privatization, 44; 45
Lats, 34; 37
Latvian Privatization Agency, 45
Latvian rouble, 54; 84–88; 245
legislation, 4; 13; 23; 29; 34; 37;
    41–50; 61; 86; 103; 167; 168;
    182
liberalization, 54; 178; 211; 257
    foreign trade, 14; 31; 32; 54;
        55; 62; 76; 96–111; 253–58;
        265
    political liberalization, 2
    price liberalization, 8–10; 14;
        18; 24; 30–39; 68; 81; 169;
        217–219; 224; 232; 246; 271
    SLP approach, 3; 15; 223; 229;
        263

LIPSP, 50; 51
Litas, 36; 38
Macedonia, 268
macroeconomic efficiency, 14;
    211
macroeconomic management, 70
market socialism, 150; 163; 254;
    255; 263
Marx K., 255
McCallum R., 119
Meri L., 34
Mises L. v., 251
monetary overhang, 53
monetary policy, 33–39; 53; 70;
    82; 90–93; 243–47
monetary reform, 7; 68; 70
monetary union, 93
moral hazard, 203
mutual funds, 264
North D., 22; 99; 184; 188; 270;
    273
Nuti M., 255
OECD, 98; 112; 117; 252
Optimization Postulate, 153
organized crime, 226
output gains, 211; 215; 217
perestroika, 18
personal income tax, 103
political risks, 13; 182; 188; 193;
    199; 200–204
Popular Front, 25
price liberalization, 8; 24; 34; 81;
    169; 170; 217; 271
price stability, 6; 244; 247
private ownership, 11; 39; 99;
    156; 159–63; 253; 270
privatization,
    agriculture, 25–29; 35; 43–52
    asset stripping, 44; 223; 226;
        236
    housing, 40; 43–52; 96
    large-scale, 39; 136

method, 11;151;152; 156; 167; 173; 175
programmes, 150; 167; 232; 237
reprivatization, 35; 40
small-scale, 39; 42–52; 260
times sequencing, 11; 152; 167; 171; 178; 266
production possibility frontier, 214; 216
production system, 18; 39; 61
Property Reform Act, 198
property rights, 10; 99; 182–206; 230; 256–66
public expenditure, 5; 111
public ownership, 253
real interest rates, 182
reconstruction, 6; 10; 222
recovery, 56; 59; 160; 267
redistribution, 3; 29; 114; 163; 179
reserve currency, 73
restitution, 43; 44–47; 51
restructuring, 6; 10–16; 32; 56; 57; 61; 93; 112–14; 134; 135; 159; 171–76; 256; 259
risk insurance, 13
Roemer J., 255
Romania, 268
rouble, 7; 9; 29; 36; 37; 54; 66–79; 84–93; 242–48; 271
rouble zone, 7; 9; 37; 66–71; 93
rublis, 88
Russia, 24–40; 54; 60; 62; 69; 75–79; 85; 89; 93; 127; 131; 146; 175; 191; 217; 223; 227; 229; 234; 239; 268–72
Sachs J., 260
Savisaar E., 23; 24
seigniorage, 69; 243
sequencing, 11; 152; 167; 171; 178; 266

shock therapy, 233; 249
Slovakia, 194; 268; 269
Slovenia, 40; 267; 268
SLP approach, 3; 15; 224; 232; 233
social engineering, 253; 255; 264
social safety net, 231
social system, 3; 19
socialism, 16; 150; 151; 163; 233; 250; 254; 255; 261; 263; 270
socialist economies, 11; 150; 151; 155; 159; 173; 175
SOE, 36; 50
South Korea, 101
Soviet Union, 7; 9; 17–19; 32–38; 48; 54; 57; 71; 89; 140; 141; 148; 162; 191; 228; 234; 249; 262; 271
Spain, 127; 267
spillover effects, 14; 175; 212
stabilization, 5; 10; 28; 52; 219; 246; 265
and economic efficiency, 14; 211; 254; 263; 266
and economic independence, 29; 71; 73; 83
budgetary policy, 100; 113
macroeconomic policy mix, 18; 35; 38; 53; 60; 70; 231; 233
programmes, 31–39; 62–67; 79; 86; 150; 229
shock therapy, 233; 263
state enterprises, 48; 51; 98; 100; 101; 110–14; 226; 256; 257
state ownership, 39; 99; 168; 172; 256; 257
structural adjustment, 14; 211–20
structural reform, 14; 16
supply shocks, 252
Supreme Soviet, 23; 41
sustainable growth, 5; 13

Sweden, 1; 32; 54; 127; 195; 272
Switzerland, 125; 227
Tajikistan, 146
Talleks, 198
Talonas, 37; 54
tariffs, 27; 33–38; 104; 108
taxation
    income distribution, 108; 111;
    114
    income tax, 79; 98; 102; 103;
    113
    optimal taxation, 108; 215
    profit tax, 29; 97; 103; 104
    retroactive taxation, 191
    tax base, 5; 6; 108
    tax burden, 103
terms of trade, 24; 29; 32; 35;
    104; 246
third way approach, 16
trade liberalization, 14; 219; 258
trade pattern, 9; 129
trade unions, 33
Treuhand, 42; 50; 193
Turek O., 261
Turkmenistan, 146
turnover tax, 79; 98
Ukraine, 34; 64; 68; 89; 169; 172;
    222
uncertainty, 12; 13; 47; 52; 88;
    194; 197; 251
unemployment, 6; 10; 14; 58–63;
    110; 151; 213; 251; 260; 266;
    267
unemployment benefits, 6
unification, 217
USA, 19; 112; 125; 259
Vähi T., 24
valuation, 78
value added tax, 29; 103
value system, 21; 255
vested interests, 169; 194
Visegrad countries, 251; 272

Visokavicius M., 38
voucher, 25; 26; 28; 41; 43; 44;
    46; 47; 48; 50; 51; 175; 176
World Bank, 37; 65; 97; 103;
    104; 110; 118; 128; 130–41;
    149; 238; 267